Some Remarkable Men

FURTHER MEMOIRS

SOME

REMARKABLE

MEN

FURTHER MEMOIRS

JAMES LORD

FARRAR STRAUS GIROUX

NEW YORK

Library of Congress Cataloging-in-Publication Data
Lord, James.
  Some remarkable men : further memoirs / James Lord.
    p.   cm.
  Includes index.
  ISBN 0-374-26655-7
  1. Biography—20th century.   I. Title.
CT120.L597   1996
920.71—dc20   *96-28637*
                                                       CIP

The author gratefully acknowledges that the letters from
Sir Harold Acton are published with the kind permission of
his literary executor, Michael Mallon, and the letters from
Jean Cocteau with the kind permission of his heir
and executor, Edouard Dermit.

Portions of this volume have appeared in somewhat different
form in The New Criterion *and* The Yale Review.

FOR GILLES ROY-LORD

CONTENTS

The Cost of the Villa

[H A R O L D   A C T O N]

The obituaries were lengthy, laudatory, international, appearing in the most prominent newspapers and periodicals of the United States and most of Western Europe, especially, of course, in Italy, though probably not, alas, in China. The legendary recipient of these numerous notices would have been pleased but hardly surprised, because he had expended an exceptionally long, privileged, and rarefied lifetime upon meticulous elaboration of the legend; and had it ever been insinuated that certain vital aspects of it might, in fact, have been difficult to verify, he would doubtless have murmured, "My dear, don't we all know that the fabric of history is woven upon the loom of conjecture?"

This person was Sir Harold Mario Mitchell Acton, Commander of the Order of the British Empire, born on July 5, 1904, in Florence, Italy, at the Villa La Pietra, the palatial residence of his parents, where he died eighty-nine years later, on February 27, 1994.

Long before Harold's time, the name Acton had acquired honorable luster in Italy. For twenty-five years at the end of the eighteenth century, Sir John Acton was minister of state to the King and Queen of Naples, lover of the Queen, and much assisted in his administration of Neapolitan intrigue by the notorious Lady Hamilton. The grandson of this statesman was born in 1834 in Naples but, being of British nationality, spent most of his life in England, where he became a noted historian, member of Parliament, and close friend of Gladstone; ascended to the House of Lords; and achieved enduring fame as author of the celebrated observation that absolute power corrupts absolutely.

Little is known with certainty concerning the antecedents of Sir Harold's father, Arthur Mario Acton, born in 1874, but what does seem verifiable is that his son's persistent intimations of familial ties to the illustrious Neapolitan and English Actons is without basis in fact. Anyway, Arthur Acton had nothing of the grandee about him. Swarthy, well-built, smoothly suave in manner, he could never have been mistaken for a young milord making a belated grand tour. The most interesting thing about him is that he aspired to become an artist, and, though his resources must have been limited, he contrived to make his way to Paris, where he took up the study of painting. This pursuit brought him less gratification than the pursuit of attractive young women, an occupation in which he engaged with outstanding success and gusto during most of his lifetime. Also in Paris at this moment, which must have been during the late 1890s, was a young fellow from Chicago named Guy Mitchell, likewise attracted by the allure of artistic fulfillment but indifferent to young women. His father, with an infallible sense of timing, had founded in Chicago shortly after the Civil War the Illinois Trust and Savings Bank, an institution poised to profit prodigiously from the explosive postwar expansion westward. Arthur and Guy became friendly, and the Anglo-Italian was invited to America for a vacation. There he met Guy's sister Hortense. Several years older than Acton, pretty but not a great beauty, she possessed exceptional allure, however, as an heiress. He proposed and she accepted. They were married shortly after the turn of the century. Why they determined to make their home in Florence nobody today could probably guess. It was still then a fashionable haunt of rich expatriates, mostly English and Russian, who lived in lavish grandeur in the magnificent villas built upon surrounding hillsides by Florentine nobles and merchants during the centuries of their city's overpowering wealth and prestige. In addition to this society of lotus-eating but highly proper foreigners, there were many serious students of the incomparable artistic patrimony to be seen in Florence's museums, palaces, and churches, and the most eminent of these throughout a very long lifetime was Bernard Berenson, himself a legendary figure, known to all as B.B., a friend whom Harold in his own way may have aspired to emulate.

The Villa La Pietra stands above the city hard by the highway leading across the mountains toward Bologna and takes its name from the stone pillar which once indicated its precise distance from the ancient city limits. Built in the latter half of the fifteenth century, the villa was viewed even then as a sumptuous showplace, and its splendors were enhanced by successive owners, including the Actons, who moved in in 1903. The husband's sometime aspiration to become an artist was forgotten, his efforts now entirely expended upon making La Pietra the envy of Florence and acquiring for its inhabitants a prominent place in local society, all of this made relatively easy by the deluge of wealth issuing from Chicago. Two sons were born, Harold first, William a couple of years later. The father seems never to have been much interested in paternity. What he cared about was buying rare paintings by the primitive masters of the Tuscan School, statuary, tapestries, splendid antique furniture, and fine carpets. His greatest pride, however, was his garden, which had been "Anglicized" in the nineteenth century and which Arthur Acton, with the indispensable assistance of a professional landscape architect and creator of imposing gardens named Paul Chalfin, painstakingly restored over the years to its vast, original, Italianate condition, with fountains, colonnades, staircases, balustrades, urns, marble benches, and more than a hundred magnificent statues gathered—some say pilfered—from all over Italy. The proprietor of this admirable restoration, however, was known as a strategist of sharp practice and an accomplished driver of very hard bargains, a man easy to distrust and quarrel with. But he didn't seem to care tuppence for the esteem of others, so long as they accepted his wife's invitations and were adequately impressed by the splendors of La Pietra. Besides, he was kept reasonably busy by the clandestine pursuit of amorous affairs in the town, an activity not unrelated to the passion for collecting art and which resulted, incidentally, in a certain number of illegitimate half brothers and half sisters to Harold and William.

Hortense Acton, a small woman, always exquisitely attired, gracious, and demure, was at the same time a person of stern character and indomitable resolve. She soon learned of her husband's infidelities and, in keeping with the convention of that era, tolerated them with severe composure. Her pleasure was to be a great hostess and a devoted mother, approximately in that order of preference. Her maternal devotion was directed principally toward her second son, and that was no secret from the first. Perhaps she had from the beginning some vague presentiment that William was destined for disaster and hoped that a surplus of adoration might avert it. Arthur, too, insofar as he made very much of his children—compared to his collections, gardens, and mistresses—favored William. He may have found Harold a trifle too clever to be doted upon, for even as a young boy the elder son was the inventive, witty, precocious one. At the age of ten he started to write poetry. That his future would be brilliant seemed almost aggressively to be taken for granted—by him and by the adults whose company he overtly preferred to that of other children.

In due time and conformity with elegant convention, the two boys were packed off to prestigious English schools. It was at Eton that Harold emerged from his adolescent chrysalis as a fully developed, gorgeous, outrageous aesthetic gadfly. His closest crony was a scandalous, highly affected but sophisticated and clever youth named Brian Howard, homosexual like Harold and William, destined to be one of the most talented and spectacular failures of his generation. Together Harold and Brian produced a volume of poetry by Eton authors, themselves the most prominent contributors, entitled *The Eton Candle*, and saw to it that this came to the notice of avant-garde writers and critics, especially their idols, Edith, Osbert, and Sacheverell Sitwell. Edith wrote a favorable review, singling out Brian and Harold for particularly laudatory mention. This led to an appreciative letter from a London publisher and the appearance, while Harold was still an undergraduate at Oxford, of his first book of poetry, *Aquarium*, a volume which does not repay attentive scrutiny today. But the die was gloriously cast. He would be a poet. His parents would have preferred preparation for the diplomatic service, but the summons of the pure ·Hippocrene was more imperative. Twenty-five years later he thought his parents might have had a point. In his first volume of memoirs he wrote, "I would have made an ideal ambassador," an appraisal wide open to debate.

It was while he was at Oxford that Harold's star attained its strongest, gemlike brilliance in the galaxy of his contemporaries. Never again would he appear quite so astonishing, promising, illustrious, or conspicuous, and luckily he had every reason to assume that the future could only get better. There was, however, one flaw in the delectable aspect of happy, satisfying decades to come. Harold happened not to be handsome, and for a homosexual that unfortunate fact usually makes for a lifetime of emotional inferiority. The brilliant intellectual can never believe himself to be on terms of equality with the handsome, thoughtless lords of the playing fields, and the aesthete, ever mindful of physical imperfection, may easily view himself as a hapless victim of circumstances. Harold was not ugly, merely plain, exceptionally tall, with an oblong face, small eyes and nose, and a pursed mouth. For a dedicated lover of beauty who at the same time is both gifted and ambitious, the lack of looks may be compensated for by a calculated extravagance of behavior and attire. Harold was never afraid of calling attention to himself, even when the attention risked attracting physical hostility. He wore a gray bowler, a stock instead of a necktie, let his side-whiskers flourish, and sported jackets and trousers of unconventional amplitude, which were soon copied by other undergraduates anxious to be thought sophisticates. *Aquarium* having been published and having made something of a splash, the provocative poet delighted in reciting his verses through a megaphone from his balcony in Christ Church. A self-declared, unabashed—and lifelong—aesthete, he made it his business to mock the philistines and do battle against everything artistically démodé. His weapon was a publication subsidized by himself entitled *The Oxford Broom*, intended to whisk away the fin-de-siècle cobwebs, outrage old fogies like A. E. Housman and Walter de la Mare, and exalt the Sitwells, T. S. Eliot, and Rimbaud. He invited Gertrude Stein, whom he had met in Florence at the villa of her brother Leo, to lecture, an audacious initiative, but the overflow audience which had come to jeer stayed to cheer, won over by Miss Stein's imperious, no-nonsense elocution. So it was presently an acknowledged fact that in all of Oxford there was no undergraduate as widely known, admired, and envied as Harold Acton, a status doubtless accepted by him as gratifying evidence of natural selection. And perhaps Harold's legend has been perpetuated to such an extent that no other undergraduate since his time has equaled that fame. William Acton, the favorite in Florence and the more handsome of the two sons, was rather overshadowed at Oxford by his extravagant brother. Aspiring to become a painter, he made something of a name for himself as a swashbuckler and heavy drinker, once throwing himself out a third-floor window, though whether from drunken impulsiveness or suicidal melancholia remains problematical. Luckily he landed on a plot of grass and broke no bones, but he was taken unconscious to a hospital and suffered some internal injuries.

Satisfaction of a variety more immediately pleasurable and exciting than any to be provided by poetry was also available at Oxford in those romantic days. Though the noxious Oscar Wilde scandal, barely a generation in the past, remained mordant in the mind of any homosexual as a warning that fulfillment of his desires was a crime punishable by imprisonment, love affairs among the undergraduates were frequent and intense. Harold's celebrity made conquest easy, and eloquent endearments were probably a passable substitute for good looks. In his memoirs Harold boasts of having "kindled flames in Elgin marble breasts," recalls "showers of burning kisses," and evokes numerous ecstasies. At the same time he is rather coy, because he never quite acknowledges that these passionate affairs were with other youths, and not once does the word *homosexual* appear in either volume of his memoirs. In conversation, of course, he was less discreet and reveled in dwelling on the long-ago delights of Oxonian romances. At the same time, however, he wrote in *Memoirs of an Aesthete* that as a boy he had seen lovers lingering in the lane behind La Pietra and had wondered whether love would someday affect him in the same way, adding, "Now that I know the answer, I envy them." His firmest friend and favorite lover during the Oxford years was a young fellow by the name of Evelyn Waugh, whom Harold envisaged as a wild faun. This was during Waugh's brief homosexual phase, so feelingly evoked many years later in *Brideshead Revisited*, and Harold frequently sighed over the memory of rolling about on the floor of his study in the embrace of the fledgling novelist.

However intoxicating the pleasures of Oxford, no aesthete in the mid-twenties could deem himself entirely of age until he had become well acquainted with the cultural resources and ferment of Paris. The Sitwells, T. S. Eliot, the National Gallery, and Covent Garden were all very well, but Paris had not only the Louvre and the Opéra, it had André Breton, Tristan Tzara, Pablo Picasso, Sergey Diaghilev, Erik Satie, and Jean Cocteau. Harold went over frequently and grew to feel honest fondness for the French and their culture. He met Cocteau and had his portrait drawn by the wrong Spaniard, Pedro Pruna, a saccharine pasticheur of Picasso, whose creations Harold airily dismissed. He enjoyed the café life, the boulevards, and the backstage intrigues of Diaghilev's ballet company. But he never became committed to the cultivation of life in Paris. His true spiritual and intellectual attachments were to Italy and England. Or so he thought when he came down from Oxford and found himself compelled to make his way in the wide world.

A son of rich parents often turns to them to smooth his way if he perceives that it could prove arduous or the destination doubtful. Acton *père* and *mère* had their doubts, but as neither of them had ever done a stroke of work and they lived among people to whom the very idea of gainful employment connoted eccentricity, they couldn't very well say no. They granted Harold a liberal allowance but attached to it the somewhat inhibiting proviso that he must "make good" within three years. If he failed, the allowance would stop. Now, just what it means for a literary aspirant to "make good"—in three years or in thirty—is a very debatable issue, subject to the most variable and hypothetical of criteria. But Harold's parents weren't interested in literature. What they wanted was public recognition of their son's talents, which would in turn reflect creditably upon them and, if possible, bring in enough cash to prove that making good, nicely in accord with the precedent of Harold's grandfather, meant making money. But the young aesthete scorned worldly success. All he yearned to do was erect a "lordly pleasure-house" for his soul, and that undertaking, however laudable, is rarely a paying proposition.

Not knowing quite where to turn, Harold finally settled around 1925 in a comfortable Parisian apartment at 29, quai de Bourbon on the Ile St.-Louis. He had spent his life so far among ex-kings and ex-queens, grand dukes, princes, sons of peers by the score, not to mention eminent literati like Lytton Strachey, Somerset Maugham, Norman Douglas, Aldous Huxley, D. H. Lawrence, and the Sitwells; so Harold was as accomplished a snob as could have been expected under such circumstances, and all his life he delighted in rubbing elbows with the famed and titled. In this realm, at least, he "made good" with exemplary panache. The literary pinnacle was of far more difficult access. He had plenty of poems on hand and a fable in prose called *Cornelian*, which he showed to his friend Gertrude Stein, who said that she saw in these works just what she was looking for: the rhythmical connection between his writings and his personality. That was all very well, but fables and poems, published though they were to esoteric but very faint praise, did not satisfy the parental criteria. The only thing able to do that, Harold realized, would be a popular novel like *The Green Hat*, which the author of *Cornelian* considered trash; but he thought that if Michael Arlen, an Armenian refugee, could pull it off, then there would be no reason why the most eminent Oxonian of his generation couldn't do better. And so, although the task was from the beginning "repulsive" to him, he lay down in bed and began writing his first novel, to which, as if asking in advance for mortification, he gave the rashly ill-conceived title *Humdrum*. Willie Maugham tried to give professional advice, but Harold was far more interested in accompanying him to an establishment where boys loitered at the bar waiting to be escorted upstairs to private rooms, and the elder novelist much impressed his young colleague by accompanying four different youths in the space of a few hours.

Meanwhile, Harold's boon companion at Oxford, the little faun called Evelyn Waugh, who had no rich parents to subsidize his ambitions, had taken a job teaching school, an occupation he detested, and was also at work writing a novel. Dedicated to Harold "In Homage and Affection," it was called *Decline and Fall*, a brilliant, savage, hilariously witty satire, lampooning the demise not of the Roman empire but of the British. Propelled by universal praise, it ascended like a rocket into the stratosphere of fame, where it still deservedly gleams sixty-six years later. Unfortunately for Harold, *Decline and Fall* was published simultaneously with *Humdrum*, which was drubbed by the critics and sank like a boulder into the sea of public indifference. Cyril Connolly, who had been at Eton with Harold and knew both authors well, reviewed the two novels together for *The New Statesman*, writing a panegyric of *Decline and Fall* and denouncing *Humdrum* as the jejune production of an incompetent scribbler. It requires no imagination to realize the effect of such notices at La Pietra. Harold was crestfallen and bitter, and the razor edge of his resentment had not been blunted when he came to compose his memoirs twenty years later. Indeed, he also found it impossible to conceal a snide satisfaction at the failure of the little faun's first marriage, an occurrence that wounded Waugh for life. This was not the only failed marriage among Harold's friends, and as he contemplated these wrecks, he said, "I could congratulate myself on having remained a bachelor." As if the option had been exercised after dispassionate contemplation!

Not knowing quite what to do next, Harold went back to London, took an apartment in John Street, engaged a Chinese cook, drank great quantities of green tea, ate with chopsticks, and grew plump. Then Arthur Acton proposed setting up his sons together in an enormous mansion in Lancaster Gate, filled with the furniture that he compulsively continued to buy, and encouraged his sons to give lavish parties as a stratagem for selling the furniture. The parties were a great success; all the bright young things of the era flocked to them. But not a stick of furniture got sold, and so the irascible father shut down the house, compelling his sons to return to Florence. William, who still had aspirations as a painter, felt frustrated and disappointed but was coddled by his adoring mother. Harold, having decidedly failed to "make good," was keenly aware of the disapproval, amounting sometimes, he felt, virtually to dislike, on the part of both parents.

Norman Douglas, one of the many older men with whom Harold became friendly—then famous as the author of *South Wind* and *Old Calabria*, books almost forgotten today—advised Harold to get out of Europe and go to the Far East. But Florence exerted its spell, and the frustrated author determined to compose some sort of tribute to his native Tuscany; so he sat down to write "a monument of Baroque prose" to Gian Gastone de' Medici, the last member of that extraordinary family whose magnificence and liberality had made of Florence the most stupendous repository of European culture since the Athens of Pericles. Decadence and instability inevitably set in, however, and by the time of Gian Gastone the city was vulnerable and impoverished. Harold related this tale in a style as elaborate as that of the seventeenth century which he was writing about, and though *The Last Medici* was dismissed by some critics as "an entertaining scrap of rococo history," it is still today considered a valid work of reference.

The Cost of the Villa

Hortense Acton's brother, Guy Mitchell, homosexual like his two nephews, had given up painting for a life of leisure in California. A generous and affable gentleman, he was possessed by a fanatic passion for footwear, owning a nearly innumerable variety of shoes. One day as he sat on a sea-front bench in Santa Monica, a good-looking young fellow happened to stroll past and, by one of those uncanny, almost supernatural interventions of fate, was moved to remark, "That's a very handsome pair of shoes you're wearing." Seized by astonishment, pleasure, and appreciation of both the youth's appearance and discrimination, Guy Mitchell invited him to sit down. They had a pleasant conversation and spent the rest of their lives together. The young man's name was Edward Eberle. He later opened an antique shop in Hollywood and outlived his lover, who left him his entire estate, a bequest which Harold sometimes enviously deplored. He had good reason nonetheless to feel affectionate and grateful toward his uncle Guy, for it was he who, at the critical juncture in Harold's life, gave him enough money to do as he pleased, an act of selfless generosity which would never have been forthcoming from the captious proprietors of the Villa La Pietra. So Harold traveled about the United States, visiting grand and notable personages whose acquaintance he had made in Europe; went on to Honolulu, where a cousin reigned over local society; thence took ship to Japan and wandered about the Far East, just as Norman Douglas had advised him to do and as his friend Willie Maugham had done before him. But in his heart he felt that Peking was his destination. "I had made mistakes and wasted my talents," he later wrote, "but I looked upon my failures as stepping-stones toward the more beautiful and the most beautiful." He had not, in fact, wasted either his talents or his time, for his true gift, already perfected at Oxford and refined throughout the decades to come, was for the creation of a captivating personality, borne upon flights of dazzling conversation capable, it seemed, of elevating the most trivial topic to the heights of exquisite discourse. As for his failures, they were not stepping-stones toward any degree of beauty but heterogeneous confections which could eventually serve to project the likeness of a literary career.

Peking in 1930 was everything that Harold had dreamed it might be, and more. He felt intoxicated by the city's atmosphere and light, enchanted by the friendliness and—to his eye—good looks of the young men, and overcome with admiration for the Imperial Palaces. "Within our time," he wrote, "no handiwork of man has achieved such a dignified and spacious harmony of buildings." Not only the city but also the surrounding countryside seemed so beautiful and calming to Harold's eyes and nerves that it surpassed anything he had ever known before. Having come to the other side of the world, as far as possible from Florence, Oxford, London, and Paris, having parted from his parents, the Sitwells, Cocteau, and T. S. Eliot, having put behind him everything that was inhibiting or oppressive, especially the odious compulsion to "make good," Harold for the first time in his life felt perfectly free to be himself as he recognized himself truly to be, and this, as he repeatedly told us all in later years, was his sole experience of genuine ecstasy. Of course, an appreciable modicum of luxury made ecstasy all the more ecstatic. He was able to set himself up in an elegant and spacious house with fine gardens and a swimming pool, to buy exquisite antique furniture, and to collect ancient scrolls, golden screens, and rare statuary. He was also ecstatic to experience the willing and eager embraces of Peking's innumerable young boys, to whom he evidently appeared a thrilling and exotic embodiment of desire. He delighted in their silken skins and tiny penises. Here he was able to lead an openly homosexual life unthinkable in Europe. In addition to all these avenues to ecstasy, he discovered the bliss of opium, became a cautious addict, and remained so intermittently for the rest of his life.

He immersed himself at the same time in intense study of the Chinese language and culture, attended the theater, made friends with professors, intellectuals, members of the ancient nobility, and Peking's smart set. He found to his delight that his reputation as a literary figure had made its way even to Peking, so he was invited to lecture on English literature at the Peking National University, a job he undertook with delectation. He felt that he had attained perfect happiness, that he had never before been so powerfully lucid, that the life he had led in Europe had been superficial and frivolous, his energies wasted in pursuing will-o'-the-wisps; and he bid farewell to the caricatures of his past.

His past, however, turned up now and then. Even Osbert Sitwell, accompanied by his boyfriend David Horner, came for a visit, extolling the *douceur de vivre* Harold had impulsively abandoned in faraway Europe. And there was a young Englishman named Desmond Parsons, "tall, fair and Nordically handsome," who moved into a house very close to Harold's. Of all the men to whom Harold became romantically attached, his friends felt that young Parsons was the only one with whom he was truly, deeply in love. This may be, but it was an intermittent affair, because Desmond was restless and, though his health was fragile, often set out upon difficult journeys to remote, almost-inaccessible places. Eventually these expeditions wore away his strength; he fell ill and had to return to London, there to die, aged only twenty-six, after a prolonged and traumatic struggle with Hodgkin's disease. Harold was profoundly saddened, feeling that Desmond had identified him with the more intense life to be found in China, and he reproached himself for not having returned to London to be with his friend while death approached. "Man is not made for happiness on this earth," he wrote.

During all the years that Harold spent in China, the country was in a state of uninterrupted turmoil amounting virtually to civil war, pitting the Nationalist troops of Chiang Kai-shek against the Communists led by Mao Tse-tung; and this inner strife, which weakened national unity, was seriously aggravated by the Japanese invasion of Manchuria in 1931 and of China proper six years later. Harold, a British citizen, had no cause for worry, though he was concerned about the safety of his Chinese friends. While lecturing, collecting, and studying the art of calligraphy, he idled away some of his time by writing a novel called *Peonies and Ponies*, a frivolous bit of fluff describing Peking and some of the people he frequented there.

Lurid gossip about Harold came to circulate in the foreign community of Peking. Perhaps this was in part because he took no trouble to conceal his contempt for fools, of whom there must have been plenty among the diplomatic wives—husbands, too—and in part because, always the aesthete, he kept very much to himself and a small circle of refined, aristocratic friends. So he would naturally have aroused animosity, nor did he bother to disguise his arrogant indifference to it. However, in so limited a milieu, it cannot have been possible to conceal the fact that this patrician lover of beauty was also an habitué of the opium pipe and a libertine lover of pretty young boys. Such knowledge does get about and, spite being what it is, vicious talk can seem to corroborate vice.

The Japanese invasion of mainland China continued apace, and it seemed foolhardy to expect that disunited and poorly equipped Chinese forces might succeed in repelling the invaders. Common sense, moreover, persuasively argued that affairs in faraway Europe were also growing daily more worrisome. Harold had been away for more than five years. He had grown bald and put on weight. Enjoying the ecstasy of life in China, he had not been too concerned about what was happening on the far side of the world. Now, though, he made up his mind to travel home for a short visit and so set out in the autumn of 1936.

To his astonishment he found Florence enchanting, though in his memoirs, speaking of this visit, there is not a single reference to the Villa La Pietra or its inhabitants. The beauty of the city, its exquisite setting, and its marvels of art and architecture had not lost their old power to enthrall the consummate aesthete. He delighted in reunions with friends like Norman Douglas, the Countess Rucellai, and Reggie Turner, the faithful comrade of Oscar Wilde in his final, pitiful days. After a time he went on to London, where his brother, William, had taken a studio and was busy painting glossy portraits of society ladies in a style evocative of Helleu and Boldini, with a dash of Surrealist whimsy thrown in for good measure. Harold's greatest friend in England was Emerald Cunard, the famous society hostess, whose charm, intelligence, sympathy, and imaginative good humor he extolled at length. "Her sweet presence," he wrote, "was a passing benediction whose influence did not pass: she offered one the chalice of her own eternal youth." But he found that his European friends were not at all interested to hear about his experiences in China. Some of them thought that he had become an Oriental. He had acquired a large gold ring set with a cabochon of the finest imperial jade which he wore until his death, and perhaps it was his fluency in the Chinese language that affected his manner of speaking, which was a sort of lilting semiwhisper that could rise and fall, sometimes audible enough to carry across a large room, sometimes so sotto voce that one had to strain to catch a mocking allusion to the turpitude of persons he disliked, who were numerous. He was annoyed to find that the myth of his own depravity had preceded him, and there were those who could not be convinced that prolonged residence in the land of the Yellow Peril might be due to anything but some secret vice, some enslavement of the senses. Consequently, despite his devotion to old friends both human and artistic, it must have been with some relief and great pleasure that he once more set out for Peking after an absence of more than six months.

Hardly had he settled back into his exquisite house amid the treasures fastidiously tended by faithful servants during his absence than the threat of disaster became a reality. The Japanese attacked the city with airplanes and tanks, while its desperate defenders possessed no comparable weapons. Martial law was proclaimed, a strict curfew enforced, trenches dug, barricades thrown up, and sandbags piled at strategic corners. Refugees fled by the tens of thousands. In vain. The city was surrounded and soon fell. Wounded soldiers were cared for in a makeshift hospital behind Harold's house, and he went every day to read to them, giving whatever help he could. He himself had nothing to fear and stubbornly stayed on, devoting himself to the translation of Chinese poetry into English—no simple task—and visiting with friends who likewise remained in Peking, most of them because they had nowhere else to go. All tried to put as brave a face as possible on a situation that literally called for bravery. The Japanese conquerors behaved with what was for them relative restraint. They wanted to pretend that conquest was in reality the pursuit of good-neighborly common interest. There was the run-of-the-mill quota of atrocities but nothing to compare with what happened six months later during the Rape of Nanking, when 300,000 persons are said to have been slaughtered. It is hard to understand how the contemplation of antique scrolls and the recitation of esoteric verse can have made for any peace of mind, not to mention the slightest sense of ecstasy, when the whole structure of an age-old culture was disintegrating before the eyes of one who had profoundly loved and understood it. But while in China, Harold had made a serious study of Buddhism, and its teachings of detachment from the life of suffering, sorrow, and dissatisfaction gradually pervaded his view of human experience. Born a Catholic, however, he did not repudiate the Roman theology of his upbringing but felt that he had achieved within himself a harmony of the teachings of both Christ and Buddha. Such harmony must have made it easier for him to accept the terrible times through which he was living and that threatened soon to grow infinitely worse.

Hortense Acton fled from Florence to Switzerland when the Czechoslovakian crisis began to look like another Sarajevo. Her husband stayed behind, unable to abandon all the treasures he had collected during the past three and a half decades. He had made astute use of his wife's money, amassing a considerable fortune of his own. It must have come in handy in order to facilitate extramarital affairs. He had also purchased real estate in Florence, including the Palazzo Lanfredini on the Arno, and had added to the La Pietra estate five other villas of considerable size, the entire property now comprising fifty-seven acres of olive groves, formal gardens, and a large kitchen garden planted with delectable vegetables, of which all the seeds were sent from America. The value of the entire estate and its collections of sculpture, paintings, furniture, tapestries, and rare manuscripts would have been nearly impossible to assess. Hortense returned from Vevey when Neville Chamberlain and Edouard Daladier cravenly caved in before the gangster intimidation of Hitler and his loutish accomplices. Optimism in those days was an opulent luxury, but maybe the Actons felt they could afford it. The very rich invariably have a hard time imagining that any misfortune can befall them.

Harold possessed more foresight than his parents. After the partition of Czechoslovakia he realized that a European war was inevitable and prepared to leave Peking. He was not quite foresighted enough, however, because he never imagined that Japan would participate in the worldwide catastrophe. Expecting one day to return to Peking, he decided that his collection of bronzes, scrolls, rare furniture, and golden screens would be safer where they were, tended by his well-trained servants, than exposed to the dangers of bombing in an English warehouse. Still, he bade them a mournful farewell and said good-bye also with reluctant sadness to his few intimate Chinese friends, none of whom he was ever to see again.

He returned first to London, where he found his younger brother set up in a large studio in Tite Street with a portrait of the

Duchess of Kent on his easel, but he sensed that William was disappointed by lack of recognition and subject to fits of depression.
Fortunately the ineffable Lady Cunard was, as usual, on hand to
dispel melancholy with her brilliant, unpredictable conversation,
which occasionally brought forth such remarks as, "Tiberius must
have been charming. Why are so many historians against him?"
Then the war began. Harold was thirty-five years old. Younger men
were wanted. The lack of any patriotic employment preyed on his
mind. Like his friend Waugh, the little faun now mature, famous,
and remarried, Harold enjoyed a good scrap, was physically fearless
and eager to prove himself useful in time of national crisis. He
appealed to influential friends to find him a post well adapted to
his abilities—obviously, he thought, something that would profit
from his experience and knowledge of China. It would take time,
he was told, and was advised to be patient.

Having lorded it over Florence for so long, the Actons must
have assumed that exceptional consideration even in drastic times
would be granted them. So when Italy entered the war, they made
no effort to flee in haste toward the Swiss border. This was a mistake.
One evening while Mrs. Acton was entertaining a few friends, a
police official presented himself at the villa and requested her to
accompany him to headquarters. This was a mere formality, he
explained, having to do with her passport. She was surprised and
upset—with reason—and protested that she had no means of trans-
portation, as her husband was absent with their automobile and
chauffeur. The official said that he would escort her to headquarters
and bring her back, a brief inconvenience. Now, for some preposterous reason, Hortense Acton had tampered with her passport,
altering the date of birth to make herself appear a decade younger.
Why she should have cared what customs officials and frontier police
knew her age to be is a mystery, but a very significant clue must be
looked for in the vanity and arrogance of the lady in question. Tampering with a passport, even for such a frivolous reason, may be
considered a serious matter, and the police official escorted Mrs.
Acton not to headquarters but to the central prison, where she was
peremptorily placed in a holding cell along with prostitutes and other
female offenders. There she was forced to remain for three days and

three nights, during which she refused to lie down, eat, or sleep, though she must have dozed occasionally on the hard chair provided. That this confinement was petty vindictiveness aimed by Fascist bureaucrats to humiliate those who had thought themselves above the common herd goes without saying. After three days Mrs. Acton was released and allowed, without further trouble, to proceed to Switzerland. She said that the experience had aged her beyond her years (she was already over seventy) and swore that she would never again set foot in Italy.

Arthur Acton had similar trouble with the police, but he was no stranger to the uses of corruption and suavely bribed his way across the frontier to join his wife in Vevey. Unlike her, however, it was heartrending for him to leave behind La Pietra, its glorious gardens, and all the treasures within the villa itself. Everything on earth most precious to him was now vulnerable to the perils of war, of which one of the most fearful is man's delight in sheer destruction and vandalism, a delight that surpasses mere human malice and requires explanation in some cosmological or even religious way. So it was not for nothing that Mr. Acton's nerves were so sorely tried during those uncertain years, especially when the shooting war finally reached Florence. He was never afterward quite the same man.

For most people who are caught up in it, a war is the most intense and vital experience of their lives. Harold was no exception. Having pulled every string available, he was delighted to learn of his acceptance as an officer in the Royal Air Force. In *More Memoirs of an Aesthete*, his second volume of autobiography, he wrote, "To leap from a sedentary life into a world of Homeric heroes, *mutatis mutandis*, was a form of self-renewal which I welcomed. Since we were all at war was it not preferable to be present 'at the focus where the greatest number of vital forces unite in their purest energy?' And couldn't it be said of the R.A.F. that its spirit burned with a 'hard, gemlike flame?' " He was assigned to the Intelligence Service and hoped to be posted as soon as possible to some place in China, where he felt that he could be of the greatest use and whither, of course, personal yearnings powerfully drew him. But it was the very strength, and intimacy, perhaps, of his yearnings that brought him furious frustration and bitter resentment. As usual in the army, accidents, confusions, and delay were the rule. At last, however, a year after joining the Royal Air Force, he reached India. China, he felt, could not but come next. This was not to be.

He was first posted to a small place called Barrackpore. There he irritably studied maps, aerial photos, and reports of interviews with prisoners, work which he deemed futile drudgery. His senior officers were so secretive that he had little idea of what was going on. He was never asked to attend conferences, and the work assigned him seemed like a hunt for the missing pieces of an insignificant jigsaw puzzle. Presently he came to have the disagreeable feeling that he was not trusted. Then, he says, by chance he came across a file emanating from an embassy official which constituted "a gross libel on my character." It stated that he was not persona grata in China and was by no means to be allowed to proceed there. It is very difficult to believe that "by chance" anyone comes across a document damning to his character, especially as the document was unsigned but official and secret. However that may be, there can be little doubt concerning the "gross libel" on Harold's character contained therein. Gossip does get about. He was enraged, but there was nothing he could do save apply for a transfer. In time he was transferred to Delhi to serve as a liaison officer with the press. This brought him once more into close and exhilarating contact with R.A.F. pilots, and once again he felt introduced to a world "so different from any I had known that I longed to be as much part of it as my circumstances permitted." Apparently the gross libel did not follow him here, and it is easy to understand how the highly cultivated, and slightly effete, middle-aged aesthete was thrilled by association with the dashing young fliers who apparently thought nothing of risking their lives. It doubtless never occurred to Harold that he might be risking his own. But he was.

For some time he had been subject to violent attacks of nausea. Having always been in excellent health, he thought nothing of them. They persisted, however, and when he finally consulted a doctor it was determined in those pre-penicillin times that only the removal of a kidney would save his life. The operation was performed in August 1943 in a military hospital in the Himalayan foothills by a surgeon aptly named Colonel Carver. Recovery was very slow. At one point he appeared to be dying and received extreme unction from a Catholic priest. After that, his condition gradually improved. It was two months, however, before he could leave his bed, and during that time he felt no desire to read, only to dream about the masterpieces he would one day write.

Of, or from, his parents in Switzerland he heard nothing. He had no news either of his younger brother, who had been drafted into the Pioneer Corps. And reports of the progress of the war were scarce, unreliable.

In the late autumn he received permission to leave the hospital for a period of convalescence, after which he was recommended for repatriation to London. The medical officer thought he should be pleased, as many men would have been. But not Harold "I felt cheated and defeated," he wrote, "as one who had lost the race through twisting an ankle. To return to England now would be a mortifying check to my wishes and ambitions." Such sentiments strike one as bizarrely incongruous when expressed by a self-proclaimed, peace-loving aesthete, one whose lifelong desire had been the undisturbed contemplation of beauty and who, while still in his Chinese ivory tower, had felt that he was "an escapist in a vacuum from which all jarring elements were excluded. Why not when there was so much vileness to escape from?" Clearly there existed a profound dichotomy in Harold's temperament. What were the ambitions and wishes to which the return to England would be a check? And why in the world—most particularly in *his* world—should such a check be mortifying? Evidently there was something he needed to demonstrate, if only to himself. Can it be that he honestly desired to participate actively in a war? For those who do so, it is probably the most terrible experience of their lives, but it is something else as well, equally terrible: the most exhilarating and liberating adventure of a lifetime. Why should Harold have felt cheated and defeated? Was it only because he had failed in his desire to return to China? Or was he trying to prove to himself— and to others?—that he was what he was not? He had had a glimpse of something that he admired and envied in the glamorous, fearless conviviality of the young R.A.F. pilots. Is it conceivable that he failed to realize that he had lost the race not because of a twisted ankle but because of a twist in his psyche? The war he needed to wage and to win was within himself, and he seems never even to have declared it. This disposition for appeasement, I think, provides much of the interest and pathos of his story, embellishing the exquisite fabric of his legend.

Frustrated as he may inwardly have felt, the return to London in the spring of 1944 was made enjoyable by reunion with old friends, especially the indomitable Lady Cunard, who continued to entertain important and witty guests as though half the world—her own in particular—did not lie in ruins. "War's so vulgar," she remarked. Also there was old Norman Douglas, who had been obliged to flee from Italy because of his persistent attentions to a boy of about twelve, whom Harold in his memoirs prudishly transforms into a girl. And plenty of new acquaintances were easily to be made. This was a time when the word *gay* connoted only merry freedom from care, but those who congregated in the Ritz Grill knew it to be the gayest place in London in the now-current connotation of the word. Harold was often to be found there. Another jolly, though not necessarily so gay, meeting place was a bookshop in Curzon Street run by a charming fellow called Heywood Hill. One of the principal attractions of this establishment was the presence there as a saleswoman of a highly entertaining, irreverent, and brilliant lady named Nancy Mitford, one of six sisters, all of whom had been portrayed by William Acton. Five of them were to become famous for wildly varied reasons: Unity as a friend and confidante of Hitler; Deborah as duchess of Devonshire; Jessica as the wife of a Communist lawyer living in California, where she wrote scathing critiques of American mores; Nancy as the author of novels and biographies; and Diana, also companionable with the Führer, as the wife of Sir Oswald Mosley, the British Fascist, both of whom spent the war years in prison.

Among the many entertaining and attractive habitués of Heywood Hill's bookstore was an American sergeant named Stuart Preston. Cultivated, well-mannered, and handsome, Preston enjoyed an unparalleled social success in London during the war years. Known to everybody who was anybody simply as The Sergeant, as if he were the only person in the U.S. army to hold that rank, Stuart was a favorite of Nancy's, and she did much to further his social career. He had no trouble striking up intimate friendships with men as handsome and personable as himself, whether in uniform or not.

He became so well known as the supreme darling of London society that when a person of note arrived late for a reception at Buckingham Palace, and Stuart happened to be in hospital for some minor ailment, King George is said to have remarked, "Never mind. I suppose you've been to St. George's Hospital to see The Sergeant." Inevitably Harold and Stuart became friendly, though just how friendly is unclear, and Harold also aided Stuart's ascension into the social stratosphere, introducing him not only to Lady Cunard and her circle but also to Evelyn Waugh and his. When Emerald criticized The Sergeant for never saying anything memorable, Harold objected that he was a character out of Henry James. There is some truth in this, but Stuart's story would have turned out to be one of the Master's more melancholy. In any case, those few brilliant, exhilarating years of social glory during the war laid up a heavy burden of nostalgia for the decades to come.

"It was with a rapture of relief," Harold wrote, that he learned of the complete withdrawal, after fierce combat, of all German troops from Florence by August 24, 1944. Damage to the historic center of the city had been great, though not catastrophic. Not long afterward news came from a friend who had visited La Pietra that the villa and all its contents, including the servants, had come safely through the fighting, some of which had taken place in the gardens surrounding the house. The five other villas on the estate had not all been so fortunate—some had been occupied by SS troops—and much rare antique furniture, many tapestries and ornaments had disappeared. Into whose possession was unclear. But no matter. The great villa was intact, now occupied by polite British officers, and all the fabulous treasures within were safe. If Harold's reaction to this happy news was rapture, one may imagine with what overwhelming joy his father learned of it. His possessions were ultimately what he lived for. Had they been destroyed, it does not seem farfetched to assume that his vital raison d'être would also have perished. Another donnée for a tale by Henry James.

In October, to his delight, Harold was transferred to Paris. His parents remained in Vevey, for the war in Europe was far from over. The French capital, however, was as festive as if no enemy soldiers had ever been seen there. Gertrude Stein and Alice B. Toklas were the center of an admiring crowd of GI's. Harold invited the two ladies to dine at his mess, where Gertrude created a sensation and was besieged for autographs. She advised her host to write his memoirs. Marie-Laure de Noailles gave smart luncheon parties and took Harold to visit Picasso, whose works the Florentine aesthete considered worthless, though he prudently kept his judgment to himself. He saw a good deal of Cocteau, whose talents he preferred, and was introduced to Christian Bérard, a painter of authentic talent who had wasted it on decoration and who, like Harold, was a devotee of the pipe. It was in Bérard's incredibly untidy lodgings that Harold made the acquaintance of a remarkably handsome youth in the uniform of a French lieutenant. He and his brother had run away from school in the United States to join the Free French and as paratroopers had performed authentic feats of heroism. Patriotic idealists, they had become confused and jaded among the cynical epicureans who welcomed them as heroes but tempted them with drugs. François was the name of the young lieutenant introduced by Bérard, and Harold more than once risked his rank and reputation, flying back and forth as he often did between Paris and London, to bring opium to the beautiful soldier. They daydreamed together of ecstatic sojourns in the Orient, but François, after all, was too worldly-wise for such flights of fancy and was presently taken up by the extravagant husband of a granddaughter of John D. Rockefeller, the Marquis de Cuevas, who provided a life of flamboyant luxury for both brothers.

After the end of the war in May Harold was reassigned to duties in Germany with an Air Information Unit at a place called Minden. It was there after years of silence that he received a letter from his brother, William, who had been able to visit Florence and go to La Pietra, where he was greeted with tears by the servants, loaded down with flowers and fruit, and overjoyed to find the property unscathed. This letter seemed to the older brother a reassuring omen after what must have been miserable years for William as a private in the Pioneer Corps, and it bore no trace of the morose despondency which had worried Harold during William's last, frustrating efforts to prove himself as an artist in London.

Consequently the shock must have been devastating when several weeks later a telephone call brought the news that William had died in Ferrara. As to the cause of death, Harold in his second volume of memoirs baldly states that he never discovered it. I can't think why. True, he had an acute sense of what social convention may deem shameful, and yet nobody more relished scandalous gossip in conversation. Perhaps it is enough to say that he was conditioned by a Catholic and Victorian upbringing. And yet the iconoclastic editor of *The Oxford Broom* proved loath to sweep away the cobwebs in obscure corners of his own existence when an accounting fell due. All the people I ever met who knew the Actons, and I met many, invariably said, when the subject of William's death was mentioned, that it had been a suicide. Harold wrote that William had been found unconscious in his bath. The people who must have been in a position to know said that the unhappy man had thrown himself out of a hotel window. An aged family retainer arranged for his burial in Florence, and it is doubtless true that fifty years ago a suicide would not have been deemed fit for interment in the very proper Allori Cemetery, where both his parents and elder brother were at length borne to join him.

Hortense Acton was prostrate, inconsolable. She shut herself up in her hotel room, refusing to see anyone. Whether or not she returned to Florence no longer made the least difference to her.

Not until late October 1945 was Harold finally demobilized and able, after a wearisome, difficult journey, to reach the gates of La Pietra. After years in India, Ceylon, London, Paris, and Germany it can only have been with deep emotion that he trudged up the long avenue of cypresses toward the Baroque façade of the palatial villa, gleaming in the sunset, where he had been born forty-one years before. It was unchanged. The great circular hall stood hushed save for the dripping of the marble fountain into a basin where goldfish hovered. In the immense *salone* beyond, Harold found his mother wrapped in a blanket and outstretched upon a velvet sofa with her eyes closed. He hesitated to disturb her. The sorrow of her expression when she looked up at him was alarming. She did not smile or pretend to be pleased. He realized that she could not bear to speak of William or allude to the profound difference it would have made for her if he had come back in Harold's place. Mrs. Acton was not a woman of large and gentle heart. Her husband took his son aside and questioned him about the death in Ferrara. That is what Harold wrote in his memoirs, asserting that he knew less than anyone, adding nonetheless that the servants who had seen William when he visited La Pietra had found him terribly changed, his complexion mottled, his manner incoherent and vague, altogether unlike his former self. It is possible that some phenomenal intervention in extremis might have saved him. No one will ever know, and speculation is idle, but Arthur Acton all the same spoke as though Harold should have been responsible for his brother's welfare. Be this as it may, the true cause of William Acton's death cannot conceivably have been a mystery to the Italian authorities or, consequently, to his family and their friends. I can imagine only one reason that may have been persuasive when it came to concealing the truth: perhaps William had not been alone in his final moments. If that had happened to be the fact, then a resolve to avert scandalous speculation would be understandable. An ironic twist to this unhappy misadventure came forty-six years later when Harold, having already affirmed in black and white that he knew nothing of the circumstances of his brother's death, asserted in an interview that William had been killed in action.

At this already-vexed and disconcerting moment, another reason for chagrin fell to Harold's lot. It contributed to his legend but diminished the satisfaction he derived from it, causing him annoyance to the end of his days. And never could he have foreseen that the author of such displeasure would be none other than his playmate from the golden days of Oxonian glory, the little faun, Evelyn Waugh. The two had always remained on friendly terms, no small testimony to Harold's tact, as the faun became notoriously irascible as he grew into a rubicund, stout, and frequently inebriated celebrity, a convert to Catholicism, the father of numerous children, and daredevil strategist of antic heroics during the war. Therefore, it can hardly have been with any sense of foreboding that Harold sat down to read Waugh's latest novel, *Brideshead Revisited*. Suffused with nostalgia for a vanished world, it begins at Oxford during the years when the two young authors were romantic dreamers together. Very soon, however, Harold must have grown uneasy. As described by Waugh, the rooms of Lord Sebastian Flyte, a beautiful but effete *fin de race* and one of the principal characters of the novel, were obviously those decorated to Harold's highly original taste, and at once there appears upon the scene a precious, outrageous, epicene individual called Anthony Blanche, poet and aesthete par excellence, given to such ostentatious expressions of his disdain for the philistine hoi polloi as bellowing *The Waste Land* through a megaphone from the balcony of his room, just as Harold had done on the occasion of a garden party honoring the League of Nations. Blanche appears periodically throughout the novel and eventually is viewed as a decadent and cynical, though wickedly comic, personage. Harold realized at once that readers who knew him would assume that he had been Waugh's model for this character. Familiar as he was with the background, he felt that the character was a composite, the other model being his old school flame and co-igniter of *The Eton Candle*, Brian Howard, who had spectacularly failed to fulfill his early promise and become a drunken drug addict, an habitué of squalid dives. He could still be very funny, but the laughter had a macabre ring, and he committed suicide in 1958 after the accidental death of his Irish boyfriend. Brian died and was forgotten, but Harold lived on, became legendary, and all his life was identified with Blanche. It galled. He referred to it as "the Blanche smear" and for nearly forty years felt compelled repeatedly to assert that he was *not* the character depicted by Waugh. But his friendship with the world-famous faun was too important to him to allow of any complaint addressed directly to the author of *Brideshead*, whom he consistently praises in his memoirs, although he skirts literary judgment of the novel, not one of Waugh's best albeit his most widely known.

All in all, as 1946 ushered in the atomic age and the tense decades of the cold war, Harold had every reason to feel a gnawing discontent with himself and his circumstances. As an author he had failed. Bald and overweight, at forty-one he looked a good deal older than his age, a fact which Acton *père* was only too pleased to point out. He had no idea what to do with himself. At La Pietra, his birthplace, he didn't feel at home. With his parents, he wrote, "I seemed to be talking as a stranger to indifferent strangers." His mother, not yet reconciled to her bereavement, remained glumly withdrawn. His father, restored to the love of his life, at once got busy trying to trace and retrieve the contents of the five other villas he owned, which had mostly been emptied by thieves when not wrecked by vandals. Suspicious and secretive, however, he did not invite his son to assist in this obsessive pursuit, which occupied him for several years to the exclusion of all else.

If return to Peking had been possible, Harold might very well have gone back to China, but that world was as lost as Atlantis. London beckoned, of course, for he had carefully kept in touch with old friends dating back to school days: Sitwells, Mitfords, Waughs, and others. And Uncle Guy generously offered a house in California and much more to go with it if the nephew would agree to change his nationality. But Harold did not find the United States to his aesthetic taste. The parental purse strings must have been somewhat loosened, for he was able to travel and was often abroad. But the question of a permanent residence nagged. And then there were his parents. They may not have loved or approved of him, but there they were, growing old in their enormous house, to which the gracious, entertaining, aristocratic friends of a bygone era would never again return. How would it look if their one remaining son went off to live elsewhere, leaving them all alone to die amid their deathless treasures? And then there was the villa. What was to become of La Pietra and its contents and its gardens when the present proprietors were gone? Arthur Acton never discussed this matter with his son, but Harold assumed that in the absence of any other logical claimant he would most probably fall heir to everything. What would be the likelihood of this inheritance, however, if he elected to live elsewhere? And then there was the city of Florence itself. More than any other, even Peking, it offered spiritual reconciliation and sustenance to the sad and indecisive aesthete. Looking down from the garden toward the towers and cupolas in the valley, he wrote, "Whatever constraint embarrassed me with my parents evaporated when I stood and gazed at this familiar view. To its potent harmony I felt I owed the vein of poetry in my nature which has never been adequately expressed." So it would inevitably be Florence and La Pietra that were to become the glorious, life-sustaining fixtures of the second half of his existence. He had asked the advice of his old friend Osbert Sitwell, who told him, "You owe it to the villa to stay on."

But what was he to do? Remembering Gertrude Stein's admonition, and mindful perhaps that her autobiography had brought both fame and cash, he decided to write a volume of memoirs. His motives, however, were, to say the least, mixed. He had not forgotten the "gross libel on his character" which had thwarted his ambiguous military ambitions. That wound had continued to fester. "My *Memoirs* was an act of vindication," he wrote later. And then, of course, there would be the delectable opportunity to settle a few scores, for Harold had the memory of a mastodon when it came to recalling slights, however trifling, or the want of zeal in others' appreciation of his talents. So he sat down and started to write.

At this juncture, having noted that Harold's motives were mixed, one may profitably take time to consider what manner of ambition is likely to animate a forty-two-year-old author who undertakes a work of autobiography. His life is in all likelihood but half lived, yet he must consider that first half to have been of sufficient singularity, vivacity, and superiority to justify its preservation from vulgar forgetfulness, including his own. He must in true humility regard himself as a rarity upon earth. And, to be sure, that is what he is, because few people take the trouble to write at all and even fewer dare to write about themselves. For a writer to do so is virtually tantamount to risking his life, because in order to maintain his integrity and his individuality the autobiographer must be willing and able to compose an accurate narrative of his past. Accuracy is all. To lose the fine and fragile thread of accuracy is to compromise the virtue of the outcome. And an ambition without virtue is like a schooner without sails; it is its own master, not the helmsman of an idea, much less of an ideal; it is at the mercy of the tides; it is a painted ship upon a painted ocean, an image rather than a reality. Harold's autobiographical ambition was of this variety. It was as an aesthete, the ferocious foe of the philistines, that he had crafted the Actonian legend, and *Memoirs of an Aesthete* is clearly meant to sustain and aggrandize that legend. It toys with the truth, trifles with candor, dwells upon all that is prestigious and sublime, leaving accuracy to drift in the doldrums of wistful speculation. Wistful because Harold could have been an author of noble attainment if he had had the fortitude to look the truth in the face and quite candidly account for what he saw. After all, Gide had done as much a generation before. But Gide cared nothing for the Lady Cunards and palatial villas of this world. Harold was deeply committed to appearances, and they make flimsy foundations for ambition. His memoirs are, in short, a fabrication, not intended to deceive but to create a vision satisfying to the middle-aged man obsessed by the memory of his glorious youth and to convince him that the image he gazes upon in the mirroring pool is the very same one that was so beguiling at age nineteen.

Since Harold was never one to be reticent about his doings, word of the work in progress got about, and the next time he ran into Evelyn Waugh the faun snapped, "This is probably the last time I shall speak to you," evidently fearful that Harold would recount embarrassing details of the Oxford days and vent spleen over "the Blanche smear." But he misjudged the versatility of Harold's scruples. Still, he had had cause to raise a cloud upon the horizon, for he knew very well what weight the truth would have in the scales of professional responsibility were he in his friend's place. When the book appeared, he wrote a letter of nearly effusive commendation. Other old friends were not so favored as the faun. Barbs abound. Philistines were punctiliously drawn and quartered. Among them, had he been daring, Harold would probably have included his own father, who resented his writing as an unprofitable hobby, remarking, as George III supposedly did to Gibbon, "Scribble, scribble, scribble." The remark was rude and ridiculous, all the more offensive, indeed, because Harold surely knew, as his father doubtless did not, that Gibbon, a writer of genius, the author not only of the magnificent *Decline and Fall* but also of an autobiography rightly admired as one of the most subtle and interesting in the English language, received little recognition in his lifetime, was personally ugly, affected in manner and speech, and a figure of ridicule. Paternal contempt and maternal indifference notwithstanding, Harold presently finished *Memoirs of an Aesthete*, concluding the final chapter with his departure from Peking in 1939. He felt that he had produced a competent, vivid, accurate history of his life and times, an opinion to which he enthusiastically subscribed once and for all. It is only fair to say that as a period piece the book possesses valid elements of interest and entertainment even today, for it is still in print, forty-six years after publication. It is dedicated to the memory of his brother, William.

If Harold thought well of his memoirs, however, this judgment was not shared by all and sundry, including some of his close friends.

Raymond Mortimer, who had written charitably of *Humdrum* and who was described in print by Harold as one of "the best of our younger critics," could not contain himself this time and wrote in *The New Statesman and Nation*,

Well off, precocious, cosmopolitan, devoted to the arts . . . Mr. Acton cannot hope to be forgiven by the enemies of promise . . . His memoirs are disfigured by pimples of malice hard to excuse in one who has been so fortunate . . . Perhaps so whole-hearted an aesthete cannot face the drudgery of writing as a professional. He skates over experiences instead of plumbing them.

And Nancy Mitford, so intimate with Harold as to be considered by him almost as a sister, wrote in a letter to her sister Diana, "Of course I agree with every word of Raymond's review. It makes me *cross* that Harold doesn't do better and so naughty all that slipshod writing, really inexcusable. Still I did like the book and so did Raymond." If so, they both enjoyed the dubious fun of hypocrisy.

Few distractions were to be had in Florence, and even less excitement. The latter existed, of course. In the environs of the fortress or among the groves of the public gardens, one could easily encounter lonely, penniless soldiers only too willing to provide pleasure for the price of a few packets of cigarettes. But so long as his parents lived, Harold was undoubtedly fearful of doing anything that might provoke gossip, much less scandal. And his mother's experience with the police served as a vivid reminder of the humiliating treatment liable to be inflicted upon rich and haughty foreigners insufficiently sensitive to Florentine vainglory. Though not easily intimidated, Harold tended to be prudent.

His friends in Florence were almost all much older than he— the closest, most interesting, and eminent of these being Bernard Berenson, the ineffable B.B., for whom Harold felt an affection close to veneration and whose Villa I Tatti in Settignano seemed more a home to him than cheerless La Pietra. Born in 1865, B.B. could have been Harold's grandfather, but he was spry and intellectually alert, interested not only in art but in physics, entomology, finance, and almost everything under the sun, including licentious gossip. He, too, despite his brilliant writings on art, felt that he had not fulfilled himself as a creative personality. Maybe he was too preoccupied by glory and money, though the devious intricacies of his dealings with the rapacious art dealer Joseph Duveen were not yet public knowledge. Harold and B.B. found much to talk about as they went for long rambles around the Tuscan countryside, admiring vistas that might have provided backgrounds for the paintings of Sassetta, Benozzo Gozzoli, or Pinturicchio. There were also a few princesses, countesses, plus a commoner or two whose company Harold found agreeable. But he longed for companionship more intimate, exhilarating, and heartwarming than any to be found—or sustained—in Florence. So he set out to travel. He went to London, to Ireland, to Mexico, to Yucatán, and all around the United States, and everywhere he made it his business not only to study art and architecture but also to meet interesting, entertaining people who were friends of friends or of relatives, who had heard of him from this person or that, who might even have read a book of his or an article about him, who knew or assumed that he was an individual of consequence, acquainted with the noble and famous of the world, a rather legendary figure, in short. So he was made much of, and the truth is that Harold repaid attention wonderfully well, because he was witty, original, erudite, a bit indecorous, with his towering physique, quavering elocution, jade ring, and slightly off-center gait when walking. There was nobody else like Harold Acton, never had been and never will be. He was uniquely unique, knew it, and knew how to let others know it.

2

The Sergeant returned to New York from the years of social renown in London as soon as the war was over. His brilliant reputation, slightly dimmed by transatlantic shipment, proved nonetheless considerable in Manhattan, where he established himself in a stylish apartment at 330 East Seventy-first Street on the Upper East Side and easily assumed a prominent place among the social and homosexual elite. And why not? Though he had begun to go bald, he was still handsome, witty, a considerate and entertaining host, anxious to please and well able to do so with felicitous versatility. He presently began to write art criticism for *The New York Times*, which added to his prestige, and his articles were polished, urbane, and crafted to please. They suffered, however, from the same defect to which Lady Cunard had objected in Stuart's conversation: they never said anything memorable or contributed penetrating and authoritative comment upon the revolutionary artistic developments of that very memorable era. But critics like Clement Greenberg did the job. And nobody much cared whether Stuart made a lot of difference to Pollock, Rothko, de Kooning and Co. so long as his bland and fluent articles week after week confirmed his status as a cultivated gentleman and a chap to be cultivated. It was art, appropriately enough, that brought the two of us together. I haunted the New York galleries for my pleasure, he did so for his profession. It is easy to strike up a conversation and an acquaintance with the help of Picasso or Cézanne. It was in December 1950 that I first met Stuart. He invited me to dinner.

I saw a good deal of him after this, learning with pleasure—or should I say because of it?—how extensive and compelling his charm could be. In addition, he was very kind to me, invited me to his own parties, took me along to others, and introduced me to a quantity of people: Tom Prentiss and Zane Rhodes, Peter Mitchell, Keene Curtis, Ruth Ford, Cliff Baron, George Platt Lynes, Monroe Wheeler and Glenway Westcott, who in turn introduced me to Kenneth Clark, Marianne Moore, and the antique Ava, Lady Ribblesdale. And through people I can't remember I met Edward James and Tilly Losch, Onni Sari, Andres Devendorf, Sheila St. Lawrence, Alan Shayne, Ima Ebin, Malcolm Dekker, Gene Waterbury, Joel Bennett, and many others. Notebooks filled with names. Diaries of lunches with Stuart, dinners with Monroe and Glenway (once with Dr. Kinsey), movies with Bill Miller, the handsomest man of his generation, evenings at the Blue Parrot Bar with Tennessee Williams, numerous nights with boys whose names I never learned or wrote down: all those people, some of whom no longer have any faces, many of whom had no identities, to whom I today, be they by any chance alive, mean no more than they to me, nonentities summoned from a lifetime conditioned by rash trust in the kindness of strangers. I had a very good time, and all this while, living at my parents' home in Englewood, New Jersey, just across the river from Manhattan, I arrogantly kept on working to prove myself as a writer.

The Cost of the Villa

On Saturday, February 3, 1951, I went to New York to see the Italian film *Riso Amaro*, a mediocre melodrama of the neorealist category, and after dinner and visits to a few bars made my way to one of New York's most notorious bars. There I ran into Stuart and a man named Bernie Weinbaum, a friend of everybody's friends. We were amused to meet in such surroundings and had a few minutes' chat before pursuing our salacious objectives. Stuart mentioned that he was giving a party the following evening for his old friend Harold Acton and invited me to come. Having read both *Brideshead* and *Memoirs of an Aesthete*, I knew very well who Harold was and what he represented. It was, and always has been, my keen desire to become acquainted with men and women who have contributed to the artistic history of my era. To have known Picasso and Giacometti, to have met Stravinsky and corresponded with Thomas Mann, for example, means far more to me than if I had been familiar with President Roosevelt, Albert Einstein, or one of the popes. Painters, writers, composers—I can't tell why—were from my early youth the objects of my longing to feel, and to express, emotional and intellectual admiration. Consequently, I was delighted to accept Stuart's invitation. I don't think I ever told Harold of the indelicate locus in which it was extended, but if I had, I imagine he might have said, "My dear, what an auspicious purlieu from which to embark for Cythera!"

I arrived precisely at the specified time and was rather taken aback to find that all the other guests were already present. These, in addition to Harold, were Tom Prentiss, a lanky, handsome lad with Titian hair; Bernie Weinbaum, fleshy and talkative; and a shy young fellow named Robin. So we were six. Harold easily dominated the soirée, being the largest, oldest, and most eminent individual present. And he clearly took it for granted that, as the party was in his honor anyway, he was expected not only to dominate but also to distinguish the occasion. That's what he did, and he did it with such polite and natural gusto that one would have had to be a fool not to sit back with composure and enjoy the performance. So much has been written about Harold's conversational brio that it seems almost impertinent to add another word, but I will. He hovered over his elocution like a hummingbird, darting from one brilliant rhetorical blossom to another with exquisite modulations of tone, a flash of the eye, a wave of the hand, and he invited lucky listeners to join in the appreciation of exotic nectars. One didn't necessarily care too much about what he said. Oh, he was interesting, erudite, and all that, of course, but his talk was a kind of music. It could be wicked as well as witty, too, and he relished discussing the ins and outs of sexuality, what people did to each other in bed or, for that matter, chained to radiators or naked in the parks of Peking. He hated New York, despised the contemporary painting which was flourishing there, and yet he was excited by the frantic rhythm of the city, the blaring radios, the neon signs, the stampede of traffic, and the casual fever of intimate encounters. We all had a very convivial time, laughing, drinking, and behaving like naughty but clever schoolboys, which is how homosexuals often enjoy behaving when among themselves. As it happened, my parents and grandmother had gone off to California the previous Friday, so I was all alone in their house with amiable and capable servants. And I impulsively thought that nothing would be more fun than to duplicate this party in Englewood the following Saturday. Everyone else found the prospect agreeable, and the date was set. Since I had to drive back to New Jersey, I got up to go at about midnight, whereupon Harold, who had paid me no exceptional attention till then, asked if I could drop him at his hotel. I gladly consented. He was staying at the Blackstone just off Park Avenue on Fifty-second Street.

As soon as we were in my car, Harold delighted and flattered me by saying that he had been much impressed by a short story of mine published just a year before in *Horizon*, the English review edited by Cyril Connolly. "Now we all know," he added, "that Cyril is an appalling shit, said to have emptied the cash box at *Horizon* every time the travel bug bit him. People tell me he's obsessed by the beauty of his private parts, compensation, I suppose, for possessing the physiognomy of a baboon. But he has the taste of an angel when it comes to literature. A tribute to your talent, my dear."

I thought it only fair to respond by saying how much I had admired and enjoyed *Memoirs of an Aesthete*. Harold was self-deprecating, remarked that Cyril had hated the book and that, in any case, he himself had neither the ambition nor the ability to compete with stylish but styleless authors like Norman Mailer and Gore Vidal, for whom he felt nothing but contempt. His writing, he added, aspired only to please a public attuned to the discrimination of Pater and the coherence of Strachey. So he could hardly hope for bestsellerdom, which, of course, was the high road to oblivion. When we got to the hotel, he said that he would be happy if I could dine with him the following Thursday. Then we could talk more at leisure. I accepted with what was surely unbecoming haste.

We met in the lobby at eight, Harold already there before me, very dapper in a rather Edwardian way, wearing a long overcoat and carrying a black Homburg and gray suede gloves, all smiles. As we went toward the door, a tall, willowy man of about Harold's age came in. They greeted each other with evident surprise and Harold said, "My dear, what on earth brings you to this Babylon?"

"I've come to b-b-buy a b-b-blast furnace," said the other.

The man, when Harold introduced us, proved to be Michael Duff. He was in a hurry and went off after a limp handshake, promising to call Harold in the morning. He was, I was told, the owner of vast estates, coal and iron mines in Wales, and lived in splendor in a great mansion called Vaynol Park. His mother, Lady Juliet Duff, had been one of the principal patrons of Diaghilev during his great London days. The stutter was amusing, and used for effect, rather like that of Mr. Maugham, and I wondered whether Waugh had taken from Michael Duff that idiosyncrasy of Anthony Blanche, because Harold had no trace of a stutter.

We went to a very elegant and expensive restaurant called Le Pavillon. Harold put himself out to be charming, and he was very, very good at that. He talked about Italy, about B.B., Norman Douglas and the Sitwells, Evelyn Waugh, and members of the Manchu dynasty he had known in China. He told stories about highly respectable gentlemen who yearned to be pissed on in public; he described immense temples in Ceylon. I couldn't list all the things he spoke about. But he didn't talk in the least to the exclusion of my presence. He was expert at drawing one into a discourse that had nothing whatever to do with one's own experience, so that when he described the wonders of the Forbidden City, one was invited to respond as though all those fabulous palaces were as familiar as Rockefeller Center. I was dazzled, as no doubt Harold meant I should be. But on both sides there was nothing wrong about that. The dazzle, however, needless to say, was not being ignited for nothing. The assumption on both sides, I suppose, was that sooner or later this would lead to a pounce. And why not? Harold was a sensitive and cultivated gentleman, so there was no reason to suppose that the pounce would be savage. He was not attractive to me physically and seemed, it's true, older than forty-six. As I was then twenty-eight, the difference counted. However, I'd already been to bed with men even older and less attractive because I liked them personally. This entailed no sacrifice. I was glad to give pleasure without myself enjoying much, and it occurred to me at the time that when I grew older, I'd be pleased if attractive young men occasionally did as much for me; and that, indeed, is how it has turned out.

The wine was excellent. We drank two bottles and were both a bit tipsy when we left the restaurant. On the way back to the Blackstone, Harold told me about all the marvelous chiantis he'd drunk while on walking tours with Scott Moncrieff and Norman Douglas, who could not be kept from fondling little boys in every village they passed through. He leaned on my arm as he talked, and we weaved a bit walking down Park Avenue, making something of a spectacle of ourselves, I suppose. When we came to the entrance of the hotel, I thought he might invite me to his room for a nightcap, but he didn't. He merely said that he looked forward with delight to the dinner party at my parents' home in Englewood. He had hired a car and would bring the whole group with him. I provided precise instructions on how to reach the house. And then I thanked him for the marvelous evening and went off into the night.

The party, I thought, was a great success, described so, anyway, in my journal. At least, there was plenty to eat and drink. I've no idea what my guests might have thought of the conventional and rather Victorian domicile of my parents, but they were polite. When I later became familiar with La Pietra, I reflected that Harold must have considered the house in Englewood a bourgeois hovel in execrable taste. I thought it pretty plain myself, except for the carpets, all of which were beautiful, bought perchance by Granny, who had no eye whatsoever for quality in interior decoration. After the dinner and a few more drinks, we all went back to New York in Harold's limousine and ended our evening at the Blue Parrot.

The next day, Sunday, I had lunch with Harold, Stuart, and Tom Prentiss, at whom Stuart gazed romantically. We went to the

Frick Collection, to two cocktail parties, and I had dinner alone with Harold. The dazzle was again as vivacious and beguiling as before. But there was no pounce. It came the following Tuesday afternoon, just eleven days after our first meeting. It was pleasurable enough, and there was no doubt that Harold enjoyed himself thoroughly. I was glad of that. There were expressions of endearment, slightly embarrassing since I couldn't very well respond in kind, but that didn't seem to matter. At all events, we spent an agreeable afternoon and had tea in Harold's room.

I had decided by that time to return soon to Europe, leaving only ten days later on the *Queen Mary*. Harold expressed regret at my imminent departure, but anticipated that by mid-April he would be back in Florence and hoped that I might come to visit him there. I said the prospect seemed delightful but that travel would depend on my resources. So we'd see.

The following Friday we dined with Michael Duff, who was having difficulty obtaining the b-b-blasted furnace and was annoyed with his mother for living with a far younger man called Simon Fleet, whose name wasn't Fleet at all but who had been in the navy during the war and assumed that name afterward because he thought it euphonious. "S-S-Simon Cheap," said Michael. But he was pleased because the Aga Khan had given Lady Juliet a golden elephant encrusted with gems. He invited me to visit him in Wales, but after that evening I never saw him again.

The next day I had lunch with Harold and a lady named Mrs. Costa, a literary bluestocking, who invited me to a party at her home the following Friday, during which W. H. Auden would read some of his recent poems. I accepted gladly. Afterward Harold and I went back to the Blackstone, where we spent most of the afternoon pleasantly enough, then took a taxi to Stuart's for tea. We dined alone together, going afterward to a party at the apartment of an extravagant fop named Peter Lindamood.

It wasn't until the following Wednesday, two days before my departure, that Harold and I again dined alone together, though in the meanwhile we had spoken daily on the telephone. By this time, which was just two weeks after our first meeting, it would be fair to say that if Harold and I had not become exactly intimate friends, we were nevertheless both intimate and friendly, and the future seemed to promise that both friendship and intimacy would fuse, making for a relationship affectionate enough to endure the test of decades.

Harold and I dined together yet again the next day, and once more the day after, going later to Mrs. Costa's party. Auden, as promised, was there and read with serene composure from his latest book, called *Nones*. One of the poems, "The Fall of Rome," made a profound impression on me. I thought it a masterpiece and imagined that hearing Schubert play one of his sonatas must have been something like that. Though I ran into him from time to time, I never knew Auden well and regretted it. I had to leave the party early to go on board ship. The farewell and "bon voyage" from Harold was fond, but we had no idea when we might meet again.

I had been absent from Paris for only four months, leaving behind my friend Bernard Minoret, with whom I had constantly corresponded during the absence, his letters alternately affectionate or fiercely irritable. I don't think I mentioned Bernard to Harold, but I did tell Bernard that I had made the acquaintance of Harold Acton, and he was adequately impressed, not by the aesthete, however, but by the social celebrity, friend of Lady Cunard and Sybil Colefax. Bernard, intelligent and subtle though he was and is, always cared much for society, the aristocracy, all the doings of the beau monde, dull though many of them were. And today they seem even duller than forty years ago.

Bernard had made plans, something he did readily in those days, whereas now it seems quite an expedition for him to leave the seventh arrondissement. The prospect of spending a rainy spring in Paris held no appeal, so he decided that we should go to Naples, where a former lover of his, a Pole named Kot, was then living with his parents—in very reduced circumstances, alas, having before the war been prominent and wealthy in Warsaw. With Kot's help, Bernard felt, we would be able to find pleasant lodgings in a pretty spot in the Neapolitan area. We would depart exactly a fortnight after my arrival.

A few days before leaving, I received a letter from Harold, the first of many written over thirty-five years. I quote in part:

The Cost of the Villa

New York
6 March 1951

Dearest James,

*Your entrancing letter has just reached me, and I hasten to
reply before launching on another day of hectic discourse . . .
Your departure was a sad wrench, and everything seemed col-
orless for a while. No doubt the color will return when we meet
again. You touched me to the core and I reveled in your company . . . However, I confess I have met a charming young artist who toils as a waiter in a Greenwich Village restaurant for
a living and I am decidedly smitten by his curious combination
of beauty and insouciance and startled gazelle air, not to mention the pathos and squalor of his conditions. I hope to be of
some use to him. I met him at a fantastic exhibition of lace at
Johnny Myers's gallery, and amid eighteenth-century fans,
black mantillas, early Victorian parasols my eyes goggled at
the artist in blue denims dreaming in the haloed background.
As usual, I fear, he prefers his own age, and I foresee an era of
desperate frustration ahead—until I see you, and by then you
will be heavily engaged, what a life . . .*

Blessings on you, and all success,

your ever affectionate,
Harold

I replied, telling him that I was about to set off with a friend
for Naples, where we hoped to find a flowery hideaway with the
assistance of our friend Kot, whom Harold, who knew everyone,
naturally had met. We traveled by train, an overnight journey, arriving at ten-thirty a.m. Kot, a charming, cultivated, worldly man,
was indeed a great help, guiding us along the coast to towns like
Vico Equense and Seiano, where unfortunately we found nothing
suitable. Bernard suggested Capri, but Kot wasn't very keen about
taking us there, because an American painter named Bernard Perlin,
with whom he happened to be having an affair, was at present on
that famous isle, and the prospect of placing in proximity a former
lover with the present one wasn't inviting. But he took us anyway,
and we were very lucky, finding a sumptuous apartment in an immense villa called the Ca' del Sole. It had a beautiful garden and

came with a good-natured lady who would cook and clean house for us. All this, moreover, approximately within our means. The proprietor, a Greek named Mitsotakis, apparently made only rare visits. So we unpacked our suitcases, and the very next day I began a novel, an autobiographical, self-indulgent, mediocre piece of work, my first book to be published, and, oddly enough, praised by reviewers.

Some days later I had a letter from Harold.

> *New York*
> *24 March 1951*
>
> *Carissimo James,*
>
> *Easter greetings! I have recently returned from Chicago with your letter in my pocket as a sort of talisman. So you are off to Naples. How wise. I wish I were with you now . . .*
>
> *In Capri you will find Norman Douglas and Kenneth Macpherson at the Villa Tuoro.*
>
> *I expect to return to Florence towards the tenth of April . . . to remain until at least the end of May, when I too hope to proceed to Naples and look for an apartment there. Why don't you come to Florence for a while? The Villa Natalia on via Bolognese (an hotel rented from my papa) might suit you. Evelyn W. and Graham Greene adored it and could work there. We might make a few trips together, but I'm personally more in the mood for settling down and concentrating on the Neapolitan area, since I also have a book to write and have idled far too long, alas. Dearest, what is this talk about a "parasite for consolation"? I love you more and more, and realize it more and more since your departure. Together we might find the bluebird of happiness. Je t'embrasse tendrement.*
>
> *Yours ever,*
> *Harold*

Life in Capri was delightful. An enormous wisteria vine in full bloom covered one end of the villa, and in its shade on the terrace below we often had lunch, prepared and served by the motherly *femme de ménage*. There were people to meet. Bernard Perlin and his friend Letitia Alvarez de Toledo, Kenneth Macpherson, whom

I didn't much like, and his guest, the aged author Norman Douglas, who was to be met almost daily in the piazza fondling some young boy. We were invited to parties, at one of which, given by a tiresome woman called Charlotte Schneersen, we were introduced to Edda Ciano, Mussolini's daughter. Kot came over from Naples fairly often. Frederic Prokosch turned up for a while. And all this time I kept busily at work on my novel. Letters arrived from Harold.

> New York
> 3 April 1951

Dearest James,

I write in haste . . . I really don't know why I have lingered so long, for I'm heartily sick of this sterilely sociable train train. *A pretty little Narcissist led me up the garden path. I had not yet discovered to what lengths Narcissists will go. If only they would stick to masturbation instead of troubling old satyrs like myself! The episode has been rather tantalizing and has left me decidedly sour. I am sorry your family is being so tiresome and do hope they will behave more generously. In the meantime,* faute de mieux, *I enclose a little cheque, which I should like to increase but for my comparative limitation of dollars. Most of my money is in England, alas . . . I hope this reaches you soon with all my love.*

> *Yours ever,*
> *Harold*

The check was for a hundred dollars, a very appreciable sum in those days, and most gratefully received. I had evidently complained in a letter to Harold that my parents did not give me enough to live on, which would have been untrue had I been prepared to live more frugally. Ironically enough, five days before receiving Harold's check, I had received one from my mother, so my complaints must have been extensive.

Harold's next letter was written from La Pietra. I had evidently written to him in the meantime saying that I would be glad to come to Florence.

Florence
16 April 1951

Dearest James,

I was delighted to find your letter awaiting me, and to hear that you are thriving. It is absurd to have qualms about a cheque. I always cash such things immediately. Should your difficulties continue, I trust you will let me know. I think I deserve your confidence, and naturally I should like to be able to oblige you.

Do you see Norman Douglas these days? I was worried to hear that he has been showing signs of wear, if not tear, and of too many liters of local wine. Please give him a hug for me. Yes, Kenneth is never extravagantly friendly, but I enjoy his company when with Uncle Norman . . . I fear me there is no chance of my visiting the south yet a while. Having just arrived, I've an Italian lecture to prepare and all sorts of local engagements. Let me know before you arrive and I'll engage a room for you at the Natalia, as my guest. My father gave me the most frigid of welcomes. After the warmth of America it was indeed depressing, but such has been my fate for years— ever since I can remember . . .

I broke with the Narcissist, whom you probably would not know, a beauty but a monster of selfishness and Greenwich Village arrogance. However, I had a couple of flings elsewhere to take my mind off the frustration he had created in me, and I'm beginning to feel calmer by now . . .

I only arrived last night, so write in haste.

Ever yours affectionately,
Harold

It sounded as though I was going to find a rather morose friend in Florence, not a very exhilarating expectation, and yet I looked forward with true pleasure to seeing Harold again and was excited at the prospect of visiting the great villa and meeting all the interesting people, including the famed B.B., about whom I had heard so much. Thus, it was with a sense of significant arrival that I came on May 9 to the Pension Villa Natalia, named in honor of a deposed Balkan queen who had resided there before the war. I found a note of welcome from Harold, inviting me to dine with him in town that evening. He came to fetch me about eight and we went down to Florence by bus. He explained that he was not permitted to use any of the family automobiles, this prohibition being but one tactic in his father's campaign of hostility toward him. Others included reading his mail, inspecting the stubs of his checkbook, and searching among his personal effects, all this to furnish ammunition for wounding remarks delivered in front of other people during meals or at tea. Happily, however, he didn't see his father very often, as he was slowly dying of cancer and spent most of his time in an enormous upstairs bathroom, drinking Champagne, shouting at the servants, and gossiping with shady antique dealers. His mother was constantly on the razor's edge of hysteria. And he himself, though yearning for escape from this nerve-racking tangle of vexation, felt paralyzed by the tension between a sense of duty toward parents who didn't care for him and his desire to make an independent life for himself and fulfill his literary aspirations. It was, I had to admit, an unhappy predicament. And I had not yet visited La Pietra, which added still another dimension to the traumatic knot. There were further humiliations, too, Harold added, as I would later see for myself. However, his natural good cheer, aided by plenty of wine, asserted itself during dinner. He told me about his visit to Chicago after my departure and all the details, some of them in retrospect honestly funny, of his imbroglio with the beastly Narcissist. We had a jolly time and after dinner sat in a café in front of the Palazzo Vecchio and drank grappa.

It was late when we got up to go. The buses were no longer running, so we had to take a taxi. Harold gave the driver instructions, then asked me whether, since the front gates of La Pietra were locked by ten o'clock, I would mind going round with him to the rear entrance, which would oblige me to return on foot down the via Bolognese to the Villa Natalia, a distance of only a few hundred yards. The taxi left us on the main road and we made our way in the dark along a lane beside the rear wall of the villa. Before we had gone very far Harold put his hand on my shoulder. Then there was some amorous, excitable fumbling in the warm May night. We lay down in the grass. I wondered whether this was the lane where Harold as a boy had seen lovers lingering and later had envied them their innocent, heterosexual bliss. Afterward Harold said, "And now, my dear, I must scale the wall. I haven't even a key to the back gate. Wouldn't you think, at the age of forty-six? My father really is a beast." When he went out in the evening, he explained, a door or window had to be left open for him to reenter the villa, an expedient which, if his father learned of it, would infuriate the old man, who lived in terror of thieves. The next morning after breakfast, Harold said, I must walk across the fields from Natalia to La Pietra and he would show me round the villa and gardens. With that, he clambered up the rather high wall with remarkable agility and, waving cheerily from the summit, disappeared into the dark. It was rather like something from *Alice in Wonderland*. I later learned that he always crossed the wall at the same spot, where handholds and footholds had been let into the masonry. Still, it *was* grotesque that an only son, the heir to this great estate, should be obliged to climb over a back wall in order to return home at night.

The next day I walked across fields awash with wildflowers under the silvery olive trees and came up to La Pietra at the end of the long avenue bordered on either side by venerable cypresses. The villa would be difficult to describe, too huge and grand, with too many statues, urns, gates. At the great front entrance I was admitted by a majordomo in navy-blue livery, a tailcoat with a silver chain and large silver buttons. He led me through a vestibule into a hall already crowded with carved chests, marble sculpture, and many paintings in tarnished gilt frames, thence to a rotunda which let dim light fall from a glass dome high above onto a faintly dripping fountain and from which a wide staircase curved upward and upward, the walls above frescoed with scenes à la Tiepolo, though not by the master himself. All this was quite overwhelming, and no doubt meant to be. Harold waited in an immense *salone* facing the gardens. Vaulted ceiling, high windows in deep embrasures, walls covered with paintings, sculptures on pedestals, red velvet furniture, lacquer tables, jeweled snuffboxes, and portraits in silver frames of royal personages who had been guests at the villa. My host was jovial, and if he perceived that I was overawed, as I was, by so much magnificence, he tactfully gave no sign of it. He escorted me round the great rooms on the ground floor, pointing out works by this artist and that, almost all unknown to me, though a small marble torso was "attributed" to Michelangelo and a marble relief of the Virgin and Child by Donatello hung in the vast dining room. Then we went out into the gardens, which were also magnificent and vast, filled with statuary and unexpected vistas, none of which I could possibly attempt to describe. Harold was an excellent guide, knew the name of every statue and often that of the sculptor. He had something to say about almost every twist and turn of the itinerary, which I learned in time to be invariably the same—both itinerary and commentary, that is. What I liked most about the gardens, perhaps, was the kitchen garden, the so-called *limonaia*, with its lemon trees in huge terra-cotta pots and its rows of vegetables, surrounded by high yellow walls decorated in rococo design with inlaid shells and pebbles. A side door led back into the villa via a corridor lined with Roman portrait busts in marble. The complete tour took almost two hours. "Sometimes I feel like a hired guide," Harold said. "But the re- muneration, my dear, the remuneration! That is another matter." I didn't yet understand just what he meant. He then explained that there were guests coming to lunch, so I would have to return to the Villa Natalia for my midday meal, as he could not take it upon himself to invite me to lunch. His mother must issue that invitation and would surely do so in time. Meanwhile, I would be welcome for tea every day if I wished and we could often dine together in town, but discretion forbade his coming to visit me in my room at the Natalia, because servants talked and would be only too pleased to tell tales to his father. "They're all Communists," Harold said. "Steal food and drink as if they were starving. Shameless. And not as if they didn't receive perfectly adequate wages—the footmen and gardeners ten dollars a month, the majordomo, butler, and chef fifteen. But it's never enough." Ten dollars a month in 1951 may have been enough for survival, but it was certainly not a lavish wage.

I went back for tea, and that was my first introduction to Mrs. Acton, a very memorable lady. She was, indeed, unusually small, with silver-white hair, pinched features, bright red lips, attired at tea time invariably in a superb Japanese kimono, of which she must have had a large collection, and wearing on her left wrist two wide, flexible diamond bracelets of the style fashionable in the thirties. Tea at La Pietra during her time—I might almost say reign—was a strict ritual. The vermeil service was set out on a large table in front of the velvet couch in the far left corner of the *salone* under the window. She poured, and two footmen in livery passed the cups around to the guests, each of whom had a small lacquer table close at hand. There were very thin, very delicious sandwiches but no cakes. Conversation was general, not necessarily elevated or intellectual, any topic not indecorous acceptable, gossip welcome. People of any note or distinction, friends of friends, and even those with the most tenuous of connections were welcome to tea at La Pietra. That first day we were six or seven, one of the others being Angus Wilson, the English writer, not yet famous, having till then published only short stories. After tea came an inevitable tour of the gardens, exactly as I had had it only that morning, with the very same commentary by Harold. He must have learned it by heart.

Teatime guests were not taken round the interior of the villa. After the garden tour came the cocktail hour, tea service and cups having meanwhile disappeared. The cocktails were always dry martinis, prepared with some ceremony by Mrs. Acton in an enormous silver shaker, proportions being approximately a thimbleful of vermouth to a bottle of gin poured over a minimum of ice, stirred but not shaken by the hostess, glasses passed round by the footmen. Mrs. Acton liked her martinis and liked her guests to like them. After the first round she would pass with the shaker, urging everyone to drink up. On that first afternoon she made a remark that gave me my first glimpse of her character. All the others save I had taken their leave, accompanied by Harold toward the front door. Mrs. Acton alone hovered by the cocktail table, and as I approached to thank her for her hospitality, she lifted the shaker and waved it back and forth. There was still some left, and she said, "Do have another."

"But I've already had three, Mrs. Acton," I protested, "and I don't think I could cope with another."

"Come along," she insisted. "It's mostly ice water by now anyway, and I don't want to leave a drop for the servants."

I couldn't very well refuse, though it was not ice water. When Harold returned, he looked startled to see me with yet another cocktail. I left as promptly as I could, too tipsy for pleasure. Harold, no shirker himself when it came to the bottle, remarked as he accompanied me to the door that he had not known I was so fond of cocktails. I could hardly explain, only protesting that by the time he came to fetch me to go into town for dinner I would be perfectly sober. Thereafter I went many times to tea at La Pietra but was never again the last to bid good-bye to Mrs. Acton. And as I thought of it I felt that if the servants were, in fact, Communists, circumstances offered a luxurious apologia for their convictions.

I saw Harold almost every day either for lunch, tea, or dinner, sometimes all three. We had very good times together, laughed a lot, and, to be sure, got drunk more than once. He was a supremely competent guide to Florence, knew every crevice of the city intimately, and sent me to see many a wonder I would otherwise have missed. He took me to cocktail parties in palaces and to dinners in outlying villas. At one of these cocktail parties, a reception really, given by the Countess Serristori in her immense palazzo, Harold suddenly gripped my arm and whispered, "Don't look round. We must leave here at once. I'll explain outside." As we walked back toward the Ponte Vecchio, he told me that a woman I had not noticed was following him through the crowd and he feared she might make some highly embarrassing scene, as she'd been known to do in the past, because she claimed to be Harold's half sister, one of Arthur Acton's illegitimate offspring. "It's too hateful of him to have inflicted this upon us, too," Harold muttered, "along with all the rest."

Then there was the ceremonial visit to I Tatti to meet the venerable B.B., aged eighty-six but spry and shrewd. I didn't like him, feeling his self-aggrandizement almost brazen and embarrassed by the sycophantic attitudes of his entourage and admirers, including Harold. He also introduced me to a quantity of other people, some of whom were delightful and became friends, like Henry McIlhenny, some of whom were vain and tiresome, like Violet Trefusis. Stuart Preston was also in town, as well as Somerset Maugham with his secretary, Allan Searle, and John Horne Burns, an American writer now forgotten, with his Italian boyfriend; and the bar at the Excelsior Hotel was a busy place every day before dinner.

It was exactly two weeks after my arrival in Florence that Mrs. Acton invited me to lunch at La Pietra. And on this occasion I had further opportunity to evaluate the lady's character. We were fourteen in all at the great round table in the rather gloomy dining room, one of the few in the villa unchanged since the fifteenth century, and to my surprise one of the fourteen was Arthur Acton. This was the only time I ever saw him, and he assuredly appeared an unattractive, peevish individual, speaking very little and scowling at the guests. But as I occasionally observed him during the meal, I noticed that his eyes would sometimes turn to the walls and the works of art adorning them, and then his features became transfigured by a sort of gentle, almost benign expression of contentment. It seemed evident that those inanimate creations awakened in him an affection and a pride which human relationships could not provide.

Mrs. Acton, indifferent for some reason to the dictates of protocol, placed me to her right, though Mr. Maugham, older, also a foreigner and infinitely distinguished, deserved the place of honor. To her left was placed a woman rather than a man, and it is true that more women than men were present at the table. This woman, like Mrs. Acton and myself, was an American, whose unconventional origins and picturesque past would have provided excellent material for Edith Wharton. Unfortunately her story is too long to be related here. She had married a British peer named Lord Bateman, lived part of the year in London, part in Monte Carlo, and every spring visited Florence, where she stayed at the Grand Hotel and almost daily gave lavish luncheon parties, followed by afternoons of bridge. She was a favorite of Willie Maugham, a skilled devotee of that game. At all events, during the meal she related a bit of recent Monte Carlo gossip. It appeared that a very rich elderly woman who spent most of the winter at the Ritz in Paris and most of the summer at the Hôtel de Paris in Monte Carlo had recently surprised her friends by selling her Rolls-Royce to a Monegasque garage but keeping on her chauffeur and renting the automobile from the garage. And then one day she was found dead in her suite, a suicide. It came out that she had lost or squandered her fortune but was determined to go on living as she always had until the very last penny was spent, then end her life.

"And how did she do that?" asked Mrs. Acton, who had listened to the story with concentration.

"Pills," said Lady Bateman.

"Oh, I think that's so very sensible," exclaimed Mrs. Acton, "so very much more sensible than all those ridiculous men who throw themselves out of windows.''

After that statement I could think of nothing but her own son throughout the rest of the meal. I'm sure Harold didn't hear it, as he was seated on the far side of the table near his father. I naturally never mentioned it to him, and left La Pietra immediately after coffee to hurry back to the Natalia to write down what had happened.

Bernard had returned to Paris, whence he wrote captious letters insisting that I meet him in Austria no later than mid-June. It was obvious that I couldn't stay on forever in Florence as Harold's guest, nor did I honestly desire to. And Harold himself longed for a vacation near Naples, a change from the oppressive and humiliating routine of life at La Pietra. But first he wanted to go with me on a little trip to some peaceful spot where we could be entirely alone together. I was happy to agree. He selected Lucca, a town of much beauty and unparalleled charm where I later spent several delightful summers. We went there by bus on Thursday, June 7, and stayed for a couple of days at the Hotel Universo in the center of town. Harold knew Lucca nearly as well as Florence and showed me all the wonders and curiosities of the place, which were many. In the evening before dinner we sat on the terrace of the café at the corner of the Piazza San Michele, drank white wine, and smoked cigarettes as the sun went down beyond the extraordinary church and the house where Puccini was born. After dinner we strolled under immense syca-mores along the fortified ramparts of the city, intact round its entire circumference, and Harold told me the entire history of Lucca from Roman times onward, stories of strife between Guelphs and Ghi-bellines, wars with Florence and Pisa, the rule of tyrants like Castruccio Castracani, the transformation of the place from a republic to a principality by Napoléon for his sister Elisa and brother-in-law Felice Baciocchi, and so on. The people and events he described he seemed to have known and experienced personally. Entrancing to listen to, he made an ordinary anecdote extraordinary by nuances of intonation and vocabulary that seemed inexhaustible. Being with him, one felt singularly privileged, because he had been everywhere and known everybody, and the keen sense of privilege one felt in his presence amply confirmed that fact. The next day we went to a nearby town called Collodi, and there, hidden in the gardens of the Villa Garzoni, Harold showed me a beautiful little Baroque bathhouse where chamber music had been played centuries before from a discreet, curvaceous balcony while the lords—and ladies?—of the villa splashed below. It was a happy time that we spent together in Lucca, taking the bus back to Florence on Saturday.

At tea that day Mrs. Acton herself invited me to go with her and Harold to the opera the following afternoon to hear a sensational, as-yet-little-known soprano called Maria Callas in an opera by Haydn which, for some unexplained reason, had never before been performed. It was about Orpheus and Eurydice, gracious and charming but not a great work. Callas, then still fat, sang superbly and received an ovation. Afterward we went to Doney's and had tea. Mrs. Acton was very pleasant that day, but I don't think I misjudged her. The inner Hortense was hard as nails. I always wondered what she could have thought of my presence as Harold's "guest." Did she realize that we were more friendly than friendship is usually supposed to be? My guess would be that she did and didn't care, the awareness swallowed up in her deep indifference to the well-being and self-fulfillment of her eldest son. She later had occasion to meet friends of Harold even friendlier than I had ever been and seems to have accepted them with remote aplomb.

Only three days then remained before my departure for Innsbruck and Vienna, where I was to meet Bernard. I was sorry to go. The stay had been pleasant (save for the nightingales, which warbled so madly in the cypresses that I often had to get up and close my windows in order to sleep). I had done a decent amount of work on my novel, had met a lot of unusual people, and had made of Harold a lifelong friend. Before I left, he gave me a photo of himself taken by Cecil Beaton, which he inscribed on the back, "To dear James, hoping for happy excursions in worlds of beauty, together, from his affectionate Harold."

We had lunch in town on Wednesday, the thirteenth, and afterward Harold came with me to the station. We embraced and I said that surely I would come back to Florence soon. It would be five years before I did. The fond freshness of our affection, however, was sustained by correspondence and also, I'm sure, by the spontaneous sympathy and sharing of interests that had drawn us together in the first place.

The letters from La Pietra were usually wan and weary, if not somber. For example:

> *Florence*
> *25 July 1951*
> *. . . As for me, I've been very low, but I need not go into this . . .*
>
> *I'm not exactly unwell, but I'm certainly not happy. On the tenth of August, D.V., I shall visit Clotilde Margheri near Naples, and then go with Alda Anrep to Forio d'Ischia, but I'm told the lack of plumbing may drive me away (it wouldn't in China).*
>
> *I wish you were in my arms.*
>
> *Your loving*
> *Harold*

As soon as he got away from La Pietra his spirits immediately improved.

> *Naples*
> *12 August 1951*
> *En route for Ischia I already feel a new-made man . . . It is a heavenly change after the sultry oppressiveness of "family life."*

> *Forio d'Ischia*
> *23 August 1951*
> *This place delights me and I never felt better, reveling in the pleasures of the flesh . . . Auden and Co. are here, but I bathe and drink the excellent wines regardless of all and sundry. Impossible to work amid the noise.*
>
> *Love*
> *Harold*

By mid-October, after a sojourn in Venice, he was settled with his friend Clotilde Margheri near Naples, hoping to find an apartment in the city, because he had determined to write a history of the Bourbon rule in Naples and needed to do a great deal of painstaking research. "It required much energy," he wrote, "to transfer myself here in the face of family opposition, but I had to get down to work again and in Florence that is impossible." Before long he found an apartment at Via Posillipo 37, a few rooms hanging above the bay with a superb view, where he continued his research and read numerous books "of a shattering verbosity and dullness." But he was happy: "The difference to my health and humor since I've been here is almost miraculous. In Florence I was beginning to feel quite ill, but I shall have to return to all that gloom for Christmas and New Year. However, I expect to be in Naples, off and on, for many a month yet."

Ten days later the dread of an imminent return to La Pietra had become formidable.

> *Naples*
> *15 December 1951*
> *. . . Next week I return to Florence for ten days or so. Oh dear, the gloom of it! . . . Already I dread the meals, the conversation: being told that I whisper, that I swallow my words, and repeating the same fatuous sentences. But I hope to see Berenson, and no doubt the change will cause me to enjoy the freedom of Naples all the more . . .*

The freedom of Naples. The freedom he had enjoyed to the point of ecstasy in China. Freedom! Freedom from what? From the willful selfishness and hostility of his father? From the hard and sad indifference of his mother? *They* were La Pietra. The villa, the collections, the gardens, the grandeur, the admiration of the world, everything represented by La Pietra was created and personified, above all, by Arthur Acton, who had overseen every detail, and by Hortense, who had paid for the lot. How is it that Harold can have failed to realize that freedom from La Pietra itself would be his redemption and ultimate deliverance? That question had an answer, which would be provided by time, then demand its due.

During the next fourteen months, as his father's condition gradually deteriorated, Harold went back and forth between Florence and Naples, tormented by a guilty conscience when in the south but tormented even more when in Florence. "The truth is I have become almost morbid after so long a sojourn at La Pietra, only seeing the very old, and I was half killed by the boredom of casual conversations there, the doctors' visits, the pall of gloom and resentment whenever I went out."

When Arthur Acton finally died—and one may imagine with what fierce reluctance—early in April 1953, aged seventy-nine, Harold cannot have felt much honest grief. Two months later he was "kept infernally busy with legal and other tiresome matters and yearn[ing] to get away." Still, when in Florence, he was ever conscientious in his role as keeper and guide to the gardens and collections of La Pietra, receiving visitors and giving them the ritual tour. Late in May he even received my parents and some friends of theirs who were motoring through Italy. Early in July, however, he planned to go to Naples and Ischia, in September to visit Venice for a while. In January he went to London for a fortnight, then to New York, Chicago, and Kansas City, Missouri, where by some devious miracle a few of the finest treasures that he had had to leave behind in Peking in 1939 had "turned up" at the local museum. He was moved to see them again, especially the T'ang horse, one of the largest and finest known, with its "lush Devonshire cream color." However, he allowed them to remain in Kansas City, aware that they would be as out of place among his father's collections at La Pietra as he himself had so often felt. Now that the old man was gone, and despite the affection that he professed to cherish for his mother, he clearly wanted to keep his distance from Florence. In addition to foreign travels, he spent much time in Naples, pursuing researches and work on his book about the Neapolitan Bourbons, and he could not help evoking "the former Acton palace on the Riviera di Chiaia," though no ancestor of his had, in point of fact, ever dwelt there. However, the clever and industrious activity of the brain could not compensate for a sense of withering and emptiness in the heart.

Florence
19 November 1955

My dear James,

Aha, so you're in li'l ole New York. I was wondering.
Dearly as I love Stuart and other pals there, and much as I am
stimulated by its dynamism (for the time being), it works
havoc on my health, mental and physical. I always "fall" for
some heartless cute mixed-up kid who bids the fairest of prom-
ises, under the effect of alcohol, and then—history all too
squalidly repeats itself! I dread another repetition—I'm getting
too old to take it. The last occasion has left an open wound. So
it is better for me to remain here quietly, and work, and occa-
sionally dive into the Greek mythology of the bay of Naples.
No affaires de coeur. My first long volume is finished and will,
I trust, be printed sometime next year, a great load off my
bosom. I'm proceeding with its successor . . .

In the spring of 1956 my friend Bernard and I decided to spend a
couple of months in Florence, arriving on April 4. Only a week later,
by extraordinary good luck, we found a spacious apartment for rent
on the topmost floor of the Palazzo Serristori, where Harold had
taken me to a reception five years before and been pursued by his pu-
tative half sister. The apartment came with a very sociable maid of all
work, who longed for us to entertain and began almost every day by
asking, "*Niente* cocktail *oggi?*" And in fact we did entertain frequently, as the maid was an excellent cook and no doubt made quite a
good thing for herself out of the marketing. During the entire two
months we spent in Florence, Harold was at La Pietra with his
mother, and we saw him frequently. As I then had a car, it was no
longer necessary for him always to come and go by bus. We met an
extraordinary profusion of people, made the ritual visit to B.B., whom
I thought quite as disagreeable as before; we went to the opera, were
invited to balls in outlying villas, and had a very good time. Harold always seemed to be in buoyant spirits, but his exquisite politeness was
such that he would have been reluctant ever to allow discomposure to
show, as he sometimes did in letters. He took us to excellent, out-of-
the-way restaurants, where we drank too much and Harold sang
Florentine and Neapolitan songs. He had a vibrant baritone and

knew how to carry a tune. His favorite was called "Madonna Fioren-tina." Afterward we sometimes made a tour around the fortress on our way home and struck up conversations with soldiers loitering under the trees. I had found a secondhand copy of *Memoirs of an Aesthete*, with the flyleaf torn out by the first owner—much to Harold's amusement—and asked him to inscribe it for me. He wrote, "For dear James, with love and admiration for his numerous gifts—aesthetic and physical, from his old friend Harold." Countess Rucellai invited us to a concert of chamber music in her palazzo designed by Alberti. Mrs. Acton, now well over eighty, fierce as ever, and nearly bald, still presided over the cocktail shaker, and no one could doubt that she ruled both her domain and her son. One afternoon she remarked, "Civilization is now divided between the people who have servants and the people who haven't." Lady Cunard might have made that observation. We saw something of the old Countess Serristori, aged eighty-four, who had visited St. Petersburg before the Japanese war, her brother Prince Pio being the Spanish ambassador there; she had known the imperial family and said they were really quite simple, unaffected people, with characteristically Russian, rather childlike enthusiasms and depressions, much more Dostoyevskian than Tolstoyan. We were sorry to leave on the thirty-first of May.

In the fall of that year occurred the Hungarian uprising in Budapest. I took it very much to heart, and as Picasso was the only Communist I knew, and one of the few in France who did not utter a murmur against the brutal Soviet repression, I wrote him a violent letter of protest, which I gave to the press when he did not respond. Oddly enough, almost forty years later, and after the exposure of the absolute infamy of everything to do with Communism, I'm still occasionally taken to task for the "impertinence" of that letter. I sent a copy to Harold, guessing that he, at least, would approve, though I did not foresee the deep and revealing expression of his attitude toward contemporary art that I would provoke.

> *Florence*
> *3 December 1956*
>
> *My dear James,*
>> *I hasten to thank you for sending me the letter to Picasso. Though I do not agree with your estimate of his work—for he*

has deliberately turned his back on Beauty and become the leading apostle of Hideousness—I think your letter splendid, most eloquent and moving. But I fear that Picasso is the most hardened of tough cynics with a genius for publicity. So long as he is talked about—well, you won't agree, but like the Parisian couturiers Picasso belongs to fashion more than to art, and I think we shall live to see his dégonflement and the return of art to its origins. Given his present world reputation your letter is admirable and needed to be written. I am dining with B.B. tonight and shall show it to him. I have no doubt of his fullest approval!

Janet Flanner gave me her article on Braque. It is extremely readable and very well done, but where are the aesthetic standards of such a person? Mere shibboleths, the slogans still in fashion at the moment. I don't know what to tell her in return. Never has greater nonsense been written about painting and sculpture; and it is a tonic to re-read Vasari and Winckelmann, who knew what they were talking about instead of inventing de la littérature . . .

Bestest wishes for the new novel and much love.

Yours ever,
Harold

A month later I learned that B.B. had, in fact, thought my letter "both timely and eloquent." Harold added, "But I imagine Picasso is beyond the reach of common mortals. Even Michelangelo did not enjoy such success in his lifetime." Well, such fame, perhaps, he did not enjoy, but the rare quality of his success, the veneration of his peers and admirers, was something of which Picasso could hardly conceive. In this same letter Harold for the first time complained of his health, remarking that he was leaving the same day for Naples and compelled "to travel with an entire pharmacy! The after-effects of my long sojourn in the Far East, I suppose."

The first volume of *The Bourbons of Naples* had appeared in 1956 to largely favorable reviews, and Harold's old pal Osbert Sitwell had chosen it as the Book of the Year for the Sunday *Times* symposium, so Harold felt "quite *couronné par l'Académie.*" This volume, however, like *The Last Bourbons of Naples*, which followed in

1961—both of them products of diligent and conscientious research, and replete with intricate factual detail of interest to specialists concerned with two turbulent centuries of Neapolitan history— nonetheless suffers from the same shortcomings which Raymond Mortimer had so astutely pointed out upon the publication of *Memoirs of an Aesthete*. Harold was a hard worker but not a professional writer. He skimmed along the surface of his material rather than plunging into the depths. His true talent was for enchanting flights of conversation, both witty and serious, and great conversationalists, Wilde and Cocteau proving the point, have never been literary creators of the first rank. I think Harold was aware of this, though he probably skimmed over that, too.

The depths into which he did occasionally plunge, however, were those of his own emotions and especially the loneliness and lack in his life of deep affection for any other being. Some of his closest friends considered him "a rather cold fish," and it seems likely that he feared the spiritual responsibility and need for self-effacement that enduring love inevitably entails. He dreamed of the bluebird of happiness, but it rarely flies into the grasp of one who is unprepared to take mortal risks for its sake. Still, he bemoaned its absence. In February 1958, he wrote from Naples, "I despair about the lack of 'love interest' in my life. Sex aplenty here: but *cela ne me suffit pas*. I'm always in search of deeper sympathy, mutual hobbies, etc., too absurd at my age."

Hortense Acton fell ill in the summer of 1962 and died in November. Despite her relative but lifelong lack of true devotion to him, Harold was sincerely overwhelmed with the grief which every son, especially a homosexual son, feels at the loss of his mother.

Florence
6 December 1962

My dear James,

This has been an awful year for me. My mother fell seriously ill in August (when Florence is empty of doctors and nurses), but she seemed to have recovered splendidly. I went to London for ten days. She still seemed well, then suddenly became much worse—agony to have to witness such suffering. I

*am still haunted by the horror and the shock and hope to get
to Paris for Christmas. I was hoping perhaps to see you there. It
is ages since I have been to Paris and I shall feel Rip van
Winkle-like—anonymous and incognito at any rate.*

*A few friends I need to cheer me up, for I am exceedingly
forlorn and have long been without any amorous experience—
not that I expect much at my age, though I do not feel as antique as I may appear!*

Yours ever affectionately,
Harold

His bereavement and sorrow were unquestionably sincere and
perhaps they exacerbated the craving for amorous experience, but
it was slightly surprising to hear the lament over its absence evoked
almost immediately after the horror and shock of his mother's death.
In *More Memoirs of an Aesthete* he speaks of her as an ideal of
spirituality and refinement with a rare appreciation of beauty and
discriminating intellectual finesse. There were those who knew her
well who did not concur in this opinion. As the years passed, Harold
tended more and more nonetheless to speak of his mother as someone nearly saintly. No doubt this made it easier for him to forget
that he had formerly felt life at home to be "a problem of which
flight seemed the only solution."

Now, aged only fifty-eight, he found himself alone at last in the
huge villa from which he had so often longed to flee and had, indeed,
frequently fled, once as far as China. It was his. The treasures it
contained were his. The vast gardens and five other villas on the
property were his. The palazzo in Florence was his. The fortune
from Chicago was his. Osbert Sitwell had exhorted him to stay on,
enduring the trials of family life, for the sake of the villa. He had
done so. Now that it was his, the question confronting him was what
to do with it. Or perhaps the real question was what the villa was
to do with him. A very rich man, a figure of note in international
society, an author sincerely esteemed by the happy few, he was free,
entirely and unequivocally free, to travel anywhere in the world, to
dwell wherever his whim, his imagination, his innermost longing
might lead. And freedom, to be sure, was what he had always craved.

In China he had felt—in the fragrant ecstasy of his gardens, his pipe, and his satin-skinned young friends—that he had obtained freedom. But nothing remained of that long-ago China save memories and his jade ring. Freedom is a harsh taskmaster. It demands an accounting and renders a judgment, for the seeming absence of all constraint is a dangerous illusion, as Harold had learned to his sorrow when "malicious slander" frustrated his wartime ambitions. Freedom is a vocation like any other, and the virtue of the free life is determined by the creativity of its self-discipline. Not an easy or simple proposition, and one which has perplexed philosophers since the writing of *The Republic*. Such were the matters that Harold had to ponder as he sat alone on the velvet sofa in the far corner of the great *salone* in the Villa La Pietra during the winter of 1963.

But I don't suppose there can have been much hesitation or doubt. He had been born in this house. All the anxiety and humiliation he had endured here would be banished by time. La Pietra was an integral part of the Actonian legend. Even as long ago as his days at Eton and Oxford, he had been celebrated as the inhabitant of a Florentine palace as grand as any in England. By taking Osbert Sitwell's advice he had sacrificed much; now it had come time to see how his sacrifice could be turned to benefit. There cannot have been much uncertainty in his mind. His freedom would be consummated by preserving the villa exactly as his father had made it, himself preserved—or imprisoned—within it like some gorgeous prehistoric lepidopteran in a gem of amber. Thus, he would endeavor to redeem from resentment the mortifications of the past and try to atone for the disappointments he had so inadvertently caused. It was the exacting but courageous course.

In May of this year Harold's humor must have been much improved by evidence that his legend had attained the pinnacle of social acknowledgment and that the "malicious slander" as well as "the Blanche smear" seemed to have been forgotten. On May 24, 1963, Evelyn Waugh remarked in a letter to Nancy Mitford, "Prince Richard of Gloucester is being sent to stay with Harold Acton to broaden his (H.R.H.'s) mind. Harold was examined by the Duke and pronounced most suitable." This was Harold's first personal contact with the British royal family and must have brought him intense gratification, for no one was more moved than he by the propinquity of royals. Besides, he was surely most attentive and efficient in broadening the young prince's mind, for Harold's own was prodigiously broad and stretched to astonishing lengths across the terrain of civilized achievement. More and more prestigious contacts with members of the royal family were to follow, quite intoxicating for the proud proprietor of La Pietra.

In the late autumn of that year, Harold came to New York, where I had already been living for more than a year with my friend Larry Hager. He telephoned me during the morning of the twenty-second of November, a day unforgettable for every American then older than, say, eighteen, because by midafternoon all the country, and the world, knew that our president had been assassinated in Dallas. I remember people weeping openly on Madison Avenue. The next day I had lunch with Harold. Half American though he was, the national tragedy did not distress him as deeply as I felt would have been natural. He spoke little of it, in fact, gossiping instead about old friends, discussing art, and complaining about the colitis from which he was suffering. After lunch we visited a few galleries, in most of which Harold saw nothing to admire. Some enormous paintings by Clyfford Still particularly roused his ire, and when I remarked that they might make interesting backdrops for some kind of performance, he said, "The only thing to be done in front of one of these would be to squat down and shit." Harold's tongue was not only mellifluous but upon occasion very tart. He once said to me, "I no longer care to see anything of Truman Capote." When I asked why, he replied, "Because he says such terrible things about you." I suspect that that was an example of Harold's irrepressible bitchiness, which became more pronounced as he grew older, and I doubted the truth of the story, because I never knew Capote well, saw little of him through the years, and would have been well satisfied to see less.

Two days afterward Stuart Preston, who had by then moved to a grander apartment on East Seventy-second Street, gave a luncheon in honor of Harold. It was an ill-chosen moment, being a day of national mourning, all places of business closed because of the dead president's funeral, which took place at midday. The television in Stuart's apartment was turned on, and attention was uncomfortably divided between the flighty chitchat of an all-male gathering and emotional observance of the dramatic ceremony being enacted on the screen. Harold was the only person present seemingly unmoved by the solemn ritual taking place in Washington and kept up a fairly constant stream of mostly irrelevant talk. I was somewhat shocked at the moment, but today I wonder whether, being an astute observer from overseas, he had not even then perceived that John F. Kennedy's fabled charm, brilliance, political acuity, and moral rectitude had all been something of a sham.

A couple of days after Stuart's luncheon, on the twenty-seventh, my birthday, Harold invited Larry and me to dine with him at the Plaza. We didn't mention Kennedy and had a very jolly time. Gore Vidal happened to be dining with a friend at a nearby table, and afterward they joined us for a drink. Harold couldn't have been more gracious and sociable, though I know he detested Vidal's self-important arrogance and glib repartee. This rather spoiled the evening, which I regretted, because I didn't see Harold again during that visit.

A year later, at the age of sixty, a nearly fatal calamity befell him in London. He had for a long time complained of frequent ill health, duodenal cramps, colitis, but a competent and thorough examination now revealed that he was in fact afflicted with a malignant tumor. Immediate surgery was required. The prognosis was favorable but not guaranteed, cancer being a vicious and unpredictable enemy. Harold entered the hospital on November 25, 1964, and the operation was performed five days later. It proved successful, though there were moments during the lengthy period of convalescence when the patient felt near death. Robust and resolute in his will to live, however, he survived, but a most unpleasant consequence was inevitable. Henceforth, and for the rest of his life, he would have to accommodate himself to the annoyance and indignity of an artificial anus. To be sure, many years later he was told that another operation could relieve him of this inconvenience, but by that time he had accepted it and didn't want to lie down again on an operating table. Still, it was surely a humiliating business for someone as refined as Harold, yet he bore it with unaffected composure, and nobody unaware of it would ever have guessed that he had to contend with such an inelegant and constant nuisance. And for a man of Harold's temperament, this nuisance must have been very much compounded by the fact that it could hardly help compromising the search for amorous experience. The pleasure, the happiness, the delight of a shared and enduring love, which every human being and many other living creatures crave, had never yet been his. He had repeatedly lamented its lack as the years wore on. And now he must have contemplated the continued likelihood of this lack with a melancholy sinking of the heart. Comforting compensation, however, presently came to him, or it might be more accurate to say that he acquired it.

Some eleven months after his operation Harold was back in London for observation by his physicians, who pronounced his condition excellent, recovery complete. I happened to be there at the same time, so we dined together on October 16, a Saturday. I found my friend noticeably more aged in appearance but not in the least diminished in joie de vivre, good appetite, or taste for impish, irreverent talk. He had recently, indeed, published a novel, entitled *Old Lamps for New*, a satire of shady and silly goings-on in the art world. Like all of Harold's fiction, it is a flimsy bit of artifice. He never mastered satire or, for that matter, the English language as thoroughly as his old friend the faun, now ill and despondent, preparing to die, which he did the following year. Harold and I had a fine dinner, got rather drunk, and promised each other to meet again ere long. But this was not to happen for eight years.

We kept in touch, however, writing back and forth, and I learned either from him directly or from mutual friends what was happening in Harold's life. In March of 1968 he wrote me that he was working on *More Memoirs of an Aesthete*. The wound of wartime "slander" had not ceased to fester, and in his introduction Harold wondered yet again who could have been the author of the anonymous but official denunciation. "Evidently some epicene dunderhead from the Foreign Office," he wrote. "His rage against my independent way of life was that of the perennial snake in the grass, the envious Philistine." A dunderhead the unknown author undoubtedly was, but epicene? Of which the definition in general usage is effeminate. How can Harold have been so rash as to attribute to his accuser a characteristic which must have been central to the accusation against himself? Did he actually fancy that no one knew? He describes his way of life as independent. That it certainly was, and independent to an extent, one must not forget, which at that time constituted a criminal offense. When all's been said and sifted, wouldn't it have been more sensible, more prudent, in any case, to consign the whole matter to forgetfulness? But the aesthete was vain, and vanity is possessed by a tenacious, unforgiving memory. I was asked to review the book for *The New York Times* but declined, as the second volume of memoirs was no better than the first and, unlike Raymond Mortimer, I could never have brought myself to speak harshly of someone who for twenty years had shown me nothing but kindness. Moreover, he had invariably written me charitable comments on my own literary efforts, decidedly less accomplished than his, especially approving a short book I wrote in 1964 about sitting to Giacometti for my portrait. And now—in 1968—he remarked, "I wish you would write something about your Parisian period, your visits to Picasso, etc. Your Giacometti essay was very well done and I think you should write more in that vein." But he ended that letter on a rather glum note:

> *Don't you miss Paris? I often do—but most of my friends have gone, so here I sit among the annual tourists, my health, alas, dubious.*
>
> *Much love,*
Harold

The presence in Harold's life of the person who was to share with him the rest of it had been well known to his friends for several years, but the publication in 1970 of *More Memoirs of an Aesthete* —by the slightest of hints, and only to those attuned to hints of that variety—formally introduced this man to the public. In the acknowledgments he listed the names of thirteen persons who had contributed to the completion of the volume. All save one were familiar to those who knew very much about Harold's past. The unfamiliar name was that of Alexander Zielcke, who was thanked for his "excellent photographs," which number five out of the total of twelve, four of them views of La Pietra and one a portrait of Sir Osbert Sitwell "at the end," thus taken about 1968. So it must have been sometime in the mid-sixties that the photographer became a person to whom Harold was happy to express his thanks. Nowhere in the text of *More Memoirs of an Aesthete* does the name Zielcke appear, however. The author was never very comfortable with candor. Not in print, anyway.

About someone so important in Harold's life it would be interesting to know more than we do. But what we do know—and much of it is hearsay—is probably enough, and perhaps a little too much. Alexander Zielcke, known to everyone subsequently simply as Alexander, half German, half Polish, must have been born at a time when conditions in both countries were, to put it mildly, difficult, and the somber shadow of difficult conditions cannot have made his formative years bright or easy. Good luck, however, gave him good looks. Which, when put to use with resourceful ingenuity, can prove an invaluable asset. So it was with Alexander. He must have been reared with a modicum of gentility and received a tolerably good education, because he later proved equal to the requirements of cultivated conversation and social poise; but he evidently possessed no employable aptitude or was not disposed to develop one. In any event, at an age when a young man may be expected, or compelled, to assume responsibility for his future, he found himself in Hamburg, a town whose reputation needs no introduction. Then, as now, it attracted many handsome, unemployed young men, and they tended to congregate in bars, cafés, restaurants, and other places of rendezvous where good looks might be turned to advantage. In one of these Alexander encountered an affluent gentleman, said to have been Egyptian, who invited the young man to accompany him on travels abroad. Thus it came about that Alexander found himself in Italy. His benefactor, a man no doubt of good taste as well as generosity, must have added much to the polish, cultivation, and social graces of his protégé. Just how long their relationship lasted is but one more needle in the haystack of irrelevance. They traveled about together, visiting, among other places, Florence. Almost any sophisticated man of the world, especially one accompanied by a handsome youth, was likely to know Harold Acton or some acquaintance of an acquaintance sufficiently well to warrant a telephone call to La Pietra, eliciting the ritual invitation to tea.

That is how Alexander first passed through the great gates at Via Bolognese 120, made his way along the magnificent cypress avenue, and entered the fabulous villa. Wild surmise indeed would be required to guess at his impression. To a young fellow from the purlieus of Hamburg the interior of La Pietra must have seemed like Ali Baba's cavern. And if a profound impression was made upon him, an impression—of a very different sort, to be sure, but possibly no less profound—was made upon his host. Harold's keen and experienced eye, responsive as ever to youthful beauty, glimpsed in Alexander's countenance the potential apparition, which he had so often soulfully dreamt about—to his sorrow—of the bluebird of happiness. It may not have appeared to be of the purest azure, perhaps, but in time it might nonetheless seem to an optimistic scanner of the skies to resemble the hue of heaven. However, he was far too discreet to allow any such perception to be visible at the moment, Alexander, after all, being accompanied by someone else. How soon after that first encounter the two men met again is uncertain, once more irrelevant. Alexander returned to Rome with his friend. Sometime afterward, probably not too long, the friend's affluence seems to have suffered a reverse, and he was compelled to go to London, leaving Alexander behind, aged about twenty-five, without resources or prospects. The predicament called for daring and imagination. Perhaps Alexander had observed, as young men in his position may be prone to do, the responsive glimpse in Harold's eye. At all events, he telephoned to La Pietra and undoubtedly intimated that his situation was not only altered but somewhat precarious. Harold told him to come to Florence at once. What they said to each other, what understanding was reached, what provisions for the future agreed upon, we will never know. Nor do we wish to know. From some of the intricacies of human intimacy, after all, even the most callous biographer will respectfully avert his scrutiny. Suffice it to say that for some thirty years Alexander occupied the central place in Harold's life. Central, indispensable, yet at the same time slightly off-center, a little ambiguous but vitally important. Satisfaction rather than bliss, I think, is what drew them and held them together, and satisfaction as an enduring bond is more to be trusted than bliss.

A matter which surely concerned them both was the double question of Alexander's status and occupation. If he was to be the *ami en titre*, he must *do* something. Ever mindful of Lady Cunard's criterion, Harold would have been gratified if something memorable might be done. It is a famous fact of contemporary life in the Western world that young people with no particular aptitude for the usual varieties of work frequently fall back on photography. Anybody, after all, can aim a camera and press a button, and the most mediocre results sometimes win acclaim. Andy Warhol proved that. Alexander's photographs in *More Memoirs* are not much better than amateur work, with the exception of his grim image of the dying Osbert Sitwell. But if practice does not necessarily make perfect, it can go a long way toward producing excellence. And if Harold guided and trained his friend's eye, talent is needed to profit from guidance. Only three years after publication of the memoirs a luxurious volume entitled *Tuscan Villas* appeared, with a brilliant text by Harold describing the most splendid of these villas, accompanied by Alexander's equally brilliant photographs of them, many in color. These were definitely not the work of an amateur. The collaborators were united on the spine of the volume, the names Acton and Zielcke embossed in letters of gold, and this symbolic union must have been unusually gratifying for one who had dreamed of "mutual hobbies," seeming to confirm not only their intimacy but also to hold out promise of further collaborations and an illustrious career for the photographer. Alas, this was not to be. The book was dedicated "To the Memory of Arthur M. Acton." This semblance of filial piety looks like cynicism, and yet Harold may actually have felt a little posthumous respect for the father who had treated him so shabbily but La Pietra so well. No imagination is needed, however, to guess what that nasty man would have thought of the relationship which produced the tribute to his memory.

As for Alexander's status, the question it presented was serious only for the two men obliged to take it seriously, lest they be undone by the frivolity of ignorance. Knowledge can be cruel and must respond to the facts of life with a heart of gold in order to provide for compassion. Harold, subtle as a mandarin, cannot have failed to be aware that Alexander was not by nature attracted to those of his own sex, and I suspect that this made things simpler for them both. Alexander was very kind to Harold, attentive to his wants and needs, very good, in short, *for* him. All the old friends agreed on that. They also wondered what in the world the two found to talk about when they were alone together. Harold had always been "in search of deeper sympathy." Something of that sort he surely found with Alexander, but not of the deep variety that he had so greatly appreciated with the incomparable B.B., now long since dead. Alexander was not an intellectual—the serious issues of high culture were Greek to him—and he did not enjoy the contemplation of ideas, though he was able to converse well enough with those who did. The ritual tea parties, at which Harold received multitudes of people year in and year out, complaining all the while of the inhuman boredom of it, did not appeal to Alexander, who kept out of sight. It is easy to sympathize with this reticence, because the tea parties, followed implacably by the tour of the gardens, then drinks, were exceedingly tedious to anyone who had experienced them more than a dozen times. It was Harold himself, his charm, wit, intelligence, and irreverence, who drew one always back to La Pietra, not the other guests, who were very often dull. Maybe when Harold and Alexander were alone together, it was Harold, like his old friend Gertrude Stein, who did all the talking. It would have been an extraordinary education, spiced with plenty of waspish gossip. But if Alexander preferred to keep out of sight in order to avoid tedium, and perhaps the embarrassment of all-too-knowing innuendo, Harold had him on hand whenever pleasure or pride seemed to require display of *le prince héritier*, as everyone presently assumed him to be. He never actually lived at La Pietra, however. A bedroom in the villa was technically his, but it seems doubtful that he slept there often, if ever, until the very end. An apartment was found for him in the town, and he was presently sharing it with a girlfriend. Harold certainly knew of this and accepted it as the normal assertion of human nature, which it was.

What to do about La Pietra? That was the question which had hovered over the villa like the black threat of desolation ever since Arthur Acton's death. Harold and his mother had talked about it. Both agreed that the ideal answer would be perpetual preservation. But how to achieve this utopian solution neither could guess. B.B. had bequeathed I Tatti to Harvard, his alma mater, but he had been unable to leave sufficient funds to maintain his bequest; and Harold was well aware that despite the masterpieces of painting and the magnificent library housed in the villa, Harvard rather begrudged the responsibility of keeping it going as a center for Renaissance studies. To leave La Pietra to the city of Florence or to the Italian state was out of the question, for too many were the villas which had been so bequeathed only to be left in neglect, virtually derelict, priceless collections oftentimes stolen with impunity, probably by the custodians. After Mrs. Acton's death, and as Harold's own health began to cause concern, his worry over the fate of the villa became almost obsessive. He was determined to arrange that it should be preserved in perpetuity exactly as it was, as he had known it since childhood, as his father had lovingly created it, the only true love of his lifetime. Preserved, in short, as a memorial to that love and to the man who had devoted himself so passionately to it. But . . . What thoughts, what emotions, what memories can conceivably have been his while Harold pondered the means of guaranteeing the creation of this memorial? Can he in his heart of hearts have sincerely desired to honor and commemorate a man who had so callously disregarded the feelings and integrity of both his wife and sole surviving son? Had he forgotten the slights and humiliations inflicted by the inveterate womanizer who must have known of his son's deviant inclinations and despised him because of them? Who knows? A good memory is not always one's best friend. Like B.B., Harold thought first of his alma mater. It had been at Oxford that he had long ago shone with most prestigious luster, and his own memory might shine there indefinitely were La Pietra to become an extension of Christ Church. But Oxford said no, having already more than enough to be bothered about without taking on a huge villa, however grand, in faraway Florence. Disillusioned, Harold thought of the country where all the money had come from. After diligent searching and cautious counsel with lawyers, he chose in the early seventies New York University, which already maintained in a grand mansion on Fifth Avenue a highly esteemed Institute of Fine Arts. Lengthy deliberations and scrupulously drawn contracts were forthcoming, and NYU graciously consented to accept the bequest, of which no one then, including the donor and the recipients, quite grasped the extent.

Having settled at last the fate of the villa, Harold was at liberty to consider the settling of his own. Not yet seventy years of age, he had excellent health despite the inconvenient consequence of the operation for cancer. Both of his parents had lived long. There was no reason to expect that he, too, might not do so. The question, though, was what to do with himself and his time and his talents while the wait went on. To ponder the potentialities of the future in an environment consecrated entirely to achievements of the past must seem, at least, quixotic. Had Harold forgotten how often he had felt induced to flee, as if for his life, from La Pietra, from Florence? True, he had fled largely from the spiritual tyranny of his parents. But that tyranny had not been entirely dissipated by their deaths. It had a life of its own within the villa. Every statue, painting, tapestry, every stick of furniture, every carpet, bibelot, and ashtray had had its appointed and changeless place for more than half a century, had been chosen and placed by Acton *père et mère*. And in their profuse, overwhelming duration these objects possessed the power of ghosts to haunt the premises, which Harold, master of all that he surveyed, had neither the will nor the desire to alter. La Pietra had witnessed his arrival on earth, La Pietra would witness his departure. That now seemed as ineluctable as a historic fait accompli. He no longer had to clamber over back walls in the middle of the night to enter his home, but the walls were there, and now, instead of seeming to symbolize his questionable freedom, they seemed to confine him within their splendid domain, just as the walls of his beloved Forbidden City had once confined the dying splendors of Imperial China. It must be stressed, however, that this was Harold's lucid and deliberate choice. He had always had a taste for splendor. Despite the aches and pains of boredom inflicted by tedious tourists trooping up the hill for tea, he enjoyed observing the awe which La Pietra invariably aroused, and he punctiliously conducted the tour of the gardens, even when he had to hobble about, leaning on a cane. To evade the garden tour, no matter how veteran the visitor, was not easy. As Harold grew older, as he became more venerable and legendary, La Pietra added superbly to his legend, and he unmistakably relished the sense of power, both aesthetic and social, which his property conferred. He must have felt that to have stayed on, all in all, had been not only the right but the glorious thing to do. And it would be inhumane to try to reckon the cost.

In February 1973 Harold wrote that his only journey that winter had been to the land of influenza and bronchitis, complained that his health was indifferent, but added, "The tenderness of various lads keeps me up and doing." The lads in question were mainly Alexander, of course. By June he was well enough to travel to New York, where NYU awarded him an honorary degree as Doctor of Literature, a modest token in consideration of the bonanza to come. A few weeks after his return, I passed through Florence on my way to Greece. Harold and I had dinner at a restaurant in town, because his cook had fallen ill and left him. He bemoaned the dearth of servants, good ones having become, he said, "dodo-rare." Only two in the huge villa for the moment. They wore white jackets now, the formal livery of an earlier time having disappeared after Mrs. Acton's demise.

Harold spoke a good deal about Alexander, praising his good nature and good looks, companionable loyalty and easygoing tolerance of an old man's idiosyncrasies. These, as I soon learned, happened to include a fair amount of criticism of his young friend —fond criticism, to be sure, but criticism all the same. The principal complaint was that Alexander no longer cared to pursue a career as a photographer, this being a double pity because he had proved his talent and Harold would have been able to facilitate things for him. True, he did consent some years later to photograph a number of Venetian palaces, but the accompanying text was not by Harold. What he now wanted, and had set about doing, was to become a painter. One of the upstairs rooms overlooking the *limonaia* had been transformed into a studio, complete with every necessity a painter could dream of, and there Alexander spent hours every day industriously producing canvas after canvas. And what were they like, these paintings? In a house filled with masterpieces, Harold exclaimed, where did Alexander look for inspiration? Into the void! Enormous abstractions were what he produced, huge and hideous daubs that meant nothing, evoked nothing, represented nothing. There was no reasoning with him. Besides, affection inhibited the tongue of the critic. I remembered what Harold had said in front of the paintings by Clyfford Still and hoped that the inhibition remained effective.

There was another cause for complaint. Alexander had expensive tastes, especially when it came to automobiles. I was surprised by this, because that very afternoon I had seen the young man's car, a convertible Volkswagen in a very mediocre state of maintenance. And in subsequent visits I never saw any other. If he possessed fine automobiles, he didn't drive them to La Pietra. It is a fact, moreover, that as Harold grew older he became rather stingy, a common enough occurrence among the elderly. I noticed it for the first time that evening, because he allowed me with only the flimsiest of protests to pay for our dinner, which I was happy to do. Still, I couldn't help observing that I was allowed to pay for every meal that we afterward took in restaurants. But how generous he had been to me in the past!—not only with meals, hotels, and a couple of checks but especially with his affection, his charm, his incomparable wit, and, of course, his inimitable aesthetic discrimination.

The broadening of the mind of Prince Richard of Gloucester achieved under Harold's tutelage must have made a good impression on the royals, because he was presently followed by his first cousin, Princess Margaret, who enjoyed being a guest in palaces other than her sister's. Margaret's presence brought much prestige to La Pietra, adding royal aura to the villa's legendary host; but her visit was fatiguing for him, because he could not retire until she wished to, and she liked to sit up till long after midnight, chatting and drinking whisky, of which she brought with her an ample supply of her favorite brand, Famous Grouse, in order to be sure no shortage might occur. However, it has to be said that Harold's satisfaction at her presence under his roof was such that he would willingly have sat up till dawn with his royal guest. Princess Margaret more than once visited La Pietra, but she did not become a regular guest, because the villa had no swimming pool. However, she was an appreciative and well-mannered woman, bestowing tokens of gratitude whenever due, and it seems logical to assume that she was instrumental in obtaining from her sister a knighthood for Harold in 1974. A lifelong expatriate and author of rather arcane literary works could hardly have expected that such a distinction would come to him as a natural acknowledgment of his achievements. He had been made a Commander of the Order of the British Empire nine years before, in recognition no doubt of his conscientious commitment to promote and support the British Institute in Florence. A knighthood would not in the normal course of things have inevitably followed. In any case, Harold was delighted, probably in part because this honor might seem to lend more credence to his persistent intimations that the Florentine Actons were related in fact rather than in fantasy to the authentically grand Actons of Naples. Henceforth Harold was invariably addressed by his servants as *Signor Barone*, although he was not even a baronet. But it must have seemed that La Pietra deserved a title, which yet again contributed luster to the legend, and if people chuckled behind his back, no echo of their amusement passed through the villa's gates.

It was not until the first days of September 1980, that I once more went to Florence and to La Pietra. The servant problem had evidently been resolved in the meantime by discovery of a few dodos, because I was invited to dinner the night of my arrival. Seven years had passed since my last visit to the villa, and perhaps I had forgotten the familiarity of more than a quarter of a century. I was surprised by the absolutely unchanged appearance of everything. In the vestibule, in the rotunda, in the great *salone* every single object was exactly where it had always been. The fringed lampshades, lacquer tables, rock-crystal goblets, the eighteenth-century Venetian black-amoor holding a casket from which ropes of pearls dangled in the motionless air, the velvet and damask furniture standing precisely where it had always stood, the paintings, the tapestries—everything was unchanged, and I felt that I'd stepped back into another era. The characters, I thought, from *The Portrait of a Lady* could pass through this room without noticing one incongruous thing. And perhaps the rotund author of those marvelous pages had himself actually sat here once and smoked a cigarette before the Actons moved in. As for Harold, he certainly did not appear to have been added that morning, either. But *he* had changed. He looked very noticeably older and seemed to move about with less ease than before. Still, his conversation was as lively, diverting, and waspish as ever. The person particularly singled out for his sting that evening, oddly enough, was one of the foremost art historians and connoisseurs of the era, Kenneth Clark, who had been a favorite of B.B. and sometime director of London's National Gallery. Author of numerous highly praised books of aesthetic discourse plus two well-received volumes of autobiography, famous also as a television lecturer and, moreover, a lord, he resided in a large castle adorned with important works by masters as diverse as Turner and Cézanne.

Harold called him an upstart. I'm afraid it sounded rather like sour grapes. But nobody's perfect, and Harold could upon occasion be derisively malicious.

We had dinner alone in the enormous dining room, served by an ancient butler who waited behind a screen in one corner, peeping over it from time to time to see how we were getting along. Harold remarked that he had told Alexander of my visit and that his friend would like to meet me in order to talk about painting, because he was still busily occupied, Harold added with a weary sigh, by the production of huge canvases which nobody wanted to exhibit, much less to buy. So I agreed to come for tea the following afternoon, very curious to meet the young man of whom by that time I had heard a great deal from many mutual friends.

When I arrived, the two were seated side by side on the velvet couch where Harold's mother had for so long officiated. My first impression of Alexander was not disappointing. As I'd expected, he was handsome, well built, with something slyly ingratiating about his glance, and entirely at ease in the splendid surroundings. He seemed, I thought, quite as at home as Harold did, and I could only assume that that had been both Harold's doing and his desire. Conversation was easy and spontaneous, Alexander not at all diffident about expressing opinions. Harold dwelt at some length on the worry caused him by thefts from the villa. There had been several, and the robbers had gotten away with some important pictures and objects. A highly sophisticated alarm system had now been installed and a number of the downstairs rooms were more or less permanently closed off. "It's as if half the villa had gone into an irreversible coma," Harold remarked sadly. It was he who presently brought up the topic of contemporary painting and led Alexander to talk freely about his work. The younger man did so—again without diffidence—enthusiastically and convincingly. About his sense of vocation no uncertainty seemed to reign, and, considering the sentiments expressed to me in private, I admired the attentive sympathy with which Harold encouraged his friend to affirm his seriousness and sensibility. Alexander cannot have learned much about contemporary painting within the walls of La Pietra, or even in Florence, where no galleries for its exhibition or sale then existed and young painters, preferring the more animated centers of Rome and Milan, did not congregate. His knowledge of what was going on in the art world was therefore backward. The painters he most admired were those of a previous generation, especially the abstract expressionists of the New York School—de Kooning, Pollock, Kline, and Rothko. Maybe that was all to the good, because the artists of his own age —Robert Rauschenberg, Jasper Johns, Frank Stella—never had much to offer by way of serious aesthetic development, whereas their elders, while hardly comparable in achievement to men like Picasso, Matisse, or Braque, had nonetheless significantly contributed to coherent cultural progress. I asked Alexander whether I might see some of his work, knowing that there were quantities of canvases on the floor above, but then he did turn diffident, protesting that he was dissatisfied with everything he'd done till then and had nothing worth showing. I could hardly insist, and Harold kept silent. Inevitably our talk led to Giacometti, as I was then in the midst of writing his biography, and Harold mentioned to Alexander the little book I'd written to describe the painting of my portrait. He said that he would be very pleased to have a copy, so I promised to send one. There was no tour of the gardens that very hot afternoon, thank goodness. We sat in the cool *salone*, drank whisky—no martinis since the end of Mrs. Acton's era—and chatted, and I was aware not only that I was having a good time but also that I had seldom seen Harold so serene and good-humored. There was not a whisper of malice that day. It was with some reluctance that I got up to go. I never saw Alexander again, I'm sorry to say, but I did send him the Giacometti book and he wrote a very flattering letter to tell me that he had been "thrilled" to read it.

In January of 1984 Harold came briefly to Paris to sign copies of the French translation—more than half a century since its initial appearance—of *The Last Medici*, and I gave a party for him, inviting all the best-looking young men I could find. He was very pleased to find himself the flame around which all the beautiful male moths attentively hovered. He seemed in buoyant spirits and health, prepared to burn a few wings if opportunity offered. It was hard to believe that within a few months he would be eighty.

I planned to spend the following summer in Tuscany, having rented a villa near Lucca, the enchanting town I had visited with Harold thirty-three years before, so I wrote to tell him of my plans and in expectation of visits with him, as Florence was less than fifty miles away. He replied that he meant to be all summer at La Pietra save for a few days' visit early in July to London, where Princess Margaret was to give a party in honor of his eightieth birthday. Relations with the British royal family had meanwhile grown considerably closer, for Prince Charles and Princess Diana, then still outwardly the image of fairy-tale romance, were to be guests at La Pietra the following spring. Their stay under Harold's roof must have seemed to apotheosize both the glory of the villa and the legend of its inhabitant. And yet . . . if one scrutinizes the situation from the far side of appearances and ponders the spiritual significance of both legend and glory, may it not seem, after a lifetime expended upon the aesthetic idea, that nothing particularly profound had come of it all? In any case, Harold reveled in the prestige—and the publicity—of the royal visit. He reveled, perhaps to excess, for an aide-de-camp suggested that it might be unduly tiring for him to accompany the prince and princess during their obligatory public appearances, visiting the museums and monuments of Florence. But Harold was not one to be shunted aside. "Why, nothing could give me more pleasure," he replied, "than to see once again all those masterpieces of art and beauty." So he was present at every public appearance of Charles and Diana, and as he was taller than almost everyone else, he appeared to be one of the most eminent members of the royal party. His picture with the prince and princess appeared in countless newspapers and magazines and on television screens throughout Italy. Harold was highly gratified, and his pleasure later led to further revelation of a flaw in his character which has already been sufficiently divulged. By no means a tragic flaw, merely a blemish in the legendary patina.

Princess Margaret's party was not the only honor to be bestowed upon Harold to celebrate his entrance into the ninth decade of life. A group of his friends decided to produce a volume of writings on various topics both personal and professional which would reflect the diversity of his interests and experiences and remain as a tangible memento in honor of his importance. Funds were solicited from friends and associates to defray the costs of production, and the prestigious publishing house of Thames and Hudson agreed that the volume should appear under its imprimatur. Twenty-nine poems

and articles by distinguished writers, including the British poet lau-
reate, most of them personal friends, composed a very handsome
volume, the frontispiece a photograph of Harold by Alexander. However, in this opulent accretion of celebratory ointment there nonetheless lurked a tiny fly. The preparation of the volume had been
kept secret from the one it was entirely designed to delight and
honor. Consequently *Oxford, China and Italy, Writings in Honour
of Sir Harold Acton on His Eightieth Birthday* was a fait accompli,
printed and bound, when placed in his hands as a handsome and
congratulatory surprise. It was certainly a very welcome and prestigious surprise, but with equal certainty must have turned quite
sour when the recipient came to read an evocation of his early years
entitled "An Oxonian Aesthete" by a friend of more than fifty years'
standing named Christopher Sykes, biographer of the defunct faun.
Evoking the phenomenal Harold of those long-ago years, he wrote,
"He was much as described by Evelyn Waugh in the portrait of him
which he drew in the character of Anthony Blanche in *Brideshead
Revisited*." To have the hopefully forgotten "Blanche smear" revived
by an old friend must have been galling indeed. Nor was there any
reference here to the scandalous Brian Howard, regarded by Harold
as more of a model than himself of the character referred to by the
novel's protagonist as "my pansy friend." The gall, moreover, was
probably made but more bitter by Harold's knowledge that many
more copies of *Brideshead* had been published than all of his own
writings put together. And he presently had occasion to demonstrate
that the "smear," if that *is* what it was, possessed a symbolic power
in its way more compelling than he knew how to withstand.

Nancy Mitford, Harold's witty, talented, intimate friend, had
died some years before after a prolonged, agonizing illness. Saddened by this loss of an exact contemporary whom he had known
for half a century, Harold sat down and wrote a book-length memoir
of her. It is an affectionate evocation of a lovely lady, her family,
friends, and era, written with Harold's usual somewhat precious
elegance, but it doesn't bring the woman to life and is prudishly
evasive about the deep unhappiness of her love affairs. In his introduction he described the book as "a biographical memoir of a dear
friend," and there is no doubt of his devotion, but few felt that he
had done Nancy justice. An accurate, candid, objective assessment

was called for, and a few years later such a volume was ready. Naturally the recipient of an advance copy, Harold was outraged to find himself described in black-and-white as a homosexual. This had never happened before—except perhaps in the official memo that had caused him such vexation during the war—and he determined to take action. The publisher, who happened to be a friend of Harold's, was forthwith notified that unless the offending passage was deleted, legal proceedings on grounds of libel would be instituted to prevent the book's appearance. Accordingly, the passage was deleted, but something of a flap ensued, as the publisher felt understandably indignant over having to expurgate a fact at which the plaintiff himself had so frequently and openly hinted. Word of all this inevitably got around. One of Harold's old and intimate friends asked him why he had made such a fuss when his homosexuality was virtually public knowledge.

"I don't deny it," he said. "But my position is delicate now that I'm so close to the royal family. What would Princess Diana think if she should read such a thing about me?" What Princess Diana might have thought, if she thought at all about Harold and/or homosexuality, barely appeals to conjecture. What cries out for consideration, however, is Harold's apologia. That he could for an instant have fancied that anyone in the royal family might have cared tuppence about his sexual tastes is not to be believed. He was far too experienced and cynical a man of the world for that and knew perfectly well that plenty of eminent knights were walking about free as the breeze who had been reprimanded by the police in public lavatories. What gives one serious pause is his assertion that he didn't deny what he was, because the outright denial of a vital aspect of his nature was the whole object of his threat to the publisher. Harold, in short, was at war with himself. And it is very difficult not to surmise that his better half was committed to defeat. Not to ignominious surrender but to silent, secret, fatalistic resignation. At twenty he had savored fame, and the future stretched before him like an imperial avenue lined with arches of triumph and monuments to the duration of achievement. But fame is an implacable despot, not the easygoing handyman of legend or celebrity. Fame demands fierce dedication to the absolute, self-discipline to the point of self-denial, and a character steeled against the blandishments of fame itself. Of these essential qualities Harold, alas, possessed none. Rather than face the uncertainty of a future in England, he had fled to the other side of the earth, immersing himself in veneration of the past, the pseudo-paradise of the pipe, and easy ecstasy of the flesh. And when it was too late for a grand and uncompromising apotheosis, he found himself climbing over the back wall of the villa within which he would ultimately be confined like the legendary person known as Sir Harold Acton. Shrewd and subtle as he was, he must have wondered how that person had contrived to make the cost of the villa so much higher than the author of *Aquarium* had ever possessed the means to pay. His old friend the faun could probably have told him, but he was dead, and the proud custodian of La Pietra did not condescend to turn to others for the resolution of his conundrum.

Money was much on Harold's mind as he grew older. During the summer of 1984, the first of several I spent at Lucca, I went a number of times to La Pietra. Taking a group on the garden tour, Harold complained of the extensive maintenance, repair of the pergola, restoration of the statuary, the skyrocketing salaries of gardeners. On another occasion I invited Harold to have dinner with me and five or six friends who were staying in my rented villa, a hovel compared to La Pietra. We went to a restaurant near the Piazzale Michelangelo, and as we were preparing to sit down Harold whispered to me, "My dear, you know I can't possibly pay for the dinners of all these people," whereupon I reminded him that the invitation had been mine to begin with. In succeeding years we often went to dine in restaurants, especially a very good one high up on the mountainside along the road leading to Bologna, and it was always I who paid for the meals—the very least, as I've said already, that could be expected. Still, it was hard to imagine that Harold could be in straitened circumstances. He insisted upon it, though, and there was no telling what reverses might have been inflicted by the stock market. Maybe the Illinois Trust and Savings Bank had fallen upon hard times. Nobody knew, but people were puzzled.

If he suffered from discomfort in the pocketbook, Harold's health as he approached authentic old age seemed good. No longer so nimble as he guided gushing guests around the gardens, he oftentimes brought along a cane, which he would sometimes use rather as a wand to point out magical vistas and mythological statuary. His conversation remained scintillating, witty, malicious, though the waspish sting became more like a mosquito bite. The future of La Pietra now presumably a fait accompli, Harold would sometimes sigh for carefree times long gone by. The memorable luncheon parties of Lady Cunard. The pagan pleasures of Ischia and Naples. Even the ecstasies of odorous evenings in Peking. But he seldom left the villa. And some of his faithful old friends felt that they were being avoided, for what reason they could not guess, and thought Alexander might be taking advantage of his friend's diminished vigor in order to settle things according to his wish or advantage. Who knows? Ironically enough, behind the backs of erstwhile friends, Harold complained of their stinginess, said they sent him letters without stamps and telephoned only on Sunday because it was cheaper. He did not seem, all in all, the happy Harold of yore. It was impossible to imagine him now singing "Madonna Fioren-tina" or stumbling about among the trees below the walls of the fortress in search of companionable soldiers.

One afternoon in mid-August of 1986—the heat was African, Harold said—I found him alone in shirtsleeves in the *salone*. Luckily no other visitors were expected that day. Alexander's battered VW stood outside, but he, of course, kept to himself upstairs. We had a pleasant chat, drank gin and tonic, and shared fond memories. Suddenly Harold leaned forward, put his hand on my knee, and said, "It's horrible to be so old, waiting for the end in this place that already seems like a mausoleum. You know, my dear, there are times when I simply can't understand why I did it." Then with a sigh he settled back into the couch.

Such was the sadness of his tone and expression that I felt it would be an impertinence to ask just what he meant. But I wondered. And I wonder still. What had he done—and for what reason—that he found impossible to understand? It must have to do, I felt, with his whole life and the irresistible dominion exercised over it by the villa. Was it possible, now that the future had been determined forever—now that it was too late to undo anything that had been done from the day of his birth in this house until the day of his death in it—was it possible, I wondered, that he regretted every-thing? The villa had contributed vitally to Harold Acton's legend.

But had he paid for that contribution with his life? Was that what he had done that he couldn't understand? His brother, William, had deliberately taken his own life. Is it conceivable that Harold came to feel that in some way he had done likewise? Maybe Alexander knew the answer. Maybe, indeed, Alexander *was* the answer.

We talked of other things. Rome, Amalfi, Venice, the places I next planned to visit. B.B. The Sitwells. Lady Ottoline Morrell and her formidable proboscis. No trace of sadness, no intimation of chagrin or regret recurred. I thought I might have misunderstood —or almost imagined—what Harold had said. But I hadn't and was sorry.

My last visit to La Pietra took place on a Monday, August 1, 1988. Driving over from Lucca, I arrived punctually at six. As expected, everything in the villa was exactly as it always had been. Arthur and Hortense Acton would have found nothing amiss or out of place if they had unexpectedly returned from the hereafter. Harold was again in his shirtsleeves—African heat—but this time he quickly put on an elegant silk jacket. He was very lively, having returned but a fortnight before from a visit to London, where despite the heat and crowds he had enjoyed himself, especially at a dinner attended by "our enchanting Prince of Wales." He had recently been awarded a literary prize in Naples and been made an honorary citizen of Florence. So much attention and honor did attract bores, he remarked, like ungainly bears in search of honey, but he felt able to cope with them. He had also recently completed, in collaboration with a friend named Edward Chaney, a guidebook entitled *Florence, A Traveler's Companion.* We chatted and gossiped about people and paintings, drank gin and tonic, and nibbled tiny sandwiches passed between us by a butler in a white jacket. There was no suggestion of the momentary melancholy of our previous meeting. We even talked about the pleasures and perversities of sexual desire, a topic I was somewhat surprised to find still fascinating for a man of eighty-four. It had been prearranged that I was to come for a drink only, as I planned to dine in town with friends and Harold did not want to go out in the heat. Not long before my departure, he mentioned the continuity of his arrangements with New York University to bequeath his property as a center for Renaissance studies. All the intricate legal details had been settled to his satisfaction, and he seemed glad, not sad, that he had made this decision, though with a smile he remarked, "Living here now is like living in a magic contradiction, because only my death will bring this place to life." Then, after a pause, he added, "I have no illusions. I know perfectly well that I'll be remembered for La Pietra, not for anything I've written." The observation was very matter-of-fact, not a sorrowful good-bye. Soon afterward I got up to go, kissed Harold on the cheek, as I always did, and, leaving him there in the changeless splendor, felt with regret that I was unlikely ever to see him again.

Driving back down the hill, I thought of his parting remarks and how unhappily mistaken I believed them to be. His death would not bring the villa to life. On the contrary. Only his survival had brought to La Pietra a convincing sense of living affinity with a world and a life of which all the immovable treasures and objects had been merely the ephemeral decor. The place would become a museum, and the very existence of a museum celebrates the vital benefit to mankind of human mortality, conferring, moreover, to the oncoming generations the prerogative to alter and revise, mutatis mutandis, the cultural residue of the past.

About the judgment of posterity, I felt convinced, Harold had also been mistaken. It is improbable that he will be remembered for La Pietra. The name Acton may remain more or less attached to it, but Harold as a person doubtless will not. Donors who bank on their gifts to earn posthumous renown are trifling with vainglory. Who today knows, or cares, very much about the lives and personalities of such men as Oskar Reinhart, Lord Iveagh, Duncan Phillips, or even the inglorious Henry Clay Frick? Yet multitudes of people yearly flock to visit the mansions, bequeathed as museums, in which those collectors amassed so many masterpieces of art. And they *are* masterpieces. In La Pietra, unfortunately, there is not one. There are numerous interesting and beautiful works of art that in future will attract the attention of art historians, but none of them are of the first rank or, indeed, by artists of the second. Even the supposed Donatello, of which Harold was so proud, is not accepted by competent authorities as a genuine work from the master's hand. The villa contributed greatly to Harold's legend during his lifetime, but in the future, filled either with young students or with unimaginative tourists who have never heard of the Sitwells, Norman Douglas, or

Lady Cunard, it will leave him by the wayside. Harold doubtless will be remembered, though, by scholars studying Neapolitan history and by a few people interested in the self-centered ruminations of a highly cultivated and eccentric bit player in the social and artistic spectacle of his era. It seems doubtful that posterity will be kind to his memoirs, because, as Raymond Mortimer so perceptively observed, Harold lacked the resolve to become a professional writer. He never developed a commanding, personal style, and style is posterity's strictest criterion for remembrance. His great talent was for the spoken, not the written, word, and that is a pity, because no matter how memorably he wove his tapestries of talk, they could not outlive the momentary cleverness of their invention. Even the most vertiginous flights of conversation have perishable wings; the brilliant epigrams of Wilde, the dazzling witticisms of Cocteau possess but simulated life in print, and Harold was not of that company.

He lived on in his immutable grandeur for some years still, becoming more legendary as each one passed, the sole remaining survivor of a realm that seemed to many like Lyonnesse, where luxury, beauty, and chivalry reigned. His opinions and recollections were sought by art historians, biographers, television interviewers. The visit to La Pietra became a mandatory objective on the agenda of anyone whose stay in the City of Lilies was to be regarded as having approached perfection. Harold was still occasionally able to take tourists round the gardens, following an itinerary as fixed as that of Halley's Comet, and to deliver the descriptive monologue that had not changed for forty years. Even now he was sometimes asked to write an article or book review for *The Spectator* or *Books and Bookmen*. But he almost never left the villa.

And then his vitality began to fail. Strength both of body and of mind little by little left him. He took to his bed. The legendary figure had become an old, old man, brilliant conversation reduced to a whisper, memories withered away, awareness itself haphazard. His closest friends, the few who remained, sometimes came to sit by his bedside. There were days when he recognized them, days when he didn't. Once or twice he attempted to sing an old Neapolitan song he had loved long ago, but only a pitiful croak came forth. During these last months Alexander was vigilantly attentive, supervising the visits of doctors and the upkeep of the villa. He also consulted with lawyers and notaries regarding the future of the estate, made several journeys to New York, and, all in all, people felt, acted as if he were Harold's heir, which he was not. The officials of the British Institute, housed in Harold's Palazzo Lanfredini on the Lungarno, had always assumed that the entire building would be bequeathed to them, its shops and apartments being the source of much-needed rental income. So they were unhappily surprised to find a few months before Harold's death that a number of the shops and apartments had, without warning or explanation, been summarily sold off. It seemed odd, as Harold had always been such an enthusiastic and generous supporter of that organization, to which he owed an appreciable debt for the propagation and luster of his legend. But who knows what reverses and regrets battle in the befuddled brain of a dying man?

Harold finally died on February 27, 1994, having received the last rites as befitted his Catholic upbringing, however nonobservant he had always been. The funeral took place in the Church of San Marco, filled to overflowing, with more than four hundred people present, including many Italian officials and the British ambassador, representing Prince Charles. The ceremony was beautiful and solemn, everything efficiently arranged by Alexander, with splendid flowers and appropriate music. Joining his father, mother, and brother, Harold was buried in the Allori Cemetery. He would have been pleased by the gravity and importance accorded to his demise.

By a bizarre quirk of fate, Harold's death coincided almost to the day with that of the last person alive who personified the traditions and ideals which had imbued the happiest period of his life, for in faraway Peking Prince Pu Jie, younger brother of the last Emperor of China and final remnant of the Manchu dynasty, which ruled from 1644 until 1911, died on the twenty-eighth of February. The Forbidden City, where the prince had lived as a child and where Harold had later roamed in transports of bliss, was now inhabited by the rulers of a tyrannical regime which had brutally repudiated the civilization that both men revered. The nearly simultaneous passing of the two men seems to symbolize the disappearance from the earth of values and virtues that mankind would have done better to cherish and perpetuate.

If Harold's plentiful obituaries would have pleased him, displeasure would also have been vouchsafed by the revival in several of them of "the Blanche smear," which named him yet again as the model for the "decadent" character in Evelyn Waugh's novel. As long as *Brideshead Revisited* continues to be read, which promises to be for quite some time, Harold may achieve a kind of immortality through his identification with this figment of the faun's invention, and, after all, considering the fickle nature of immortality, that may not be deemed too bad. Much as he disliked the persistence of the notoriety, he disliked oblivion even more.

The details of the bequest to New York University received much attention in the press: six villas standing on fifty-seven acres of land overlooking Florence, plus the art collection and an endowment in cash of twenty-five million dollars. The last item astonished all of Harold's friends, who had observed the penny-pinching of the later years with surprise but believed in the protestations of financial adversity. A very, very rich man, Harold in his last years had become something of a Silas Marner, and that awareness rather tarnished the legend. Everyone assumed that Alexander had been generously provided for, but nobody knew to what extent, for in Harold's will he received only the jewelry that had belonged to Hortense and to Harold.

New York University was the major beneficiary. That institution had originally expressed with becoming eloquence its pleasure and gratitude at the prospect of Harold's bequest. Now that he was gone, however, and NYU authorities had an opportunity for close inspection of their impending inheritance, second thoughts arose. By the terms of the original agreement, a period of some latitude after Harold's death had been granted for the university to decide whether, in the end, it would accept or refuse the bequest. If it refused, La Pietra would be offered to the Art Institute of Chicago, the city where, after all, the money had come from. Upon inspection, it became apparent that Harold's obdurate resolve to change nothing in the villa had been a drastic, if obsessive, mistake. La Pietra, the building, its contents and gardens, all were in a state of grave disrepair. Plumbing and electrical wiring had not been touched for more than sixty years. Priceless tapestries hung in shreds. The antique furniture creaked ominously when one sat down. Exquisite carpets lay threadbare. In the gardens the statuary, balustrades, pergolas, urns, and benches were cracked and overgrown. Harold would have done well to spend a million or two in order to leave behind an estate viably in keeping with the reverential idea of preserving everything exactly as it had been. Is it possible that he failed to notice the decay—and loss—gradually overtaking all that he supposedly held most dear? Some of the contents of the villa had, in fact, actually disappeared despite the elaborate alarm systems. All of Evelyn Waugh's letters to Harold, for example, the invaluable record of forty years of literary and personal intimacy, were gone. Who can have known that they were precious or, indeed, where Harold carefully stored them? Then a lot of silver, too, was missing. And while Harold lay semiconscious upstairs, the servants noticed that small objects sometimes were placed where they had never before been seen, then were presently seen no longer. One can't help wondering what motives, made powerful by unhappy memories dwelling in the cellar of consciousness, led him to disregard in the end the well-being of the patrimony for which he had sacrificed so much. Perhaps, precisely, he had sacrificed too much.

There was another quandary confronting potential administrators of La Pietra as a center for Renaissance studies. Even if the villa, gardens, and outlying buildings were properly restored for student use, what specifically academic materials would be available for their study aside from the mediocre art collection and, of course, the incomparable riches of Florence itself? B.B. had been sly when bequeathing unendowed I Tatti to Harvard, because in addition to certified masterpieces of art he left an incomparable library of fifty thousand volumes, many of them unique, and no university official with any sense could have turned down that lure. But La Pietra had neither library nor masterpieces. It had only its beauty and the haunting evocation of a way of life now seemingly almost as remote as the Renaissance itself.

Harold meant his twenty-five million dollars to be held in perpetuity intact, the interest alone available for upkeep of villa and grounds. Will this be enough? Nothing is supposed to be sold, and two of the other villas are leased to the Olivetti Company, which in principle must surrender them within a couple of years. But relinquishment of a lease can in Italy prove to be a very tricky business, especially if the occupant is an outfit as powerful as Olivetti. The president of New York University has evaluated the entire bequest as being worth between five hundred million and one billion dollars. That is a great deal of money, an amount, indeed, large enough to make any claim, however flimsy, upon a portion of it seem worth pursuing. Thus, Harold's dread of illegitimate cupidity has turned out to be well founded and has further complicated the eventual settlement of his estate. The supposed half sister from whom Harold had fled at Hortensia Serristori's reception has initiated lawsuits in Florence and New York demanding half of the estate. Should she win, villas, land, and works of art will have to be sold to settle matters once and for all. New York University would hardly care to cope with leftovers, and an official of the university has stated that it would not be prepared to spend for the maintenance of La Pietra funds that might be used for student scholarships. Who would? Is it possible that La Pietra itself will become an unwanted, tumbledown vestige of Harold's ambivalent and second-rate dream? The decades to come, not to mention the centuries, will tell whether or not all those evaluated millions may be enough to pay for enduring remembrance, and thus determine in the end to what extent the monetary outlay was commensurate with the human cost of the villa.

2

Inside Santo-Sospir

[J E A N   C O C T E A U]

One morning on the beach at Golfe-Juan, Picasso said to me, "Have you ever met Jean Cocteau?" When I replied that I hadn't, he added, "You should. It would be useful for you as a writer. And then, after listening to his monologue, you wouldn't have to bother to read his next book." He laughed loudly at that last remark and drew the face of a clown in the damp sand where we were seated at the water's edge.

This was in mid-July 1950. I was spending the summer at Villefranche-sur-Mer, a town twenty miles away which was as yet unspoiled, and rode over often on my motorcycle to visit Picasso, Françoise Gilot, and their two small children, Claude and Paloma, either at Vallauris, where they lived in a very modest house called La Galloise, or on the beach at Golfe-Juan, where they went almost every day to swim. My companion in the mediocre apartment we had rented in Villefranche was a young Frenchman named Bernard Minoret. He did not enjoy riding on the rear seat of my motorcycle, as he felt that it was both undignified and unsafe, but he came along occasionally, in particular if I were going to see Picasso. So it happened that he was present when Picasso suggested that I make the acquaintance of Jean Cocteau. I was diffident.

"But how could I meet him?" I protested. "I couldn't just go to his house, even if I knew where it was, ring the doorbell, and expect to be made welcome, could I?"

"And why the devil not?" cried Picasso, laughing. "That's what you did with me, and look how well it's turned out. You tell Cocteau I sent you, and you'll see, everything will be just fine."

"Maybe," I said, though I felt less presumptuous now. "It would be awkward," I objected. "I wouldn't know what to say."

"So much the better," exclaimed Picasso. "Cocteau does all the talking. He is staying at the villa of a rich lady called Weisweiller somewhere on Cap-Ferrat. That's not far from Villefranche. If you found me, you can certainly find him. Ride over there on your motorcycle and say that I sent you. Cocteau will be happy to see you. I can promise you that."

"Well," I said dubiously, "maybe I'll do it if you say so."

"And when you see him," Picasso added, "be sure to give him my warmest greetings. It's been such a long time since we've met. He was one of the witnesses at my wedding. Ancient history. The others are dead. And maybe he would like to go for a ride on the back of your motorcycle."

"Why, even Bernard hesitates to take that risk."

"Well, there's no risk Jean wouldn't take for a sip from the fountain of youth. Maybe you'll meet Jean Marais, too. But I think there's a new boyfriend now. Not that it matters. They're all the same person."

Picasso resumed drawing grotesque faces in the damp sand, every successive wavelet washing them away, and to my relief there was no more talk of Cocteau.

I had no desire to become acquainted with the famous author, which was odd, because from an early age I had dreamed of meeting men and women who were known for great creative achievements, and I had not long before taken the trouble to arrange through a mutual friend a meeting with Somerset Maugham, who also resided on Saint-Jean-Cap-Ferrat and who received me at some length with sympathetic courtesy. It is strange, too, that I sensed nothing untoward in Picasso's suggestion, since he had sent me to meet Gertrude Stein and afterward scolded me for liking her; but part of Picasso's magic was to make every invention or persuasion seem entirely unpremeditated, therefore innocent.

Anyway, Cocteau at that time meant relatively little to me. I had seen some of his films, admiring their technical innovations and modernist romanticism while feeling that they had no deep or durable aesthetic distinction. Of his literary works, I had read—at Bernard's insistence—but a single one, *Le Grand Ecart*, which,

though stylistically impressive and seemingly wise, had in the end
impressed me mainly as a display of wit and ingenuity for its own
sake. What I knew most about Cocteau was what I liked least: that
he was an international celebrity, known by everybody because he
knew everybody. Picasso, to be sure, was even more famous than
Cocteau, but I wanted at that time to believe only that *his* fame was
the noble and natural outcome of genius. I had seen too many
excessively mannered photographs of Cocteau in fashion magazines,
and I was aware of much pseudo-poetic posturing in public.

And yet, being homosexual myself, I might have found it appealing that Cocteau had lived all his life openly as a homosexual;
for to do so then, as I knew only too well, was far less easy and
common than it has now become. Still, what I knew about Cocteau
as a homosexual—his ambiguous romance with Raymond Radiguet,
his well-advertised liaison with Jean Marais, the coy publications
of erotica, and so forth—led me to assume that this aspect of his
life was also subject to the imperatives of affectation and notoriety.
As a matter of fact, I had had an opportunity to observe the man in
person only a few months before, having found myself at a party in
Paris where he appeared briefly. He was accompanied by an exceptionally handsome blond youth, and both of them were wearing
identical camel-hair polo coats which, though the room was crowded
and hot, they neither removed nor opened. The party was largely
theatrical, I having been invited by my friend Arletty, so Cocteau
was naturally acquainted with most of those present, whom he
greeted in terms of effusive and chic endearment—"My darling,"
"My angel," "My sweet"—kissing many on the cheeks. The handsome young man kept very close to Cocteau, speaking almost not
at all, though he was pointedly introduced to everyone Cocteau
spoke to. It appeared to me nevertheless that he was treated and
produced, so to speak, as an impersonal adjunct to Cocteau's own
performance, and his expression I thought both withdrawn and sullen. I was not introduced to either of them, but the opinion I formed
that evening did not arouse any desire to meet Jean Cocteau.

Bernard, on the other hand, felt decidedly otherwise. Having
been present on the beach when Picasso made his suggestion, he
assumed that he was quite as entitled to ring Cocteau's doorbell as
I was. No sooner had we left the beach than he began urging me

to act upon Picasso's proposal. I was evasive. From our apartment in Villefranche, Cap-Ferrat was clearly visible a few miles across the bay, its opulent villas set amid terraced gardens, a lush, luxurious enclave, richly evocative of wealth, fame, and a life of sumptuous but nonchalant elegance. As a locality and as a symbol, it represented conditions of existence capable of generating the most sybaritic fantasies. I could not believe in their relevance to myself, whereas Bernard felt that vulgar chance alone had prevented him from living in high style. Consequently it seemed eerily fitting that our meeting with Jean Cocteau would soon take place by chance and through Bernard's initiative.

One afternoon as we were strolling about in the old quarter of Villefranche, Bernard suddenly whispered, "Look! There's Cocteau."

Not far from us lingered a group of three people, two men and a young woman. The older man was immediately recognizable as Cocteau, while the other was the handsome youth of the party in Paris, though his hair had ceased to be blond and become brown. He must have been about twenty-five, was broad-shouldered and well built. The young woman was slender and slight, elegantly attired in slacks and silk shirt, with long blond hair and scarlet lipstick.

"I'm going to speak to Cocteau," said Bernard, striding toward the unsuspecting trio. I lingered behind, not wishing to appear responsible for any brash familiarity. But now that a meeting which I had done nothing to bring about seemed imminent, one, moreover, in which I could appear as a politely reticent accessory to Bernard's *démarche*, I began to feel that it could be gratifying, after all, to become acquainted with Jean Cocteau.

As I watched from my safe remove, I saw Bernard present himself to Cocteau with that air of obsequious condescension and superior politesse by which the French bourgeois asserts his right to deference. Cocteau responded in kind, but with such expert flourishes and felicities that even from a distance I could see Bernard beguilingly put in his place as one of the innumerable youths whose very raison d'être might be defined by a passing encounter with the great man. Gestures were presently made in my direction, and though I went to join the little group with a suitable diffidence, I was able to welcome the situation all the more easily and pleasurably because I did not appear to be responsible for it. That enjoyably childish misconception was an appropriate beginning to my friendship with Jean Cocteau.

Bernard introduced us, explaining that I, in fact, was the friend to whom Picasso had recommended this meeting. The operation of Cocteau's famous charm was powerfully persuasive as he shook hands with me, made polite exclamations of pleasure, and asked for news of his old friend. I replied that Picasso had especially desired to be warmly remembered to one who had been a witness at his wedding. Cocteau appeared pleased by the remembrance but did not neglect for its sake to introduce me promptly to the young woman, whose name was Madame Weisweiller, and the young man, Edouard Dermit. Some minutes of practical talk followed, explanations of where Bernard and I were living, the expected duration of our stay in Villefranche, and so forth, all with the obvious purpose of determining how it might most conveniently be arranged that we should meet again, because this chance encounter could hardly seem to satisfy the impressive purpose signified by the fact that it was Picasso who had decreed the desirability of our meeting. At the same time, Cocteau himself, without any perceptible effort to do so, contrived to impart to the very haphazardness of the moment an aura of surpassing distinction and pleasure, not only, one felt, by virtue of his participation but also because of our presence. The entrancing naturalness by which these intimations were conveyed and these impressions received was the apparent guarantee that this brief meeting offered a rich promise for the future. It was accordingly agreed that late the following afternoon Bernard and I would call at Madame Weisweiller's villa, named Santo-Sospir, at the end of Cap-Ferrat, for a drink. And so we parted there in the street after less than five minutes' talk.

We were elated. Each of us felt that Cocteau's prompt, cordial invitation must portend the sort of distinction that we supposed his friendship could confer. So we got onto my motorcycle the following afternoon and rode over to Cap-Ferrat, a distance of no more than three or four miles, finding the Villa Santo-Sospir without trouble at the very tip of the peninsula, adjacent to the lighthouse, just down the hill from Maugham's Villa Mauresque. Cap-Ferrat in the fifteenth century had been called Saint-Soupir—Holy Sigh—and the

Weisweiller villa had presumably been named Santo-Sospir by its
original owners—Spaniards?—in order to commemorate that fact.
Set on a steep slope, the last house overlooking the sea, Santo-Sospir
was not an imposing residence. Pure white, standing amid luxuriant
shrubbery, the exterior, as a matter of fact, appeared unusually modest and architecturally undistinguished compared with the magnificent villas hidden nearby among the pine trees. There was a
spacious gravel car park in front of the villa. We left my motorcycle
there and rang at the front door. Cocteau himself, attired in a white
terry-cloth dressing gown over blue slacks and shirt, came to admit
us, exclaiming with such enthusiasm over our arrival that it might
almost have been interpreted as a surprise. I grew accustomed to
this later. Passing an airy hallway, we came into a salon which,
though not large, gave an impression of vastness because it opened
directly onto a terrace that offered an unobstructed view of the Med-
iterranean all the way to the horizon. The furnishings were simple
but exotic: wicker chairs of unusual design, flimsy side tables, flow-
ered rugs and draperies, kitsch vases on the mantelpiece, all of which
conveyed an unexpected and rather bizarre aura of eccentric luxury.
Cocteau had already begun to paint the walls of the villa, which
little by little he transformed into a total showplace of his personal
imagery. Even the lampshades were eventually painted with profiles
of brooding youths.

In the salon we were greeted by our hostess, Madame Weisweiller, whom we were invited to address by her forename, Francine,
and the handsome Dermit, who went by the name of Doudou, in
keeping with Cocteau's habit of inventing somewhat infantile nick-
names for his lovers. We sat outside on the terrace under an awning.
Below us, gardens rich with variegated flowers fell toward the sea.
Here and there in baroque vases stood enormous bouquets of tuberoses, their heady fragrance saturating the late afternoon with further languor. Cocteau mixed the drinks without inquiring what
anyone might or might not want: tall, frosted glasses with fruit juices,
ice, and gin, delicious. Sipping slowly, while the smoke from our
cigarettes lazily wafted across the slanted sunshine, we seemed to
be suspended in a never-never land of privileged civilization.

Picasso was right. Cocteau did all the talking, pausing only
occasionally to allow somebody to agree with him, and thus provide

a possible springboard toward a variation in the monologue. It was enchanting, spirited, witty talk, and the audience, though not encouraged to provide anything more than token participation, was nonetheless made to feel indispensable, illuminated by Cocteau's brilliance, and consequently borne upward with him into the historic empyrean. I felt that all this was quite dizzying and delightful. Bernard, however, presently gave signs of feeling otherwise, of feeling, in a word, left out. Once or twice, when Cocteau's talk briefly came to an intersection, Bernard endeavored to introduce views of his own, which would have carried the discourse along a track of his choosing, compelling Cocteau to board a train of conversational give-and-take not engineered by himself. Now, of all the men I've known, with the possible exception of Charles de Noailles, Jean Cocteau was without quibble the politest. He was also an unparalleled master of verbal quicksilver, so that with perfect courtesy he was able to introduce Bernard's views into the momentum of his talk while at the same time allowing to hover the diaphanous intimation that an ever-so-slight detour had unnecessarily been traversed. This was so subtle as to be virtually imperceptible, and in fact I was altogether unaware of it until Bernard with some asperity pointed it out later. I didn't consider it anything to think about twice, but I, to be sure, had never read Saint-Simon, knew nothing of protocol, and did not regard myself as an arbiter of social and intellectual nuance. While the afternoon exquisitely dwindled, the scent of the tuberoses seemed to grow still more odorous, then the sun trailed orange streams over the sea, a hush fell upon the gardens, and, alas, it was time to say good-bye. Cocteau invited us to return, insisting upon our meeting again soon, perhaps for lunch at one of the waterfront restaurants in Villefranche, where he had spent happy days a quarter of a century before. He wrote down the telephone number of the villa—251-28—on a slip of paper, adding his forename only—Jean—accompanied by a little star. We promised to see one another soon. Francine and Doudou were equally friendly. One almost had a sense of their being a bit lonely in their fragrant paradise. Only some time afterward did I discover what fragrance was in fact their antidote to loneliness and their sure access to paradise. In the silvery twilight Bernard and I got onto my motorcycle, skidded on the gravel, and sped away.

At the time I knew next to nothing about Jean Cocteau, but Bernard knew next to everything and told me as much as I needed to know. At the age of eighteen Cocteau had contrived to make himself well known in Paris by having his poems read to a select audience by some of the most noted actors of the day. The poetry was poor stuff, never reprinted, but the fame was the real thing, and that was what he wanted. He aspired to be recognized as a genius, a poet of worldwide renown, a man who could transubstantiate the humblest material or medium through the poetic creativity of his imagination. And that was very much what he had done. Poet, novelist, dramatist, film writer and director, draftsman, designer of posters, pottery, tapestries, mosaics, costume jewelry, and heaven only knows what else, he grew to be a byword for artistic celebrity. Avant-garde innovations and overt romances with handsome young men: everything he did readily accepted because of his extraordinary wit and charm by the social elite he tenaciously cultivated. His idols were Diaghilev, Stravinsky, and Picasso. It must be acknowledged that he had an infallible sense of what was best, and he worked his way into convincing semblances of friendship—and even collaboration—with all three, but there were ups and downs en route. Fashionable and successful, lionized by an ever-multiplying public, he also liked to scandalize, to find out, as he said, how far he could go without going too far. He smoked opium, underwent well-publicized, unsuccessful "cures," was occasionally summoned by the police, and flaunted the deviant fete of his private life at a time when such license was still discountenanced by the authorities. But he deemed that no authority need be heeded by a poet, save his own sublime prerogative to create, to do whatever his muse might prompt in order to beget the delectation of the multitude.

Bernard's admiration of the famous author was not so unconditional, however, that he failed to criticize a certain frivolity in the overpowering passion to please at any price which had led Cocteau to praise too many mediocrities, to make compromises motivated by the compulsion to enhance his own reputation, and to avoid commitment concerning the imperative moral issues of his desperately troubled era. About the boyfriends, of course, Bernard saw nothing to blame except, perhaps, that some of them had so sustained Cocteau's addiction to drugs that at times he had been unable to write. Jean Marais, the sensationally handsome actor who had preceded Doudou, had not been one of those; he had, in fact, probably been the most sincerely devoted, beneficent, and altogether decent of all.

Neither Bernard nor I then knew much about Francine Weisweiller, although it was rumored that she had worked in a beauty parlor before marrying the immensely rich Alec Weisweiller, whose fortune flowed from Shell Oil. The facts were commonplace enough. Born into a well-to-do Jewish family named Worms, Francine had married at seventeen, wearied of her husband after two years, and divorced him, outraging her family, who more or less disowned her. Left to herself, she did find employ in a beauty parlor, and it has been said that at this time she began to smoke opium. Being exceptionally attractive, she found rich suitors, Guy de Rothschild and Alec Weisweiller among them, both, unfortunately, married. But Alec was so smitten that he deserted his wife and married Francine. That this union would prove no more compatible than the first became apparent even before two years had elapsed, though it begot a daughter, Carole. Divorce from a husband as rich as Alec, however, does not appear to have been an option appealing to Francine, so the two went their separate ways.

Cocteau came into the life of Madame Weisweiller because of her fortune. In 1949 he was deeply involved in the production of a film based on his novel *Les Enfants terribles*. Some of the filming had taken place in the palatial Weisweiller residence at 4, place des Etats-Unis, as Francine happened to be a cousin of the leading actress, a young woman named Nicole Stéphane, née Rothschild. Life as a rich young lady about town had begun to seem less satisfying than Francine had hoped, and this may in part be because she had not been accepted in the elite social and intellectual circles of the capital. Meeting someone like Cocteau, whose entrée and celebrity went without saying, must have looked like an opportunity not to be squandered, so she politely let it be known that she would be happy to offer material assistance for the production of *Les Enfants terribles*, should difficulty arise. Providentially, it did. Francine donated a large sum. She did more. When the production was finished, she invited Cocteau and his leading man, who happened to be Edouard Dermit, to rest from their cinematic labors at Santo-

Sospir, her villa on the Riviera. They came for ten days and stayed, off and on, for ten years. It was to express his gratitude for such extravagant largesse of hospitality that Cocteau started transforming his hostess's villa into a microcosm of what he liked to call his "graphic poetry." Francine was delighted. Famous people came to call on her famous guest. The telephone rang all day long. Stacks of letters arrived, every single one of which Cocteau answered. They were invited to amusing parties. There were balmy outings on Francine's sailing yacht. And Doudou, as well as Jean, turned out to be a pleasurable companion.

The itinerary which led Edouard Dermit from his birthplace near Trieste to the Villa Santo-Sospir was far more circuitous, not to say devious, than the routes pursued by his two companions. Born in 1925, the offspring of a working-class family, he was taken by his parents while still a child from northern Italy to northern France, where his father found employment in the coal mines. He received sufficient education to be able to write an acceptable letter and speak French correctly, but that was all. He knew nothing of what are called the humanities, and not much humanity attended his up-bringing and early youth. At the age of fourteen or fifteen he followed his father below ground into the pits, where the labor was grueling, fear of fatal accidents ceaseless, and care for the well-being of miners negligible. Added to these hardships were the odious difficulties of life during the Nazi occupation, when decent food was nearly im-possible to come by and social pleasures in the grimy, ugly mining towns nonexistent. Whatever personal initiative, resolve, or joie de vivre may originally have been latent in the young Edouard must have been pretty effectively ground out of him by the time he turned twenty. But he possessed an asset which, with a modicum of inge-nuity and a maximum of good luck, could transform a lifetime, as if nature wished occasionally to compensate for cruel hardships so often insurmountable. He was exceptionally handsome, with the face of an angel—a fallen angel, perhaps, sullen and brooding at times, but always beautiful—and hard work had added to the fine head the classical physique of a Hellenistic athlete. But so much physical favor added up to little practical benefit in the grim envi-ronment of the mines. His advantages, such as they were, required display against the teeming, competitive, anonymous, and ambiguous backdrop of a metropolis. Paris, in short, beckoned as the only destination which could offer reprieve from a backbreaking and heartbreaking future. To risk the uncertainties of the great city, however, called for daring, and the youth to whom nature had been so prodigal did not possess the strength of character to complement his physical strength. Perhaps the netherworld of the mines had sapped his moral and spiritual fortitude. His nature, at all events, was malleable and passive, and this prepared him ideally, if an ideal had anything to do with it, for the role which circumstances presently proposed. Having found the courage to leave the north for Paris, he looked around for some kind of employment. But jobs were hard to find in a capital still struggling to recover from the ravages of a war, and the young newcomer, aged about twenty-one, had no skills save those learned in the mines, and these were useless in Paris. Not afraid of hard work, he found that his most useful advantage, being simply his splendid appearance, required next to none. For a time he drifted from one experience to another until good luck led to a meeting with a publisher and bookstore owner named Paul Morihien, whose shop was in the Palais Royal. A friend of Cocteau, who, as it happened, resided nearby, Morihien introduced young Edouard, aged twenty-two, to the famous fifty-seven-year-old author. Infatuation appears to have been instantaneous, like Hadrian beholding Antinoüs for the first time. Cocteau's liaison with Jean Marais, moreover, had by then waned in intensity, and the actor was living on a houseboat in the Seine with an American ballet dancer named George Rech. Not long before, Cocteau had acquired a fine house in the small country town of Milly-la-Forêt, barely forty miles from Paris. He suggested that Dermit go live in Milly and take care of the author's garden, which, in fact, consisted mainly of a considerable lawn and a few hedges. This proposal must have seemed more creditable than those which the young man had thus far encountered, so he accepted. From Morihien Cocteau had naturally learned the details of Dermit's Parisian sojourn, and it is doubtful that he honestly foresaw a green-thumbed future for the beautiful youth. In next to no time Doudou had moved from the garden into the house and been assigned a small role in the film adapted from Cocteau's play *L'Aigle à deux têtes*. A considerably more important role came in the next Cocteau film, *Orphée*, and one may assume that the role in Cocteau's life had become by that time even more important. They were to be inseparable for sixteen years. Doudou was awarded the starring role in *Les Enfants terribles*, playing opposite Nicole Stéphane, and this performance demonstrated conclusively that he had no future as an actor. When they went south to Cap-Ferrat, Jean suggested that Doudou might take up painting as an avocation, which he obediently but rather languidly did.

Not wishing to appear too impetuous or pushy, I waited some days before using the telephone number Cocteau had given me. Bernard, moreover, seemed in no hurry for a return engagement with the author he nonetheless sincerely admired. Less than a week had passed, however, when I called the Villa Santo-Sospir. Cocteau suggested that we have lunch two days later at a waterfront restaurant in Villefranche. He knew the people who ran the place, of course; they were thrilled to receive their famous client, and complimentary drinks were served. There were no tourists in 1950, only a few French vacationers, and the Villefranche waterfront was a delightfully tranquil spot. Cocteau pointed out a gnarled, weather-beaten man mending nets at the water's edge and said, "You can't imagine his beauty twenty-five years ago." Nearby was the Hotel Welcome, and Cocteau told us of his sojourns there, smoking opium, writing some of his finest poetry and a script for the play of *Orphée*, and competing with prostitutes from Nice for the attention of sailors when the fleet dropped anchor in the bay. It was lovely in the hot sun; with some delicious fish and lots of white wine, we were all three a little drunk, and Cocteau insisted that we must henceforth use first names only. Of all the people I've known, he was one of the most prompt to adopt the outward forms of familiar friendship. Ironically enough. So we became Jean, Bernard, and James. And the more intimate second person singular, *tu*, was not to be long deferred. Jean, as usual, did all the talking, which was brilliantly entertaining. We were encouraged now and then to contribute some observation providing added momentum to his inimitable improvisations, which were so phenomenally inimitable that it seemed almost impossible to remember or record them. But, as Picasso had snidely observed, a lot of the brilliance of what he said comes vividly through in what he wrote. Still, I'm sorry now that I was not more conscientious, because the spoken words benefited from a singularly spirited and sometimes frivolous freedom which I might occasionally have caught but which Jean himself was too clever to allow on the printed page. But perhaps it was precisely the elusive, singsong, rapid-fire charm of his conversation that made it too captivating to catch. Anyway, I fell very much under the spell. When we parted in midafternoon, Jean insisted on paying for the lunch, then airily added that another visit to Santo-Sospir must not be too long delayed. Once again I had the impression that perhaps the famous author craved an admiring audience more varied than the two familiar spectators in the villa, and that maybe Francine and Doudou were also pleased to welcome strangers who had not yet become apprentices to the sorcerer. I promised to reappear quickly. Then Jean was wafted away in Francine's luxurious automobile.

I was reprimanded by Bernard for what he believed to be my sycophantic and inane behavior toward Cocteau. It was a relinquishment of social dignity, he said, and a loss of intellectual scruple. It was all very well that Cocteau happened to be a creative personality of authentic merit, entitled to thoughtful respect, but he behaved at the same time like a fame-famished starlet seeking to impress the producers of a fourth-rate bedroom farce, and this aspect of his personality earned him the scorn of discriminating poets and writers like Paul Eluard and André Breton. It went without saying, therefore, that I was a fool and a toady for having failed to respond with becoming indifference to the listless siren song of the erstwhile nightingale.

It was on that day, at all events, that Bernard renounced any incentive for seeking Cocteau's friendship, whereas I, on the other hand, felt more drawn even than before to enjoy the exotic enchantments of Santo-Sospir. The next visit was made by me alone. I told some lie to explain Bernard's absence, but he didn't seem to be missed. Jean received me by himself at first. Francine, he said, was resting. Doudou was down in the lower garden, painting a still life of flowers. Jean had a pair of binoculars at hand, took them up to study the application of his protégé, and laughed, passing them to me. It's true there was something rather ludicrous about the labored concentration, brows knotted and lips pursed, with which Doudou applied one dot of paint after another to a tiny canvas—

ludicrous but poignant. Jean talked about his own painting and drawing, explaining how he had developed an original style while undergoing a cure for opium addiction. Then, of course, true to his habit, Picasso had adopted for his own use some of Jean's most distinctive inventions. Ah, that Picasso! One had to acknowledge he was a prodigy. And how was it, Jean inquired, that Picasso and I had become such friends that the painter had had the excellent idea of sending me to make the acquaintance of one he had known, portrayed, and collaborated with for thirty-five years? It was simple enough to tell the story of the American soldier who had rung Picasso's doorbell in 1944 and, as it happened, also been portrayed by him. But then must I not often visit the artist and his family in Vallauris? Yes, fairly often, I conceded. What an excellent idea it would be, Jean exclaimed, would it not, if we were to go together to call on the painter some day soon? I agreed. Why in the world not? Then the next time I was in Vallauris, said Jean, I should set a day with Picasso for our visit. I said I'd do it and never wondered for an instant why Jean needed to go along with me to call on a man he'd known for half a lifetime.

Francine presently came onto the terrace, politely exclaiming with pleasure at my presence and appearing luxuriously at peace with the world. Doudou by that time had put away his paintbrushes. He suggested that we all go for a swim before having drinks. I had not brought along a bathing suit, but Jean said that men at Santo-Sospir never wore any, as the swimming platform was absolutely private, visible only to those using it. A path led from the bottom of the garden down the rocky end of the cape to the water's edge, where a wide cement platform had been built. Jean and Doudou and I took off our clothes, and I was awed by the beauty of the young man's physique. Never before and never since have I beheld such a marvel of masculine splendor. But Doudou himself seemed quite without self-consciousness in his nudity. He can hardly have helped knowing that he was beautiful, for that fact had transformed his life, but in some strange way it did not seem to have transformed *him*. Jean also appeared indifferent to nakedness—his own, Doudou's, and mine. But he, after all, had seen scores of beautiful nude youths. I observed that for a man of sixty-one he was remarkably fit, slender, and muscular. We swam for half an hour. The water was wonderfully clear and bracing. Afterward we lay on the cement to dry, then climbed back up to the house, where Francine sat smoking a cigarette on the terrace; and there we had drinks, while beyond the fiery horizon the sun eventually set.

A couple of days later I went to Vallauris, climbed the overgrown slope to Picasso's ugly little house, and found the family, including Paulo, the son of the artist's first marriage, just finishing lunch at about half past two. I was aware that if one were to find them at home, this was the most likely hour. Picasso knew that I had been seeing Cocteau and soon inquired about him and the Weisweiller ménage. "Not too dopey from smoking?" he sarcastically inquired. Not to my knowledge, I answered, reflecting that Picasso might have refrained from sarcasm, having been in his youth heavily addicted to the pipe. I said that Jean wanted to come and pay his old friend a visit and asked what day would be convenient. Any day would be convenient, Picasso replied, but there were days when he was absent, so callers had to take their chances. If I wanted to escort Cocteau to Vallauris, I should consult my lucky stars to find the right moment. This certainly did not constitute an invitation, even less a specific appointment, but with Picasso, protocol stemmed exclusively from his dicta. I said we'd see. After a while we went to his studio on the other side of town to observe what progress had been made on the life-size likeness of a goat made from scraps of junk picked up here and there by the artist and stuck together with plaster. Picasso was very pleased with it. But then . . . when was he not pleased with something wrested from oblivion by his hands? As for myself, I disliked the goat from the beginning and still do.

To tell Jean exactly what had been his old friend's reaction to the prospect of an imminent visit was not an appealing option. So I said only that the absence of a telephone in Picasso's house made it difficult to settle on a specific day, because the artist was subject to unpredictable commitments, such as Communist meetings, though I didn't believe for a minute that Picasso could be led to comply with any agenda except his own. Jean took this in with composure and said that Picasso was like the law that governed the universe: incomprehensible and inexorable, to be accepted without understanding by one and all, including Picasso himself. The daily sunrise itself possessed no more self-determination than Picasso when he stood before a blank canvas, brush in hand. So we would willingly put our faith in the goodwill of gravity and go to Vallauris three days later, a Thursday, stopping en route to have lunch at La Bonne Auberge, a luxurious restaurant on the highway between Nice and Antibes.

When I told Bernard about these plans, he was quite anxious to come along and witness the meeting between the two great men. For once, however, I resisted. Having made the arrangements, I would witness—alone—what manner of affinity they produced.

Jean and I had a jolly lunch at La Bonne Auberge. I was flattered and entertained to hear all his stories, though I realize that they would have been exactly the same had his guest been someone else—a shepherd, policeman, shoeshine boy, archbishop, circus acrobat, cardsharp, or what have you. I felt no conviction that the advent of James Lord in Cocteau's life would modify its landscape by so much as the addition of a single blade of grass. He talked about Proust, Nijinsky, opium, Picasso, his marriage to the Russian ballerina Olga Kokhlova, Matisse and Braque, and the Empress Eugénie, who had ended her days not far from where we sat, about Modigliani and the hardships of an artist's life, about his own diseases, his solitude, his battle to survive the war with language. I tried to say the right thing at the right time. Not that I believed it made a scrap of difference. But I think I did tolerably well, because Jean bestowed a few smiles upon me and kept on talking. It was just two when we finished. Francine's car and chauffeur waited outside. Half an hour later we were in Vallauris.

Picasso, Françoise, and the two children were still at table under the grape arbor. Exclamations of surprise, pleasure, and warm remembrance of bygone comradeship were immediate. The two men embraced. Invited to sit down and have a cup of coffee, we did. Picasso said he'd heard Cocteau was present somewhere along the coast but hadn't known how to get in touch with him. Jean said the same thing. Then wasn't it a splendid bit of luck that little Lord had come along to bring together, after far too long a separation, a pair of friends who had meant so much to each other? How many memories! Those luminous Roman afternoons in 1917. Diaghilev, Stravinsky, and Bakst. Selisburg, the bon vivant lawyer. The studio in the Via Margutta. *Parade.* Their youth. And now they stood on the threshold of old age. No, no, no, said Jean. The paintings, the poetry would live forever in the midmorning of youth. All very well, murmured Picasso, but the body does not obey. Consider Cheops. Relatively speaking, he had been present on earth but a moment before, and now nobody living could tell you the color of his eyes.

Just when the conversation had become worth remembering and recording, it was interrupted by the arrival of an uninvited Scandinavian photographer who wanted to take some pictures of the famed painter. Until his last years Picasso rarely turned away photographers, because they were important to the propagation of his legend. On this occasion he willingly posed with Paloma in his arms, then ostentatiously introduced Cocteau to the photographer, who was delighted at his luck in finding two celebrities on hand instead of one, both of them, as it happened, only too happy to submit to the interrogation of the camera. By chance I had one with me as well and took a couple of snaps of the celebrated couple, all smiles. When the photographer had finished, Picasso took Jean by the arm and suggested that they go to visit his studio. This invitation seemed to include me as well, also Françoise, who left her children in the care of the *femme de ménage*. The photographer had clearly not been invited, but he asked, with what I considered some brashness, whether he might come along, and Picasso agreed on condition that he ride with Jean and me. Picasso's car led the way and we followed.

The studio, on the other side of town, had several rooms, one for painting, another for drawings, and the largest for sculpture. We visited the painting studio first. When I was present for showings of recent work, Picasso often asked me to carry outside into the sunshine the two paintings that pleased him most, both of them versions of works by other artists. The first, and, I felt, the better, was based on a Courbet of two women voluptuously drowsing beside a river; the other was a "copy" of a supposed self-portrait by El Greco. After these pictures had been admired and carried back inside, we passed into the room where a great heap of drawings lay helter-skelter on a large table. To have touched any of them would have seemed presumptuous, and as Picasso did not pause we followed along while he made his way toward the open door of the next room, which was the sculpture studio. The anonymous photographer, however, was not intimidated. Picking up from the table a large and beautiful drawing in red crayon of a centaur and a woman, he said to Picasso, "Did you do this?"

Smirking at the obvious, Picasso said, "Yes."

"Well, do you mind," inquired the photographer, "if I take it along as a souvenir?"

The rest of us, aghast at such unthinkable effrontery, held our collective breath, expecting an outburst of indignation from the art-ist. But he liked caprice and contradiction. "Take it, of course," Picasso said. "People claim I'm stingy, but it always gives me plea-sure to offer a little souvenir to someone who likes what I do."

The presumption of the photographer was not yet satisfied. "Then would you sign it?" he asked.

"Why not?" cried Picasso, snatching a crayon from the table. And he did.

Then we all filed into the sculpture studio, bemused by what everyone except the photographer knew to have been an astonishing exception to the prevailing law of Picasso's studio. Not that he wasn't generous. He gave close friends and mistresses quantities of draw-ings and paintings. But to respond with grace to the blunt request of a stranger was decidedly not his usual practice (though, to be sure, he had once made a similar exception for me).

Since my last visit, the goat had acquired more plaster round its belly, which had originally been a wicker basket, and an anus made of the bent bottom of a tin can. There were plenty of other things to admire as well. The sculpture studio, where Picasso had been expending most of his energy over the past months, was a sort of Ali Baba's cave of his works, large and small. As we stood around, admiring and exclaiming, Picasso suddenly turned to Cocteau and said, "Well, Jean, since I'm handing out gifts, I don't want to neglect an old friend like you. Not after all that we've been through together. Let's see what I can find."

He turned away toward the rear of the studio, where a shelf along the back wall was piled with objects. Jean, Françoise, the photographer, and I waited with impatient anticipation. Since he had made an admirable gift to a total stranger, it seemed natural that he should outdo himself for an old friend. And he did—but as only Picasso might have succeeded in outdoing Picasso.

He turned toward us, smiling, with his right hand outstretched, grasping an object which he held out toward Jean, who took it as we all craned forward to see what it was. And what it was was what nobody but Picasso—or a child of five or six—could ever have made into something that looked like a Picasso: a roughly triangular scrap of broken pottery from which a handle protruded like a grotesque nose, on either side of which the artist had painted a black dot with a straight line underneath, making of the discarded fragment a ludicrous semblance of some approximate human or animal countenance. In all the studio there can hardly have been an object so preposterously devoid of beauty, novelty, or artistic interest of any kind whatsoever. Cocteau looked at it with an expression of fastidious disgust, as if he had been handed a scrap of excrement, which was very nearly what, in fact, had occurred. And for once he was left speechless.

Surely sensitive to the significance of his talkative friend's silence, Picasso said, "Look on the inner side. It's signed."

And, indeed, on the curved inner side of what had once been a cheap casserole of some kind, Picasso's signature was largely inscribed.

Then Cocteau found his voice. "Ah, Pablo," he murmured, "what you've given me is evidence that there must be life outside our solar system. This fragment is like a telegram from another world, the world where everything is created from nothing, and your name on it proves that life goes on forever, that Cheops dwells among us still, and I wager you could tell that the color of his eyes is exactly the same as yours, since both of you can see beyond the confines of creation."

"Well, I knew that that was just the thing for you," said Picasso.

Françoise observed that it was time for both her and Pablo to get to work, which I recognized as the tactful means of ending a highly awkward encounter. So we went back to the car. The photographer said good-bye and sauntered down the hill, his beautiful drawing held carefully against the breeze. Jean kissed Picasso and Françoise on the cheeks and got into the car. I did likewise and we drove away, having been in Vallauris little more than an hour.

For some moments Jean said nothing as we drove down toward the main highway. I knew the outburst was coming. He sat very straight and stared at the preposterous object in his hand. I was extremely ill at ease, because for some irrational reason I felt at fault for what had happened. The longer Jean remained silent the more tense the atmosphere within the car became, so finally I blurted, "That was abominable."

Jean glanced at me, shaking his head. "No," he said. "That was simply Picasso. Abominable, yes, but he remains Picasso, immutable, absolute creation. I couldn't tell you all the abominable things he's done. A god, you know, can be a monster. Consider Apollo torturing the miserable Marsyas to death merely because he wanted to play the flute."

But he did tell me of many unkind and cruel things Picasso had done, many to women but more than enough to men, during the years he'd spent in Paris. As he spoke he became angry, his voice grew shrill, and he waved the scrap of pottery in the air for emphasis. I was almost alarmed, feeling still that somehow I must be to blame for what had happened. I didn't record all the misdeeds attributed by Jean to his old friend, but I did write down that Picasso had once broken the leg of his ballerina wife by striking her with a chair during an altercation. I've since been told that, although Olga did at one time suffer a broken leg, Picasso probably was not responsible for it, however emphatically Jean that afternoon insisted he was. The old story of Picasso's disowning his friend Apollinaire when questioned about the stolen statuettes from the Louvre also came up. It as well is probably untrue. And the allegation that Picasso had not lifted a finger to save his oldest friend, Max Jacob, from the Gestapo. There were plenty of other stories, too, enough to occupy the entire time of our drive back to Villefranche. Some of them must have been true, but I couldn't record them all, especially as Bernard continually interrupted me, wanting to know exactly what had happened. The strange thing was that Jean had never once referred to the hideous object given him by Picasso, nor did he later ever mention it, though for some time it sat ludicrously on the mantelpiece in the salon at Santo-Sospir, disappearing only when gifts indescribably finer took its place.

Several days went by before I returned to Vallauris. Picasso's car was not on the road at the foot of the path, and I found the front of the house deserted, the door closed. It was not the first time I'd made the trip for nothing. Still, I thought that the *femme de ménage* might be present and decided to have a look in the kitchen before going to the studio or the pottery, where Picasso often worked in the midafternoon. The kitchen door was at the head of a flight of outside concrete stairs that led up to a terrace. It stood open. Picasso sat alone at the table inside. I said hello. He stared at me for a long minute, then shouted, "How dare you bring that whore to my house?"

Stunned, I stepped backward and muttered some phrase to the effect of not understanding.

At this Picasso leapt to his feet, overturning behind him the chair on which he'd been seated, and shouted, "That whore Cocteau. He never would have dared to come by himself, so he used you. When I think I've treated you like a son, and you do this to me. It's intolerable. I told Françoise you'd fail the test."

"But how could I know?" I stammered. "It was you who told me to go and see him. He was a witness at your wedding. You've known each other for forty-five years."

"That buffoon," said Picasso, "that perfidious arriviste, that vampire. How many young men do you think he's destroyed? Maybe you're one of them. Has he been fucking you?"

"No, he hasn't," I said. "And he's never tried to."

"Amazing," murmured Picasso. "Opium then, I suppose."

"Not at all."

"Well, I can imagine he was pretty enraged by the gift I found for him, wasn't he?"

"He didn't say so. He didn't mention it at all."

"Ungrateful slut!" Picasso exclaimed, picking up his chair and sitting down again at the kitchen table. For some time he sat there in silence, staring at nothing, and it was as if he had ceased to be aware of my presence.

Feeling that it was time to leave, I said, "I'm sorry. I only wanted to please everyone. If it turned out badly, I'm sorry."

"Oh, don't burst into tears," Picasso said calmly. "Here. Come and sit down. Have a glass of wine. You Americans are so sentimental. Maybe that's why you think you should rule the world."

I didn't answer. The two of us sat together quietly for a few minutes, and then the voices of Françoise and the children came from outside. Picasso put his hand over mine. "Don't despair," he said. "What I told you about Cocteau is the truth. You'll find out. But he has a song. If you find the music pleasing for a while, all right. I like it myself sometimes. Now I must go and put some teats onto my goat. Come back soon." Then he was gone.

Françoise came into the kitchen with some packages. "Has he been shouting?" she asked.

"He frightened me," I said.

"He was planning on that. It's what he likes to do. As an artist, too. Very good at it. But you must never show fear. Just be yourself, then you're all right. If necessary, you can walk out and close the door."

I continued to see Cocteau, and it came to be the case that I could arrive at Santo-Sospir for a drink without even bothering to telephone in advance. I *did* find the music of his presence pleasing, though I noticed that if one saw him often there was a certain repetitiveness to the song. New melodies seemed to be composed every two weeks or so. Bernard deigned to come along occasionally, too, and was always cordially received. We had dinner at the villa now and then. And it was with Bernard and Jean that I went in Francine's car to Vallauris early in August to attend the ceremony of the unveiling of Picasso's sculpture *The Man with a Lamb*, a gift of the artist to the town he had almost overnight made famous.

The proceedings were to take place in the market square, where a raised platform had been set up facing the sculpture, which was covered with a tarpaulin. Picasso, Françoise, Paul Eluard, and a group of Communist Party officials were seated up there. The artist waved to us, but we were not summoned to join him on the platform. By good luck and some persistent shoving, aided by Cocteau's celebrity, we were able to squeeze onto a balcony behind the platform, thus able to witness all that went on. I knew that Eluard, a distinguished poet, committed Party member, and unconditional Stalinist, was a declared enemy of Cocteau, whom he considered a frivolous and narcissistic climber. The principal speaker was a thick-set Communist called Laurent Casanova, nicknamed "the French Zhdanov," no compliment by way of reference to a man known for his brutal repression of artists and intellectuals. Casanova was reputed, however, to have been instrumental in persuading Picasso to join the Party. His address, broadcast by loudspeakers to the crowded square, was by no means an airy effusion attuned to Sunday afternoon jollity. Picasso was praised for his attainments as a painter, but it was his exemplary commitment to a logical program for the benefit of mankind that excited the speaker's eloquence. There was urgent work to be done in the world, and just as art had a useful role in disseminating truth, a revolutionary artist must participate in revolutionizing society, redressing its injustices, and reconciling its disaffected elements. *The Man with a Lamb* stood for the principles of brotherhood and political progress personified by Picasso, faithful member of the Communist Party. And so on.

During this lengthy harangue, the painter sat still on the platform, his back to us. Photographs published later show him to have been smiling. One can only wonder, with a sentiment akin to stupefaction, how the man who proclaimed that his whole life as an artist was a continuous struggle against reaction and the death of art can have brazenly connived at his own humiliation. Cocteau remained singularly silent during the entire ceremony and as soon as it was over declared that we must leave. Our progress back to the car was impeded by attractive boys and girls soliciting signatures to a Communist tract, especially insistent that Jean, a recognizable celebrity, sign; and his very politest pirouettes were improvised to avoid it, the inveterate giver of autographs repeatedly insisting, *"Je ne signe jamais rien, mon chéri."*

Casanova's speech had seemed to me nothing better than cynical bile, especially since Communist armies in Korea had at that very moment overrun almost all of the south, but I dismissed it as irrelevant. Picasso, not Communism, was what mattered. Jean was decidedly not of the same mind. He was incensed, and en route back to Villefranche he delivered himself of a considerable diatribe. Picasso's politics, he said, were a travesty and a dishonor. Nobody who cared two straws for decency and justice could conceivably have anything to do with Communism, not after Gide's return from Russia, the Great Terror and the trials of 1937, treacheries in Picasso's own homeland, the Stalin-Hitler pact, the betrayal of the Warsaw Uprising, the Iron Curtain, and so much more. How could Picasso—the artist who had set art free, who had employed his genius to denounce tyranny and reaction, the painter of *Guernica*

—how could this man collaborate with the agents of a monstrous dictator and let them use his works to advertise their sordid schemes? It was worse than hypocrisy. It was ignominy. I was very impressed by this tirade and never forgot it, but I couldn't help wondering whether it would have been quite so vehement if Cocteau, instead of Eluard, had been invited to preside alongside Picasso throughout the ceremony.

During the rest of the summer, which lasted for Bernard and me till mid-September, I continued regularly to see both Jean and Picasso, the former more often than the latter because he never intimidated me, seemed actually to enjoy my company, and always welcomed me, I felt, with sincere warmth whenever I turned up. One day after lunch on the waterfront, he came to our apartment and made for each of us a large ink drawing. All my life I've had drawing paper, watercolors, India ink, and crayons on hand, because I've always done a bit of painting and drawing, none of it, however, ever taken seriously by myself or anyone else. The drawings Jean made for us were in his Orpheus style. The Orphic legend and cult were constant staples of his conversation that summer, and he maintained that he could easily imagine his own disembodied head, still singing, afloat upon the wine-dark sea to teach the arts of poetry and song to denizens of the deeps. It was no accident that Francine had named her yacht *Orpheus*. We went sailing several times up and down the coast, once as far as Monte Carlo, where Jean went to the Hôtel de Paris to have his hair cut while I waited in the lobby. When he came back, his hair was bright blue, and he said, "Léon overdid it." However, he didn't seem to mind and gladly gave his autograph to a young girl on the sidewalk who had recognized him. I said, "It must be a terrible nuisance to be so famous that people recognize you in the street." He threw up his hands and exclaimed, "It *is* terrible, my dear, but the terror isn't in the recognition, it's in the cause of it, you see."

Along the coast road not far from Antibes there was an extravagant antique emporium, with huge wooden horses from extinct carousels rearing outside amid rococo iron furniture and Art Nouveau statuary. We stopped there one afternoon, Jean fancying that he might discover some amusing gewgaw for Santo-Sospir, because he was already pondering the project of making a short film about the villa. We didn't find anything, but in the rear courtyard stood an ornate wicker chair, a Graustarkian item, Jean said, asking whether I had my camera along. I did. Then we'd do a scene, and Bernard, who happened to be with us, could be cameraman. He sat me down in the chair, standing himself behind it, and told me to gaze up at him. "With innocence, trust, a certain childlike naïveté," he said. "You know a secret which you don't know you know, and the whole plot turns on that." He took hold of the chair between delicately poised fingertips, raising to his lips the admonitory forefinger of his right hand, and said, "Camera." Bernard snapped two or three times, and one of the photographs turned out rather well. It was only for a laugh, of course, but my trusting gaze and Jean's grave expression of warning are so true to life, as it were, that later I couldn't help wondering whether *he* knew at the time what the secret was that I knew without knowing it. I found out eventually, of course, what it was.

Picasso finished his goat. He gave me a couple of drawings and a particularly ugly terra-cotta platter. He and Françoise seemed to have frequent altercations, and to my surprise it was she, I thought, who often came out on top. When I said good-bye to them at the end of the summer, it was rather with a feeling that I might never see them again. But I did.

Returning to Paris, I found all my familiar friends, also some new ones, including Jean and Doudou. Then I departed for America in mid-October to say hello to my family.

Life in Englewood, New Jersey, at 182 Hillside Avenue, where I was alone with my mother, father, grandmother, and a couple of servants, was not very entertaining after the exotic and erotic freedoms I had enjoyed in Europe. Still, I was allowed to do as I pleased, and what I pleased to do was to spend most of each day writing, then often drive into New York for the evening. I don't remember now which unpublishable novel I was working on, because my journal says only novel, novel, novel and laments the difficulty—but not the futility!—of writing it. I wrote letters as well. To my friends overseas, whither it was my resolve to return come springtime. It never occurred to me to write to Picasso, since I knew very well I'd receive no reply. But I wrote to Jean, aware that he answered every single letter he received. In his lifetime he must have written something like fifty thousand letters. Until the time of our falling out six years after our meeting, I myself received about fifty, although during that period I was seeing him fairly regularly at Santo-Sospir, in Paris, and at Milly. The very first letter that I received was sent from Milly on the twenty-eighth of November, 1950, and it was virtually a model for all those that followed. Jean's letters, no matter how short or how long, never covered more than the recto of a single page; the script was sometimes flowing and legible, sometimes tiny, arachnid, and almost hieroglyphic. Occasionally there was a drawing. Usually there were descriptions and lamentations concerning physical ailments more or less serious but seemingly incessant. There were expressions of endearment and impatience at the length of separations. But there was almost never a single phrase to suggest the innermost feelings, the personal thoughts and sentiments, the essence of the private man. One could not help suspecting that if he wrote, say, half a dozen letters while drinking his breakfast coffee, comparison would have shown such similarity between them that for the author the recipients might almost have been interchangeable. And I may say that I have been in a position to compare.

On the twenty-eighth of November he complained of otitis, announcing an operation the following Thursday. "You can imagine how much I fret and suffer in my room." On the second of January he had come out of the clinic after the operation on his ear. "Twelve days of solitude without speaking and without hearing. I was forbidden, moreover, to read. In short, we embrace you and dream that you will come back to us as quickly as possible." On the fifteenth of January the after-effects of the operation had caused outbreaks of eczema on his face. On the twenty-second he was painting large canvases. "Painting keeps one from thinking of the sick world and of one's own sickness." On the ninth of March: "I am still sick. My left hand torments me at night." On the thirteenth: "Here it's one day of sun, one of mist. The results are crises of sham colds and miseries which compel me to wear gloves while painting, which the journalists would consider an affectation."

During most of the spring, when I returned to Europe, Jean seemed to be reasonably well, sending letters to Capri ("Capri must still be mythical, thus real.") and Florence ("Florence is a city that exists only in the minds of a few aesthetes."), where I was visiting Harold Acton; but on the seventh of June he returned to Santo-Sospir "rather sick." Early in July Doudou underwent an operation in Cannes for appendicitis, returning to Santo-Sospir by midmonth. "He walks like an aged general but is feeling well."

I arrived in Villefranche with Bernard on the eighth of August, 1951. The motorcycle, now a thing of the past, had been replaced by a Ford convertible. We rented a small apartment. Arriving at the Villa Santo-Sospir, I found it in the state of well-ordered chaos that naturally accompanies the making of a motion picture. Having by this time finished painting almost every wall, and some ceilings, of the house, Jean had determined to produce a film in honor of the ensemble as a token of gratitude for his hostess and, incidentally, as a tribute to the protean talents of the artist. Consequently, an enormous truck was parked in front of the villa, while inside serpentine electric cables wriggled underfoot, the rooms were cluttered with arc lights and cameras, tracks for traveling shots were set down in the salon and on the terrace, and most of the furniture had been pushed into corners. In short, the place was a mess. But its inhabitants were delighted. They welcomed me with enthusiasm as a witness to the celluloid consecration of a miracle, it seemed, which their triple intimacy had wrought. To just what extent that tripartite relationship may, indeed, have been intimate was a matter much debated but never, so far as I am aware, known for sure by any but the three individuals concerned. Assumptions, in any case, were not lacking, and the one regarding opium appears to have been correct. Anyway, the making of the movie was an exceedingly tedious business, a fact well known to everybody who has had an opportunity to observe the process. Even for a short and modest film like this one, each little detail had to be arranged and rearranged, rehearsed and re-rehearsed before the actual filming, which itself was liable to be repeated again and again. Two or three hours could easily be devoted to a sequence that would appear on the screen for less than a minute. The privilege of observing this collective creative process is not one that provides much entertainment, however diverting and artistic may be the outcome.

I went to dinner with Picasso and his family in Vallauris. It was a pleasantly warm evening. We ate outside on the terrace. Everyone seemed in excellent humor. There were no altercations, and not a word was said about Cocteau.

The filming went on and on, but I enjoyed my visits to Santo-Sospir all the same. Bernard did not come along. One scorching hot afternoon Jean and I went down alone to swim. Afterward, as we lay on our towels to dry, he said, "It's absurd, my dear. There's something I've been meaning to do for ever so long. When we return to the villa, come to my bedroom."

What he meant to do he didn't say, supposing, perhaps, that I could guess. But I couldn't. Maybe this was the prelude to what Picasso had asked about. If so, I was not averse. When we had climbed back up through the garden, we went straight to his room, which was on the lower level of the house, beneath the terrace, and had a door opening directly to the exterior. It was cool. He told me to sit down on his bed. Having done so, I awaited with some agitation what might come next. But it wasn't at all what I anticipated. Or perhaps in a very different way it was. Settling in a chair beside his desk, he took up a sketchbook and said, "I'm going to try a portrait of you. I've had it on my mind for ever so long. Show me your profile. Chin up a little higher. There. After the swim, maybe I can see something. Besides, you're a rather good-looking boy."

He worked in silence for fifteen or twenty minutes, no longer, then handed me the sketchbook. "Will that be to your liking?" he asked.

It was and I said so. Maybe he thought I was good-looking, but I felt he had made me handsome, which I didn't believe myself to be. Still, I was gratified by the image and attempted to express my appreciation. "You can show it to Picasso," said Jean. Taking back the sketchbook, he wrote on the page:

To James
his friend
Jean
☆
Santo-Sospir
August 1951

Bernard was a bit envious but at the same time censorious, as though I had done something slightly reprehensible in order to prevail upon Cocteau to make my portrait or as if the mere possession of it were in some way discreditable. I remembered this with rather cynical amusement several years later. To have shown the drawing to Picasso was the very last thing I'd have considered doing with it. Jean never asked whether I had. Maybe he guessed why I couldn't. If so, it would have been very unlike him to allow anyone else to understand.

It was only gradually that I came to realize that Jean was an affectionate and generous friend, prepared to go to considerable trouble to make himself obliging (and to create obligations), but that at the same time he meticulously avoided the candor and responsiveness of genuine intimacy. He did not want to know anything about the deep feelings, worries, or aspirations of his friends. He was charming, polite, *serviable*, but those qualities were exhibited in order to keep people at a distance while serving a desire for popularity so great that it took precedence not only over fatigue but over judgment. When faced with the naked need or emotional stress of another, Jean by an elegant pirouette suddenly managed to achieve an incommensurable remoteness. "Let us beware," he once wrote, "of the drowning who cling to us and who drown us." An excellent swimmer in the water and in the world, he kept safely away from anyone in danger of going down for the last time, while eloquently mourning the unhappy event after the fact. It seems strange today that I was slow to perceive this aspect of Jean's character, and, to tell the truth, I didn't fully grasp it until I got into rather deep and hot water myself. Meanwhile, I enjoyed without scruple the afternoons or evenings at Santo-Sospir, drinking gin and raspberry juice on the terrace, smoking cigarettes and listening to Jean talk, all the while floating in the exotic fragrance of tuberoses, which to this day invariably recalls those enchanted moments.

In Paris Jean lived with Doudou at 36, rue de Montpensier in a two-room apartment with windows opening beneath the arcades of the Palais Royal. It was rather dim, for only the kitchen and bathroom had windows on the street side. There they were attended by a housekeeper named Madeleine Bourret, who took great pride in the celebrity of her employer, acting to some extent as a guardian-cum-social secretary. In the stairway outside Jean's door, anony-mous young men often waited in hopeful anticipation of glimpsing the great man or, even better, prevailing upon him to autograph a book or, better still, having the volume enriched by a drawing. Made-leine habitually took stock of these admirers, and her whim often determined which ones should be privileged with an audience. She was unpretentious, down to earth, and I liked her. Having been presented as an accepted friend of the household, I was always warmly welcomed by her. But I didn't go very often to the rue de Montpensier, because the place was so small that with Jean, Dou-dou, and Madeleine present, the addition of even one more person constituted something of a crowd. The kitchen often served as a waiting room. When I did go there, it was usually to accompany Jean, Doudou, and Francine to lunch at the Grand Véfour, a lux-urious restaurant just around the corner where Jean was persona ultra grata. We also had lunch or dinner sometimes at Francine's palatial residence on the place des Etats-Unis just across the square from the mansion of Marie-Laure de Noailles, who had known Cocteau intimately as a girl and later subsidized his first film. The two ladies, needless to say, had little use for each other, the vis-countess deploring the poet's companionship with a woman she deemed unsuitable.

The house at Milly-la-Forêt was far more spacious and elegant than the Paris apartment. Standing by itself at the end of a dead-end street and isolated from nearby buildings by a stream that ran through the property, the place was completely private, the house itself, two stories high with an attic above, large without being grand and mostly covered by ivy. Jean had not seen fit to transform his own residence into a total—one might almost say totalitarian—museum of his graphic poetry. That was all very well for Santo-Sospir and for the various deconsecrated chapels and public places he later decorated. His own home was designed to satisfy a lifelong disposition to make a poet's dwelling place the haunt of bizarre and arcane fantasy. He had always surrounded himself, even when poor, with outlandish, baroque objects, many of them made by himself, others liberated from the flea markets; and his various abodes had won the awe of innumerable aesthetes. To install the decor at Milly, he was luckily not dependent entirely upon his own resources, which were never lavish, as Francine logically took it for granted that she would frequently reside there. Jean had originally acquired the house in 1947. Its interior installation was not completed until several years later and included numerous strange, costly items. Center stage was the main salon on the ground floor. Victorian sofas and neo-Gothic cabinets stood round the walls, set off by two gilded, wooden fruit trees, said to have come from Versailles, and an extraordinarily large narwhal tusk mounted in bronze. The chairs were chinoiserie or composed of bison's horns. Bronze casts of Cocteau's hands lay on a table. A sumptuous Savonnerie carpet covered the floor. Against the white-and-green Art-Nouveau wallpaper hung a pastel of a ballerina by Degas and a large canvas by Bérard depicting the confrontation of Oedipus and the Sphinx. In a silver frame was the famous photo of Stravinsky and Nijinsky. It was in this cluttered, heteroclite setting that Jean received and entertained his guests. I went there often, sometimes serving as a taxi for friends without cars. One afternoon, searching for an out-of-the-way bathroom, I went upstairs and, having opened the wrong door, found myself in Doudou's bedroom. He lay outstretched on his bed, attired only in his underwear, gazing wide-eyed at the ceiling. The odor in the room was heavy, pungent. I spoke to him, but he did not answer. So I closed the door and soon found the one I'd been looking for.

It was at Milly, I think, removed from the agitation of Paris and the languor of the Riviera, that Jean was most satisfyingly and satisfactorily himself and there also that one could approach and appreciate him with the greatest simplicity and pleasure. That, at all events, was my feeling. I liked him and felt confident that he liked me. That winter of 1952, for example, I had a severe attack of the flu, which kept me in bed for more than ten days. Fortunately I was then living in the guest room of an American friend I'd known in the army who was now at the U.S. embassy in Paris. He often had to go away on trips around Europe, leaving me alone in his comfortable apartment in the rue de l'Université, where I spent mornings and afternoons writing at his dining room table. I suspected he was in the CIA but never, of course, knew for sure. Anyway, while sick in bed, I received three visits from Jean, who brought me flowers and cookies made by Madeleine. He was leaving for Cap-Ferrat the following week and invited me on Francine's behalf to come to

Santo-Sospir to recuperate. I didn't go, because I felt that it would be difficult to do any writing there. Jean, after all, had a separate studio, whereas I knew the one guest room to be small and without a desk. Still, I was touched by the visits and the invitation, believing them to be sincere evidence of care and affection.

Then in April of 1952 I once more sailed back to America, where to my surprise and somewhat to my dismay I was to remain for a year. And it was during this absence that my relationship with Jean, and his with Picasso, underwent a change. I kept on writing to Santo-Sospir, and Santo-Sospir conscientiously replied. I even received a letter from Doudou, composed somewhat in the Cocteau style though with a few grammatical mistakes. It was on the eleventh of August that Jean first mentioned the possibility that I might take on the task of translating into English some of his works, mentioning first *Les Enfants terribles*. In a postscript he said, "Haven't yet seen Picasso. Wrote to Françoise without reply." I didn't know quite how to respond to the prospect of becoming Cocteau's translator. He said that if I should accept, "it would be a dream." Writing on September 1, he again said a translation by me "would be a dream," adding, "Very difficult, but you will know how." I was flattered, of course, and allowed Jean to assume that I would be happy to give it a try. He was now addressing me as My Very Dear James and by way of conclusion embracing me with tenderness. I sent him a photograph of myself taken at the age of five or six. He replied, "With what grace you send me proof that true faces do not change but preserve childhood. Picasso was saying just yesterday that one reaches one's maximum at five or six. Afterward one strives to rejoin it. He much inquired for news of you." So Jean had apparently reestablished himself in the good graces of the contemporary he had admired— and envied—most. And exactly two months after he wrote this letter, an event occurred which would permanently secure his companionable place in Picasso's orbit.

Paul Eluard died in mid-November. On the twenty-third, Jean wrote, "The death of Eluard was lugubrious. Entirely fraudulent funereal and political pomp around a stranger made of marble or of wax who had taken his place." His place, of course, in addition to that of honored poet and Communist eulogist, had been at Picasso's side as one of his closest, most trusted friends. Death had left that place vacant, and Jean hastened to establish his right to it. If Picasso considered Jean a buffoon and a whore, characteristics which he would have had no difficulty perceiving in himself, it must be said that throughout his life he consistently enjoyed the company of such characters. And Jean, to be sure, was witty, clever, inventive, truly creative, and, above all, highly entertaining. That there may have been flaws in the foundation upon which all these qualities stood was not the issue. Picasso, a jester of genius, enjoyed having an accomplice, and he had reached an age at which he liked to impersonate in earnest the clowns he had depicted with compassion fifty years before. This was the beginning of his long, steady, and lamentable decline as an artist.

In the same letter that related Eluard's death, Jean wrote, "I dream of a profound understanding between us through a book. But I hardly dare to bother you with my fear of being badly translated except by the language of the heart." On December 6 he told me that he was sending the proofs of his latest book, a volume of autobiographical writings entitled *Le Journal d'un inconnu* (*The Journal of an Unknown Man*), adding yet again that a translation by me would be a dream and "a masterpiece because you know the soul of our language." On December 28 he not only reiterated his desire to have me translate his work but expressed the hope that I would find a publisher for it. In a postscript he requested that I send by return mail the address of Marlene Dietrich. (I didn't have it.) Two days later he wrote, "I'm certain that *only* you will know how to reveal the visage of my soul (a visage unknown)." Ten days later he advised that he was also sending *La Difficulté d'être* (*The Difficulty of Being*).

In mid-January I received the two books, which, along with several others in much the same vein, constituted what Jean expressly considered his autobiography, anecdotal, intellectual, and spiritual. I read them at once, and the more I read the more I felt the onset of grave misgivings. Autobiography induces one to consider not only what one is told about the author but everything one knows about him. As one reads Jean's autobiographical musings, it soon becomes clear, if one knows very much about him, that what one is being told and what one knows are far from the same. Contradiction and inconsistency became so ingrained with Cocteau that he virtually made his strength of them. The "difficulty" that truly confounded him was one not of being but of seeming. He was obsessed by appearances. Incident and fact abound, but he so manipulates them that he, indeed, comes to seem almost unknown. Throughout his works the device of the mirror recurs with symptomatic regularity, and the image he sought to fix forever in his eye and in ours was his own. But this was not to reveal his true nature and, by extension, human nature. It was for the aggrandizement of the image of the deathless poet, the child-angel-hero who defies fate and safeguards the divine nature of mankind, and in so doing risks destruction in the anarchy of an unappreciative world. As long as he lived, Jean was unable to reconcile his wishful, theoretical concept of himself with the existence of a self whose incongruous and incorrigible behavior he was compelled to rationalize, and this tells us why he conceived of being as difficult. The conflict between antithetic selves generated a tension that doubtless fructified his talent. Yet because he was unprepared or unable to serve the needs of that talent for its own sake but obliged it to serve needs foreign to all serious creativity, this tension ultimately avenged itself by limiting the scope of his talent and inhibiting its fulfillment. The outcome was drama of a kind and an authentic, understandable anguish.

More than any other people, perhaps, the French are in love with their language. Few have written it with such hypnotic fascination as Cocteau. He had a prodigious mastery of rhetorical effects. With superb precision and ingenuity he could present in a minimum of space and with a maximum of emphasis the essence of his visions and intuitions, many of which are indeed trenchant. His greatest talent was for brilliant photographic impressions: the description of Proust returning home from his nocturnal wanderings is lapidary, but in the end Cocteau's phrases take precedence even over the magnitude of Proust's imposing presence. Style, offering the surest passport to literary immortality, is not to be dismissed lightly. It was to the unique virtuosity of his style that Jean certainly owed the impressive reputation he early acquired and long maintained even through periods of bleak creative irresponsibility. Unfortunately, the cadenza quality of his style does not survive in translation. French, the language of the mot juste, or of the *mot tout court*, does not lend itself to the workaday verbiage of other tongues. And even more unfortunately, Jean was not content to be a stylist but wished to prove himself a thinker as well. He told readers that he stood by his ideas, no matter how contradictory. But the contradiction was in him, not in his ideas, for he had none. The serious thinkers of his era refused to take him seriously, and he acknowledged that his personality exposed his work to severe judgment. But he refused to accept the verdict, threw out quantities of glittering phrases, and went on his way, brilliant, idolized, but miserable.

Such were my opinions, reached painstakingly and reluctantly, with lengthy ratiocination and true remorse recorded in *my* journal, when I had finished careful readings of *La Difficulté d'être* and *Le Journal d'un inconnu.* It was unthinkable, needless to say, that I should express them to Jean. He had been consistently hospitable, kind, even affectionate to me. And he continued ardently to hope that I would translate at least one of his books. Toward the end of January he wrote, "How could you fail to believe that this translation would form but another bond between our hearts? The book is like a long letter that I send you. Nothing more." He fell ill with the flu in February but wrote that my translation would infuse him with the red blood cells he lacked. By the end of the month he was sufficiently recovered to lunch with Picasso. "I will embrace him for you," he wrote. On March 6 he exulted, "Stalin is dead. Picasso *reigns.*" But he returned to the issue of translation, saying, "In a certain way it's a marriage that I'm proposing. I offer you my hand through which flows the soul in the form of ink."

During these weeks I had not been so self-righteous and vain that I didn't honestly attempt to translate lengthy passages from *Le Journal d'un inconnu.* Setting aside my opinion of the text itself, I conscientiously labored to render into English the linguistic legerdemain of Cocteau's epigrammatic and histrionic style. "Not alchemy," I wrote in my journal, aping Jean deliberately, "would be to the purpose of this enterprise but, rather, the power to polish a diamond by the use of a rhinestone." I couldn't do it, but I *did* try, and my only consolation is that when *La Difficulte d'être* was at last published in an English translation after Jean's death, the work left readers wondering how he had ever earned his reputation as a stylist. As for *Le Journal d'un inconnu,* it was trounced by French critics and never found its way into English. One of its gravest flaws, of course, was that its renowned and conspicuous author really believed himself to be misunderstood, the victim of prejudice and loose thinking, a man intellectually and spiritually unknown; and this, after forty-five years of unabashed self-advertisement, seemed close to comic, if not sheerly bathetic.

So the irksome day finally came when I had to write Jean and tell him that despite my most conscientious, loyal efforts, I found myself unable to translate his work and felt compelled in all sincerity to abandon the effort. His reply was as I expected.

> *Saint-Jean-Cap-Ferrat*
> *A.M. 16 March 1953*

> *My James,*
>
> *Your letter consternates me but does not succeed in convincing me. I attribute it to your fear of doing a favor poorly. How could you do so, since you are alarmed by what others never fear? Talk further with your friends. My writing is very difficult. But it will be even more so for strangers than for you, who thinks with his heart. You need only to revise your text, to go over it with friends. We will succeed, I assure you, and I would be too sad if we were to fail. Yesterday Picasso obliged me to engrave nine platters. I believed myself incapable of it. I did it. Answer me quickly.*
>
> *I embrace you,*
> *Jean*
> ☆

I did answer quickly, reiterating with unhappy regret my conviction that I was not equal to the task and expressing the heartfelt wish that this failure would not appear a betrayal of our friendship. For his part, Jean also answered quickly, his reply dated March 25. "How could you believe," he wrote, "that I care more for a book than for you, more for an American publication than for our private rapport? Don't distress yourself . . . So all is in order . . . I embrace you from the bottom of my heart."

It was gracious, it was princely. He must have been disappointed, and so was I, but already I've said that one could not hope to meet a man more polite or more quick to grant a favor when asked. The issue of translation was not quite abandoned, however, for on May 15 Jean inquired whether I would be prepared to translate a short piece for Edith Piaf. I declined again.

In the same letter he announced that he was leaving on the twenty-seventh to deliver a lecture in connection with the large retrospective exhibition of Picasso's works at the National Gallery of Modern Art in Rome. Francine and Doudou went along, but Picasso stayed put in Vallauris. In June, however, the painter and poet traveled together to be present at a corrida in Céret, the town in the Pyrenees foothills where Picasso had executed some of his greatest Cubist masterpieces more than forty years before. If there had been coolness between the two men—and there definitely had—the relationship was now demonstrably warm, though neither of them ever forgot which one determined the temperature.

That year, 1953, I arrived in Villefranche on the second of August and remained for six weeks, as usual in a modest rented apartment, the sort of accommodation easily had in those days. This was the last summer I was to spend there. I never imagined that it might mark the end of a chapter in my life. It was only the beginning of the end. At Santo-Sospir I found everything and everybody unchanged. Or almost unchanged. Jean had gone on painting. Few surfaces now remained unadorned, and there were mosaics designed by him at the entrance to the villa in case a visitor chanced not to know the identity of the graphic poet who dwelt within. And in the salon I immediately noticed that the hideous gift of the miscalculated visit to Vallauris three years before had now disappeared from the mantelpiece, replaced by several beautiful ceramic tiles painted by Picasso. As usual, we sat on the terrace, drinking and smoking, while Jean told us hilarious stories of imaginary, eccentric, picturesque people whose ludicrous adventures he had invented to amuse Picasso. We went swimming, sailing, driving on the Haute Corniche and paid a call on Somerset Maugham, who overtly eyed Doudou in a pair of tight white shorts and was permitted by Jean *par extraordinaire* to do a modicum of the talking. In the entrance hall of the Villa Mauresque hung a large, superb Picasso of the classical period. Jean asked our host whether he knew the painter and, when Maugham said no, offered to arrange a meeting. Willie wryly replied, "D-d-does he play b-b-bridge?" It was icily clear that the two famous writers did not take to one another, Maugham undoubtedly considering Cocteau an affected popinjay, while Jean frankly regarded his elder as the facile author of light stuff to be read on the train. There was something to be said for both views.

I went to Vallauris too, finding the whole family present and apparently in excellent humor despite rumors that Françoise might leave Picasso. In the studio, however, were numerous recent portraits of her. We had lunch twice in Golfe-Juan, but by the middle of the month Picasso had gone off to Perpignan. I did not see him again that summer, and in fact was to see him only twice more the summer following.

Back in Paris in October, I had a letter from Jean in which he said, "You must have learned of the Picasso drama. Françoise has left the conjugal domicile with the kids. *But silence.* Picasso likes to do the leaving, not to be left." The drama was genuine, alas, and had an unhappy effect on all the actors.

That winter—it was 1954—I saw little of Jean, Doudou, and Francine. It was the beginning of my intense friendship with Dora Maar, which occupied me almost to the exclusion of all else. Almost, but not entirely. Jean was frequently in the south or at Kitzbühel, in Austria. Absence, however, did not diminish his inveterate readiness to do a friend a favor, and at my request he subtly intervened with an editor of his acquaintance to ensure that my first novel would be published in translation. This kindness naturally renewed my sense of remorse over having failed to translate a book for him, and knowing that he didn't hold it against me only aggravated my contrition. I did not desist from asking favors however. My friend Bernard, though not eager to show much personal admiration for Cocteau, took it into his head that he would nonetheless enjoy having his portrait drawn and asked me to ask Jean to do it. I asked. Jean inevitably agreed and set a date and time when Bernard might come to the rue de Montpensier to pose. In the evening of the appointed day I went to Bernard's home and asked him to show me the drawing. What was my astonishment and indignation to be told that he hadn't gone to the rue de Montpensier. "And why not?" I demanded. Well, Bernard flightily explained, he hadn't been in the mood to pose that afternoon, so he'd gone to the movies instead. He had not even bothered to telephone to say that he wouldn't be coming. Incensed, I maintained that such nonchalance constituted an offense not only to Cocteau but to me. Bernard dismissed the business as inconsequential. If so, I told him, he could be sure that I would definitely not renew the request or endeavor to make some sort of apologetic excuse to explain away his cavalier discourtesy. Five years later Bernard was to suffer his comeuppance in a sequel both mortifying and bizarrely appropriate.

In April I went with Dora to the house Picasso had given her in the small Provençal village of Ménerbes. While there, she suggested that I drive across the mountains to the Riviera and pay a visit to Picasso. This was a rather perverse proposal on her part, given the assumptions Picasso might have made about my relationship with his cast-off mistress, but Dora was nothing if not complex. And I was prompt to accept her whims. I had not seen Picasso since the previous August, and the prospect of a visit was beguiling. But one could never be sure of getting past the painter's box office, as he delighted in observing, so I felt hesitant. Dora said that I should write him a letter announcing my arrival, telling him that I was staying with her in Ménerbes and would come bearing a gift. Then, she affirmed, I could be certain of a warm welcome. I did as she said. It occurred to me also that I might combine a visit to Vallauris with one to Santo-Sospir, having been so often invited to stay there, my absence lamented in many a letter. So I telephoned to Cap-Ferrat, and Jean responded with warmth to the announcement of an imminent arrival, proposing that I dine at the villa and spend the night at the nearby Hôtel du Cap-Ferrat. I agreed, of course, with pleasure, keeping to myself my surprise that Santo-Sospir, after all, could not accommodate a guest. Perhaps, I thought, what went on there at night did not allow for the conceivable indiscretion of a witness, however friendly.

It was gleaming afternoon, April 21, when I set out in my little black car for the slow, tedious drive to the coast. But I was elated and sang to myself as I passed through the olive groves and ravines, across the flowery mountainsides, and came at last to the sea, thinking of that wonderful passage in Xenophon when his weary soldiers finally catch sight of the Aegean. I went straight to Santo-Sospir. The welcome was affectionate. We sat on the terrace, talked, drank.

I felt almost as though I had a home here despite the fact that there was no room of my own in it. For dinner we had an enormous sea perch and freezing Pouilly Fuissé. I recorded these details in my journal, but unfortunately next to nothing of what we said. As usual, Jean had a sparkling new repertory of anecdotes, all of them rapid, replete with quicksilver wit and accompanied by droll gestures and self-deprecating hilarity. I was conscientious about recording conversations with Picasso and Giacometti, on the other hand, but I knew they were geniuses and recognized an obligation to endeavor to keep faith, as it were, with that fact. Jean I never regarded as a genius, which, I think, was what made him easy to like. After dinner we sat on the terrace, breathing the fragrance of tuberoses and drinking *eau de vie de poire*, highly intoxicating after the wine. Jean was excited by the fact that I was to visit Picasso the next morning, almost envious, I thought, and entrusted me with pressing messages of affection which I forgot to deliver.

My visit to Picasso was bizarre and didn't seem to bode very well for the future. It was just three days later, in fact, that I saw him for the last time. But I have described all that in the first volume of my memoirs, *Picasso and Dora*. It has no place here, anyway. Jean was not present and probably never knew what happened.

That November I fell on the staircase of the Café de Flore and broke my left ankle, causing me to spend ten painful days in the American Hospital. A lot of people came to see me, including Jean, who created something of a stir in the hospital, told some funny stories, and stayed for fifteen minutes. When recovered, I returned again to America, staying at home this time for fourteen months.

While I was there, I was at last able to do Jean a favor, negligible in comparison with the many he had done for me but not, perhaps, quite negligible enough. A French literary review called *La Table Ronde* was devoting its autumn 1955 issue entirely to analyses of all aspects of Cocteau's work and career. Having by this time already published a few articles on art, I was requested—at Jean's suggestion—to contribute a text on his drawings and paintings. To refuse was, of course, unthinkable, to accept *almost* unthinkable, because it went without saying that unqualified admiration was called for. And at age thirty-two I was not—and forty years later still am not—sly enough a conjurer with words to pull the rabbit of praise out of the hat of deprecation. Not that I actually disliked Jean's drawings. He possessed an authentic flair and a style that was all his own, but the outcome was precisely too stylish and facile to allow for reasoned commendation. Even today, nonetheless, I derive an easygoing pleasure from contemplation of the several drawings Jean gave me. In 1955, however, easygoing pleasure was beside the point. High aesthetic seriousness was wanted, and sycophantic hypocrisy alone could provide it. I wrote to Jean, asking for advice. He replied, "Don't ask me for advice. Everything you do will be well done." Then he went on to describe a corrida he had witnessed with Picasso, holding Paloma on his knees and Claude on his shoulders.

So I sat down to write. I began by quoting a definition Jean himself had given of how he conceived of drawing: "To draw a living line and not tremble from knowing it to be in danger of death at every point along its way, I must sleep in a sort of slumber, allowing the sources of my life to flow down without restraint into my hand, so that that hand ends by working alone, by flying into a dream, by moving without any care for me." My own commentary after this introduction is superficial, bombastic, frivolous, maundering along about poetry and the precarious status of a poet in the modern world. I was even able to bring myself to say, "The drawings given us by Cocteau in 1923 are largely portraits of friends drawn with a fidelity to friendship and a vitality which in our time only Picasso and Matisse have been able to equal." This is nonsense, of course, but perhaps the conclusion of the four closely printed pages provided an ever-so-slight redemption:

To situate the graphic work of Cocteau in relation to his contemporaries, one thinks first of his friends Picasso, Matisse and Modigliani. But the true situation, the profound and vital rapport is altogether elsewhere, and, being poetic, is perhaps to be found precisely where one would least seek to find it. In our century the Douanier Rousseau alone has known, without knowing it—and in the same manner as Cocteau—how to make the sources of his life flow down into his hand in order to create works of authentic poetry. For the others their knowledge too visibly overrides their instinct. The

Douanier Rousseau sought not at all to make a "situation" for himself. Like Cocteau he cared only for the truth which is to be found beyond apparent reality. So one may place them side by side in the realm of graphic poetry.

I don't know whether Jean was gratified to find himself arbitrarily placed in the company of a naïve and genuine dreamer, but there could be no cavil about the Douanier's genius. And he was, moreover, idolized by Jean's idol, Picasso, who prided himself on the possession of one of Rousseau's paintings and had arranged in 1908 the famous "banquet" in his honor. At all events, I feel confident he never imagined that in order to please him I had—in a matter, to be sure, not gravely damaging to my integrity—willingly expressed opinions and passed judgments seriously opposed to what I truly believed.

Jean was delighted by my text. It came to him, he wrote, as if by carrier pigeon, adding, "I delicately raised its wing and found your good warmth beneath." In a postscript he added, "Perhaps you will also do me the favor (in relation to art dealers) to point out that this is without doubt the first time that a poet produces the work of a painter which is not merely marginal but which can survive by itself." I didn't make this addition, because I couldn't bring myself to go back over the text and felt, besides, that I'd done enough trifling with the truth. Jean's drawings are very often elegant, charming, witty, original, with a versatility all their own, but the paintings are without exception ugly, embarrassing failures, though he didn't think so and wrote to me, "I have really abandoned the graphic in order to penetrate the canvas and make my way into it without shame." But then . . . shame, I fear, was not an emotion easily, if at all, roused in the consciousness of a poet who made his myth of being misunderstood and "unknown" while never neglecting an opportunity to publicize this contradictory predicament.

It was in March 1956 that I returned at last to Paris, where I saw all my old friends, including Jean, Doudou, and Francine. They seemed somewhat changed, I thought, aged, a little worn. Doudou and Francine in particular looked older, the captivating sheen of youth erased. People said that there had been excessive indulgence in illicit stimulants. Who knows? Jean, in any case, was as convivial and urbane as ever. But I didn't see much of them, because I remained only three weeks in Paris, spent the spring with Bernard in Florence, the summer in the Loire valley, and the autumn in Holland and Germany.

So it happened that on the twenty-fourth of October, when the Hungarian uprising against Soviet domination began, I was in Munich, only three hundred and fifty miles away. For a week it seemed that this unprecedented, courageous, and noble resistance to tyranny might actually succeed. There was much public jubilation in Munich. Nobody could talk of anything else, and to my surprise I felt deeply moved, personally concerned in a way that I had not felt since the end of World War II. There was nothing, of course, that I could do, and yet I would have liked to do something. I can't say why. Perhaps it was because I was so nearby and because many of the people I knew in Munich had close ties to Hungary. The war in Korea, for example, though also a Communist transgression, had not affected me comparably.

I drove back to Paris on the first of November. On the fourth, Soviet troops, supported by tanks and artillery, entered Hungary and with ruthless savagery set about crushing the incipient revolution. Outrage and censure in the free world were unanimous, except, of course, in servile Communist papers such as *L'Humanité* in France, where the perishing patriots were denounced as Fascist counter-revolutionaries. Numerous eminent Communists, however, repudiated their allegiance, and many demanded that the French Communist Party, the most slavishly Stalinist in the West, denounce the nefarious Soviet intervention.

As the days passed and the situation grew hopeless, I began to think that perhaps there was something I might do. Even Louis Aragon, feline and amoral as he was, had managed to insinuate that maybe there were grounds for protest. From the most famous, the most prestigious, the most talented member of the French Communist Party, however, not one word had come. Picasso remained resoundingly silent. For the painter of *Guernica*, the scathing critic of Spanish Fascism, this silence seemed to me not only an outrage but a cowardly contradiction, and I felt that even so obscure and uninfluential a person as I might prevail upon him to take a stand, so I determined to write him a letter. It is a long one, which I quote in full in *Picasso and Dora*, so I will not reproduce it here. When Picasso did nothing to acknowledge my letter, I gave a copy to a leftist newspaper called *Combat*, where it appeared on November 17. Five days later Picasso's name did appear as one of ten signatories—the nine others nonentities—to a letter published in *Le Monde*, France's most distinguished newspaper, addressed to the Central Committee of the French Communist Party, soliciting clarification of "the innumerable problems which present themselves to Communists today." Not a word about the butchery in Budapest. This letter is a tissue of ambiguity and disingenuous equivocation, addresses itself to no issue, and had no purpose save to rationalize Communist self-righteousness. Picasso would have done better to keep silent than to sign such a self-serving, hypocritical document. Some weeks later he told an American journalist, "Communism represents a certain ideal in which I believe. I think that Communism works toward the realization of that ideal." That is what he said, but it cannot have been what he believed.

My letter received considerable notice, and excerpts from it were published in newspapers both in France and abroad. To my astonishment, though, I was severely criticized by many of the people I knew, all of whom, incidentally, would have suffered grim fates in the Soviet Union. Dora Maar had warned me that one could not criticize Picasso with impunity. His power, his fame, his magic were too absolute, she said. And it is true so far as I know that nobody but I ever condemned him publicly for his Communism, to which he remained committed till the day of his death.

When writing my letter to Picasso I hadn't thought about Cocteau. When I did, it seemed to me unlikely that Jean would openly condone criticism of his idol, with whom his intimacy had now become the durable feature of countless newspaper and magazine articles. But I was quite unprepared for the letter from him which I received three weeks after the publication of my own in *Combat*.

6 December 1956

My dear James,

You understand my horror of excuses and of those clumsy stains which even the cleaning fluid of the soul can no longer afterward remove. Your letter to Picasso pained me profoundly. These are things to be thrashed out between us, face-to-face, and never in public. Things of which the public can understand nothing and which allow it to hope for that sort of atrocious corrida which it loves, that being the sole stimulant of mediocrity. Let this error, unworthy of us, evaporate.

I met you through Picasso, and you have consistently shown that what you like in me is that straight and somewhat naïve line incapable of following intellectual meanders.

For nothing in the world would I wish for a dispute between us, and even less to be the victim of a weakness for allowing myself to be convinced of a point of view contrary to my own. For Picasso your letter was like seeing a weapon brandished in the hands of a comrade who had the free run of his home. By tampering with this fresh wound I would render myself unworthy of your confidence.

Jean

☆

P.S. A simple woman, one who knows nothing of us, Madeleine wept when reading your letter in the paper.

It was the public denunciation that displeased a man who all his life had constrained his versatile talents in order to please the public. And this imperious desire to please, perhaps even more than the facility which served it so well, may have been the fatal flaw that kept Cocteau from making the most of his talents. Of all desires, the desire to please at any price, whether sexually, socially, or intellectually, is the most insatiable, treacherous, and pitiless, for it can never be sufficiently satisfied even if it protests too much that it expects nothing in return. So it was all too easy for Jean to maintain that he was "unknown," misunderstood, resented, and belittled despite his recent election to the glorious French Academy, for which he had schemed so shrewdly that he could celebrate it as a joke. As a joke, alas, it was on him, because by joining the academic "immortals" he demonstrated yet again how hollow his claim to bohemian emancipation had always been. I had never told him that what I liked about him was "that straight and somewhat naïve line incapable of following intellectual meanders." What I liked about him was the highly sophisticated and slightly devious *empressement* of his camaraderie, his sense of fun, his easygoing generosity, *and* his spontaneous juggling of intellectual novelties. He didn't want to be the "victim," he said, of a weakness for allowing himself to be convinced of a point of view contrary to his own. He was, indeed, a victim, but the weakness at issue was that he had no point of view save that which was fixed entirely upon his own image and the magnification of his myth.

I couldn't help remembering the violent denunciation of Picasso's Communism delivered by Jean as we had driven away from Vallauris six years before after the inauguration of the painter's gift to the town. If Jean remembered, it made not a particle of difference now. I remembered, too, Picasso's furious condemnation of Jean as a buffoon and whore, though later they became merrily companionable. Picasso himself was not above a bit of prostitution, and he certainly loved playing the clown. He and Jean went very well together, so long as there was never any misunderstanding as who was in the possession of genius. Though I certainly would not have expected Jean to choose me before Picasso, I couldn't understand why he'd thought he must choose at all.

Not only in his life but in his works, Jean provided evidence that he suffered for the sake of the public, not for the sake of art. He was forever worrying about his position, his influence, his popularity, and there was next to nothing he shrank from doing to enhance all three. He designed the menus for elegant restaurants and advertisements for expensive jewelry stores, he eulogized music-hall performers and glorified the work of third-rate artists, his drawings appeared on dinner plates and fashion accessories. In the last decade of his life this compulsion for chic ubiquity had the effect of virtually eliminating from serious consideration any book or exhibition praised by him, and there were many. It was a pity.

I did not expect to see Jean again, but I wrote him a polite apologia the following March. He replied, as he always did, but said in closing, "I remain free and ask you only to wait until the lips of the wound can close and no longer accuse anyone."

I spent that summer at Aix-en-Provence. Being casually acquainted with a very bad painter but a pleasant person called Bernard Buffet and his friend Pierre Bergé, I was invited to a large reception they gave at their château in a little place called Rousset-sur-Arc not far from Aix. Jean was there. When he saw me, he ostentatiously circled away with the unmistakable purpose of avoiding any exchange. Annoyed by what was too obvious a reluctance to confront the consequences of a dissension which in fact had been none of his business, I went up to him and held out my hand. Prisoner of politeness, he shook it but murmured, "Not yet, my dear, not in public," and turned away. In October in a restaurant in Paris I caught a glimpse of him and Francine. We shook hands and said hello, that was all. And that was the last time I ever saw him.

A nostalgia remained, however. I was only too aware of everything that made impossible any resumption of the semblance of friendship we had shared. It had been a semblance only, but imbued with a haunting, sunset aura of romance. The expectation of being entirely cut off from this caused a slight ache. So I wrote to Jean in 1961, 1962, and 1963. All three letters he answered, of course, and the tone of his replies became more gentle, less evasive as the years wore on. I heard that he had had a severe heart attack but had recovered. And then it was said that Francine had wearied at last of being but one more mirror to reflect the glory of her guest. She wanted to shine in her own right. Alas, she possessed no brilliance. Her ten-year investment in hospitality had paid a handsome dividend in celebrity, but it was all on the surface; no gleam came from within. She took up with an aging playboy who supported himself —poorly—by writing detective stories and could not abide a rival author. So Jean and Doudou moved out of Santo-Sospir, never to return. In September 1963, I was only briefly in Paris, for during the sixties I spent the majority of my time in America. While in Paris, though, I thought of Jean—I can't say why; memories of fragrant evenings at Santo-Sospir?—and felt it would be good to speak to him again. So I telephoned to Milly. He answered himself. His pleasure at hearing from me sounded perfectly genuine. He asked me to drive out to see him, but I kept no car in Paris then and felt that a telephone conversation was sufficient tribute to the past. He was working on his memoirs, he said, though spending much time in bed. We talked for six or seven minutes, then said good-bye. A month later he died amid a blizzard of incongruous publicity. Only hours before his own death, Edith Piaf, the famous music-hall singer, had died, and he had been unable to resist joining in the public storm of mourning, recording a tribute which was broadcast at noon that day. Even as his words issued from the radio, he was called on the telephone with a request for further comment. Doudou answered, saying that Jean was too weak to respond, but the incorrigible author insisted on taking the call. As he spoke, a fatal attack overcame him, blood-tinged foam poured from his nose and mouth, and an hour later he was pronounced dead.

The funeral ceremony was not as grand as Jean would probably have wished. Members of the French Academy attended, family and many friends, including Jean Marais, a penitent Francine Weisweiller, and Edouard Dermit, probably the most grievously bereaved. Jean had unsuccessfully tried to adopt Doudou but had arranged nonetheless for him to be his sole heir. Picasso was represented by his scapegrace son Paulo. The coffin was borne to a chapel on the outskirts of Milly which Cocteau had decorated, and there was lowered into the earth, a lyre of red roses reposing upon it. At a later date, a bust of the poet by Arno Breker, Hitler's favorite artist, was placed in the chapel, a most regrettable memorial. But it was in keeping with Jean's passion to seek publicity and to please at any price, which had led him even during the Nazi occupation to praise Breker in print, and to look forward to the day when his statues of nude youths would grace the place de la Concorde.

Though dead for more than thirty years, Jean is not forgotten. That his writings are much read today seems doubtful. His films are still occasionally shown, but they are period pieces now. A play is sometimes revived, though not to much acclaim. His countless drawings bring moderate prices at auction. He is remembered as the flamboyant epitome of a certain period, which is associated mainly with the presence and creativity of Cocteau's idols Picasso and Stravinsky and the many lesser men and women, all of them intimate friends or intimate enemies of Jean, who made that period more brilliant than the lackluster era of today. Jean put his talent into his life, his facility into his work, and it can only be assumed that he got what he wanted, for he worked with unremitting industry for fifty-six years to obtain it. The sense of fulfillment, however, I suspect, must in the end have escaped him. He was too intelligent not to realize that he had erected for himself the kind of tinsel pantheon he hated and despised, but for which he had sacrificed everything.

3

The Strange Case

of the Count de Rola

[B A L T H U S]

Picasso had heard of him and had already acquired one of his paintings. Rilke had known him since childhood. Derain, Gide, Giacometti, André Breton, Max Ernst, Marie-Laure de Noailles, and a lot of the Rothschilds were his friends. Someone once said— was it Gide?—that authentic fame is being known by fifty people so long as they are the fifty whose opinions make all the difference. According to that criterion, Balthus in 1950 was famous. But his fame didn't extend very far beyond the numerical criterion. I had never heard of him, and I was passionately eager to learn all I could about the art of my time. Nobody that I knew had heard of him. He was not mentioned in the late-night, rambling talks about painters with which I and my friends sought to establish our footing on the high ground of contemporary culture. I might have chanced upon an exhibition of his work in New York at the Pierre Matisse Gallery in 1949, but I was in Europe almost all of that year, and little notice was taken of the exhibition.

In the month of June, 1950, however, Balthus became overnight a painter I had good reason to esteem. I was posing at the time for a portrait drawing by Lucian Freud in the cheap hotel room he occupied on the Ile de la Cité. One afternoon he remarked that if I cared to, he would take me along to dine and spend that evening with his friend Marie-Laure de Noailles. I gladly agreed, for at least I knew who she was.

Her mansion was stupendous, its contents even more so. In the octagonal drawing room where she received us hung paintings by Goya, Rubens, and Braque, drawings, including her portrait, by

Picasso. a Prud'hon, and a series of extraordinary pen-and-ink studies in simple frames set atop low bookcases. I had never seen any
quite like them. very strong, almost violent and yet tender, somewhat
awkward in execution but utterly self-assured in style. These were
a series of studies by Balthus, Lucian told me, for illustrations to
Emily Brontë's novel *Wuthering Heights*. I was surprised, almost
taken aback, by their overt emotional intensity. There seemed to be
something virtually aggressive about them. Before we left to dine in
a restaurant, Lucian prevailed upon our hostess to take me upstairs
to see Balthus's portrait of her. It hung in an enormous salon, a
large, severe painting in muted colors, all attention concentrated
upon the fixed and strangely haunting gaze of the viscountess, who
was depicted in a setting of barren austerity. It was a work, I felt
immediately, of truly remarkable mastery, reminiscent of Old Masters in a way that I couldn't quite define. At all events, it didn't
appear a bit out of place in the same room with an enormous Rubens.
So my first meeting with Balthus's work, though I didn't know it at
the time, was profoundly in keeping with essential aspects of both
his art and his life. And it now seems ironically fitting that my interest
in Balthus and his work should have been initiated by Lucian, for
thirty-three years later it roused his enmity, he being by that time
a famous cultivator of enemies. For the moment, however, we were
great friends, and he gave me not only my portrait—one of his finest
early drawings—but also an etching inscribed "To James with love
from Lucian." All this, of course, was long before the advent of my
grandmother's carpet, of my portraits by Balthus, of Chassy, Frédérique, the Villa Medici, and the Count de Rola.

There was a restaurant in those days called La Reine Christine
at the southwest corner of the rue des Grands-Augustins and the
rue Christine, thus about equidistant from the apartments of Picasso,
Dora Maar, and Alice Toklas. It was an unpretentious, inexpensive,
out-of-the-way place with decent food, and we used to go there
often. Only four months after my evening with Marie-Laure and
Lucian, I happened to wander into La Reine Christine for dinner
by myself and found Dora already there, seated upstairs with a man
who appeared to be about forty, lean and handsome. I greeted her
with some hesitation, as we were not yet close friends, and she
introduced me to her companion, Balthus, then invited me to join

them if I was alone. I was glad to. Dora was exceptionally friendly, which surprised me, and did most of the talking, leading both Balthus and me toward topics of conversation which would be easy and familiar, mostly about art and artists. He was polite to me, though somewhat aloof, but clearly much enjoyed Dora's company, laughing at her jokes, making a few himself, and adding a counterpoint of cultivated and penetrating finesse to the discussion of art. He spoke slowly and with a slightly nasal, aristocratic drawl. If it could not be said that he was warmly forthcoming, it seemed at the same time credible that he could be courteously sociable. Such a semblance even forty-five years ago was not what one would have judged to be spontaneously contemporary, was it? In any case, I did not see Balthus again for three years. It was in November 1953. I had just returned from a trip to Greece and Egypt, and it was then that my close friendship with Dora began. I saw Balthus with her. He gave no outward sign of remembrance but was courteous. We had dinner together. It was rather like the previous occasion. Lucian also happened to be in Paris, accompanied by his then-wife Caroline. We met several times and one evening had dinner with Balthus. It was evident that Lucian, the younger artist, felt for his elder something close to veneration. At that time, to be sure, both were committed to a concept of the painter's vocation and to a consequent mode of representation that flew violently in the face of all prevailing fashions and convictions. That lonely but indomitable stance certainly made for a powerful bond between them. What caused it ultimately to fail I do not know, but fame, that malign antagonist of fellow feeling, may have had much to do with it.

Meanwhile, I had made friends with Alberto Giacometti, his wife, Annette, and his brother Diego, with Marie-Laure de Noailles, Georges Salles, director of France's museums, André Masson, Valentine Hugo, Jean Leymarie, and a number of others, all of whom had known Balthus well and for a long time. From them, and later from his brother, Pierre, his first wife, Antoinette de Watteville, and Pierre Leyris, the intimate friend of his youth, I learned a great deal about Balthus. Also, of course, from Dora. They were particularly close just then, though it went without saying among those who knew Balthus well that there could not have been any serious intimacy between them. Perhaps they were drawn together by the fact that both were then alone in the world, Dora having been abandoned by Picasso and Balthus by the young woman who had for some years been his mistress and model.

He was decidedly not at that time a man who took kindly to the idea that anyone might learn very much about him, going out of his way, indeed, on more than one occasion to declare, "Balthus is a painter of whom *nothing is known.*" Such an extreme craving for privacy may seem peculiar, especially on the part of an artist, an individual, after all, whose overriding purpose in life is to secure public appreciation of endeavors which inevitably reflect the innermost aspects of his being. It is an odd fact, though, that many artists have been secretive. Perhaps they have feared that the overt quest for admiration was already revealing too much, betraying secrets which had best be kept from the world, and even from themselves. The very willingness to exhibit creations produced in circumstances which are the ne plus ultra of privacy presupposes a certain tendency toward exhibitionism, an inclination akin to that which impels children to seek adult approval of make-believe playthings and imaginary dwelling places. Children, too, are secretive, of course, but they seldom advertise it and tend to avoid situations whereby their fantasies run the risk of grown-up consequences. An artist who endeavors to make a mystery of himself seems to be playing at blindman's buff with the far greater mystery which it is his professional purpose to unmask. Creation goes hand in hand with revelation, and the fullest measure of the former comes from a candid profusion of the latter, while common sense advises that the creator's life is paltry stuff compared with the great existence expected of his work. Having created it, moreover, the very best thing he can do by it is to die.

Balthus was not his real name. But reality, to be sure, never very bearable to any of us, was a matter of exceptionally minor moment to him. All artists inevitably lead their lives in a continuum of imagination and make-believe. They see the world through eyes conditioned by their commitment to reveal a highly personal and unique vision of it. Balthus has been an extreme example of this disposition in an era little prepared to understand or encourage it. He was born Michel Balthazar Klossowski in Paris on February 29, 1908. That accident in the date of birth—assuming that any occurrence in the enactment of a calling can be accidental—has allowed the artist to regard his maturity somewhat as a prolonged childhood and adolescence, because the number of his actual birthdays has till now been only twenty-three. All during his early manhood he delighted in calling attention to this natal singularity, suggesting that it did, indeed, guarantee enduring access to the pristine enchantments of youth. More recently, though, he has grown chary of such intimations, the fewness of birthdays having not diminished the accumulation of years, and he has resented revelation of the date, however singular. If, as Baudelaire remarked, "Genius is childhood recaptured at will," the conquest becomes increasingly tricky as the decades grind on, because great purity of spirit and tenderness of heart are needed by an old man looking for triumph through the visual innocence of a child.

The little boy, nicknamed Balthus by his parents, was their second and last offspring, the older brother, Pierre, having been born in 1905. Their father, Erich, came of a Polish family of minor but "immemorial" nobility, and his forebears had fled abroad in the mid-nineteenth century to escape the partitions of their homeland by its neighbors. He was a highly cultivated man, wrote a monograph on Daumier, and had aspirations, though little talent, as a painter. The mother, née Elisabeth Spiro, was also Polish, though not by birth an aristocrat, being Jewish, daughter of a cantor from Wroclaw. She, too, painted and with considerably greater talent than her husband, signing her works Baladine. The Klossowskis were at home in intellectual, artistic circles. Among their friends were Bonnard, Vuillard, Valéry, and Rilke. An involuntary tribute to Baladine's creative competence was paid one day by Bonnard when he came to visit, saw a recent picture by her hanging on the wall, and said, "Hmm, when did I paint that?"

The family moved to Switzerland, first to Bern, then to Geneva, while the boys were still young, and it was there that Balthus grew up. Precocious, imaginative, given to reverie, he was coddled and made much of by his parents and their distinguished friends. In later life he used to say, "When I was young, I always felt like a little prince." So the disposition to conceive an aristocratic image of himself seems to have been ingrained almost from the beginning. It became more and more pronounced and productive as time passed. Rilke, an intimate friend and admirer of Baladine, was one of those most impressed by the boy's precocity. "One can't imagine where he gets all his assured knowledge of Chinese Imperial and artistic dynasties," he said, and volunteered to write the preface for a little booklet of reproductions of drawings of cats executed by the thirteen-year-old artist: *Mitsou, 40 Drawings by Baltusz, Preface by Rainer Maria Rilke.** The "z" appears to have been put on solely for the sake of this publication, as it did not stick, and it does add a livelier zing to the nickname, along with the suggestion that subtle adjustments of identity might be all to the good in the interests of art. The budding artist later painted a self-portrait inscribed "A Portrait of H. M. The King of the Cats Painted by Himself." Royal reverie was mingled with symbolic premeditation, for cats appear repeatedly in the works of the grown man, adding the suggestiveness of their own sphinxlike secrecy to scenes already enigmatic and sometimes menacing.

Well before their twentieth birthdays both Klossowski boys were back in Paris, Pierre determined to make a career in literature, arriving with an introduction from Rilke to André Gide, and Baltus resolved to follow in his parents' footsteps as a painter. He needed no introduction to the reigning artists of the older generation, having acquired entrée to the most exalted milieu by right of birth. Of the illustrious elders who counted for much in the outlook and career of the young newcomer, the most important by far was André Derain. Although he had been an authentic member of the avant-garde in the first years of the century, one of the wildest of the Fauves, Derain's ferocity had faded fast: while his confreres increasingly abandoned all notion of a viable rapport with traditional aesthetic values in their stampede toward uncharted territory, he beat a strategic retreat to the rear area of proven precepts and consecrated virtues. It took some courage, plus a good deal of egotism, for Derain to do that, because it was so defiant of the contemporary trend, and left him with little to show for his strategy save a display of professional skill, which went without saying anyway. But Derain was phenomenally persuasive about stating his case. A brilliant conversationalist and ingenious dialectician, he had the personal authority

* Zürich: Ortapfel-Verlag, 1921.

to make his stand seem unassailable. He presumed to be the sole
champion in his generation of the continuing relevance and vitality
of the grand tradition represented at its best by Titian, Rubens, and
Renoir. From 1920 onward, he produced myriad works in a manner
clearly derived from this commitment to the conservative principle.
His industry, however, brought forth not masterpieces but chic portraits, wooden nudes, slick landscapes, and static still lifes. The
amazing thing is that for a long time nobody questioned either the
validity of his claim or the value of the works. Even so fanatic a
disparager of all things bourgeois as André Breton, the panjandrum
of Surrealist anarchy, who categorically shat upon the art of the past,
was very slow to see the fatal error of Derain's strategy: what he
stood for was not the sustaining grandeur of tradition but the profitless triviality of convention. This, to be sure, was by no means
obvious half a century ago, especially in the commanding presence
of the artist. It is perfectly understandable that Derain might have
seemed, to a newcomer in his early twenties, an admirable contemporary likeness of the great masters of the past. That is how Baltus
appears to have seen him, and a profound impression was plainly
made.

The youthful painter seems to have decided from the beginning
to retain as the adult appellation of his artistic career the nickname
he had been given as a child, signing his early works "Baltus." The
"h" was added a few years later, and it is, of course, a great addition,
evoking more explicitly the homage of the wise man to a miraculous
child. By signing his childhood name to grown-up works of art,
Balthus was making a point which presumably could not be made
in any other way, a point somewhat similar to the one made by the
fewness of birthdays, but more insistent and telling, because an
artist's signature represents a commitment no man can take lightly,
binding him beyond the extent of his own lifetime to the prospective
perpetuation of his good name. The means by which Balthus set out
to affirm the integrity of that bond had much to do with nomencla-
ture, and in due time he once more made the point by insisting on
his entitlement to a name not his own but which again suggests a
childlike fixation on the make-believe. As to the aesthetic course
and creative aims he was destined to pursue, the untried artist seems
never to have entertained an instant's doubt. His work was to be

resolutely, and one might well say defiantly, figurative from start to finish. Though he sometimes questioned his power to attain fulfillment according to the exalted standards he had set for himself, he disdainfully dismissed the relevance of any others. His were those which had stood the test of time and guaranteed the eminence of masterpieces of the past. He revered Piero della Francesca, Velázquez, Seurat, and, above all, Gustave Courbet. He traveled to Italy especially to copy works by Piero on the spot, and in the works of his maturity it is astonishing to see figures that might have stepped straight from the frescoes of *The Story of the True Cross* in Arezzo. While in Paris, he devoted himself so painstakingly to the study of the masters he admired that their vision became almost second nature to him. Such infatuation with the past is all very well so long as it inspires a creative passion capable of self-transfiguration in the future.

Lacking in technical virtuosity, Balthus's youthful paintings yet show an instinctive grasp of spatial and structural relationships, and reveal the artist's haughty inclination to make his work reflect the world within him more vividly than the world around him. It is, in fact, almost uncanny to see how early, how positively, and how permanently Balthus's creative demiurge took control of his talents and turned them to compelling account. He obviously worked as hard at his craft as he looked at the prototypes meant to consecrate it. The lesson of the masters was learned the hard way, self-taught, by the sternest discipline and command of self, though the imperious pupil made lavish provision for the dictates of self-expression. Balthus never crossed the threshold of an Ecole des Beaux-Arts. If he was to become a master, it would be entirely by his own doing and on his own terms. At age nineteen, he was a beginner; ten years later he had already painted a number of the pictures upon which his future reputation would stand or fall, having developed a highly personal style and adapted it to the exploration of subject matter even more personal. Neither subject matter nor style were to evolve very much during the half century to come, as if to demonstrate yet again that Balthus had found himself and his art once and for all in the experience and vision of youth. It is a peculiarly intimate vision but at the same time strangely aloof in its attitude toward the experience. Pubescent young girls became the painter's preferred

Harold Acton in his library, 1950 [*James Lord*]

(top) La Pietra, the Florentine villa Acton inherited from his father [*photographer unknown*]; *(bottom left)* La Pietra seen from the cyprus drive [*James Lord*]; *(bottom right)* Alexander Zielcke in 1977, about ten years after meeting Harold [*photographer unknown*]

(top) Jean Cocteau with the author, in a pose devised by the playwright, 1950 [*Bernard Minoret*]; *(bottom left)* portrait of James Lord by Cocteau, August 1951; *(bottom right)* Edouard "Doudou" Dermit and Francine Weisweiller aboard the sailboat *Orpheus*, 1950 [*James Lord*]

(above) Balthus, self-portrait, 1942; *(opposite top)* Château de Chassy [*James Lord*]; *(bottom left)* third portrait of the author by Balthus, 1959; *(bottom right)* portrait of Frédérique Tison asleep, by Balthus, c. 1957–58

Alberto Giacometti, c. 1952 [*Abisag Tullmann*]

Diego Giacometti, 1985 [*Martine Franck*]

(top left) Alberto's wife, Annette, in 1954 [*Ernst Scheidegger*]; *(top right)* Silvio Berthoud [*photographer unknown*]; *(bottom)* Bruno Giacometti, Gilles Roy, Odette Giacometti, and the author in Munich, 22 November 1994 [*Isolde Ohlbaum*]

subjects, portrayed with obsessive diligence and frequency, often
nude, daydreaming or asleep, with cats alongside them, and sometimes in situations of overt eroticism from which an element of the
sadistic is not absent. Their poses, their very expressions frequently
refer back to identifiable works by the masters he most admired.
The dream of youth is a haunting nostalgia for the noble certainties
of long ago. An aristocratic reverie pervades Balthus's paintings.
However effete, however irrelevant the criteria of the past may have
seemed to his contemporaries, to Balthus they remained incorrupt-
ible and sublime, it seems, precisely insofar as he could prove himself
worthy of them and live up to the proud vindication of their legacy.
That, as it turned out, would take some doing.

What saved Balthus from becoming a mere pasticheur of the
past, however great his talents and high his standards, was the very
down-to-earth integrity of his obsession with his subject matter. It
took precedence over the display of painterly skills for their own
sake. It presided over the creation of the never-never land in which
girls, boys, and cats, even landscapes, vases of flowers, and bowls
of fruit, hover outside time, outside everyday reality, bathed in an
aura of ambiguous tranquillity, motionless, speechless, and yet
aquiver with the vital certainty that they will dwell forever in a realm
secure from the rude intrusion of common mortals. The very other-
worldliness of Balthus's world and the arrogance, the downright
hauteur, with which he pictured its configurations and inhabitants
were what saved him from seeming passé and drew the attention
of his contemporaries. He deigned to accept it, as it was merely the
most prestigious then obtainable, bringing the offer of a one-man
exhibition from Pierre Loeb, the favored dealer of the young avant-
garde, a man who had already made a market, and a packet, off his
carefully nurtured reputation for aesthetic clairvoyance. The first
one-man exhibition of paintings by Balthus took place at the Galerie
Pierre in the spring of 1934, when the artist was just twenty-six years
old. Though sales were not many in that period of financial crisis,
people of discernment were impressed. They wondered what sort
of man had created these works so hauntingly evocative of the past
and yet so powerfully present in their overt depiction of fantasy and
malaise.

Balthus was a loner. A self-made artist, he felt free to devise whatever inventions seemed essential to the making of his name and to invest them with the passions most profoundly relevant to himself. That was his contemporary side, promptly and appreciatively noticed by the Surrealists, committed as they were to unbridled indulgence of the unconscious. They would have been glad to welcome Balthus to their group, and it went without saying that they believed no young artist could aspire to greater distinction. Balthus didn't think so. He was disposed to accept their homage but clearly could not be bothered to participate in any of their "nonsense," and would never have submitted to the aesthetic dictates of another man, be he even so commanding a personality as André Breton. Besides, the Surrealists were very mixed up in politics: they talked revolution, preached Marx, and were on speaking terms with the Communists. That, to be sure, was the dernier cri for young intellectuals in the mid-thirties. From the imperturbable vantage point of his devotion to the ideals of other times, however, Balthus viewed all this brouhaha with unmistakable distaste. As for the moral challenge inherent in the social issues of those days, he seems to have deemed it simply too vulgar for notice. His idol, Courbet, had mistakenly identified aesthetic revolution with political revolution, had left his studio, and taken to the streets, whereupon he paid for his errors with a stint in prison and death in exile. Balthus, by contrast, had a lordly, romantic view of his calling and thought of the artist as a heroic, mythic figure, one still prepared to dedicate himself to a noble idea in an age which made a mockery of chivalry, a man with the spiritual fortitude to pursue a lonely, lofty path rather than mingle in the lamentable plodding of the masses. His view was, in a word, Byronic. He had read *Don Juan* in its entirety in the original when only twenty and had been profoundly influenced by the lyrical, cynical masterpiece of an aristocrat too proud to bow before public opinions he despised. The Byronic view, moreover, was nicely self-sustaining, as luck would have it, since Balthus maintained that by some far-fetched familial coincidence he was related to the English lord. Affinity of spirit, in any case, was quite authentic enough to transcend the prosaic happenstance of genealogy. Unfortunately, however, the Parisian painter had no title, no fortune, and no fame.

The artist-hero in the image of Lord Byron was not the only source of inspiration vital to Balthus in the genesis of his persona.

There was another, also literary and also English: the masterpiece of somber beauty and passionate imagination by Emily Brontë, *Wuthering Heights*. Heathcliff, its protagonist, is a romantic, almost demonic character, proud and moody. A waif, he is encouraged to frame high notions of his birth in order to compensate for its obscurity. For a time he attains the height of joy by sharing with the adolescent daughter of the man who has saved him from the gutter a wild fantasy of everlasting bliss, only to have it shattered when he overhears her saying that she would feel it degrading to be wed to one so lowly, whereupon he flees the scene, eliminating himself from the eventuality of further humiliation.

Balthus was fascinated by *Wuthering Heights*. The obsessive, overwrought, almost perverse relationship between Heathcliff and Cathy struck a chord of primal feeling that reverberates throughout the artist's life and work. Once again, the commanding vision of creativity comes from the past. Balthus clearly identified himself with Heathcliff, for in 1933 he made the extraordinary series of pen-and-ink drawings illustrating various scenes from the novel and gave his own features to the brooding hero. The identification, moreover, goes beyond these particular works, extending into the future as a source of emotional and thematic revelation—Balthus and Brontë bound forever, as it were, in the idealistic dream of two young people romantically out of touch with reality. The *Wuthering Heights* drawings set the style, and established the very schema and poses, for paintings that would not be executed until many years later. It has been noted that only the first third or half of the novel, concluding with Heathcliff's frustrated love and disappearance, engaged the artist's attention. The latter portion, when the onetime foundling reappears miraculously transformed into a wealthy gentleman of fashion, if not a genuine aristocrat, obviously did not possess the same passionate potential for identification. Or, perhaps, possessed it too much.

Balthus fortunately had the right physique for the role of the romantic artist-hero: slender, almost gaunt, with angular features, dark eyes, and intent gaze, he was handsome. Even his good looks, though, were those of another era, and his few self-portrait drawings seem to call for the accessories and attire of a more formal time. They are the best and most accurate images of him that we have, because he long fought shy of the camera, as of so many things contemporary, distrusting its mechanical "eye." The handsome, sensitive, moody young artist aroused passions. He was greatly appealing to women, but the passions he aroused seem to have been wanting in some essential ingredient needed for mutual satisfaction. Maybe the prospects appeared a bit too easy, and that viewpoint, too, might have stemmed from a nostalgia for the Byronic notion of love as an impossible longing for an unattainable ideal. However it may have been, until he was twenty-five no decisive emotional attachment had come between the artist and his valiant devotion to his craft, though he did pay court for a time to Lelia Caetani, the daughter of a very grand Roman family, and painted her portrait. To no avail.

Aristocratic in character as well as by the concept of his vocation, Balthus felt drawn to the company of those who were aristocratic by birth. His own, of course, might have seemed so, on his father's side at least, but his paternal antecedents were remote and obscure, lacking in self-evident grandeur, while the maternal origins were definitely not designed to gratify a class-conscious temperament. Despite her charm, her intellect, her talent, and perhaps in part because of all that his own endowments owed to her, Balthus felt ashamed of his mother. To be sure, it was not easy for the grandson of a cantor from Wroclaw to assume that he was the social equal of a direct descendant of a noble house dating back in an unbroken line of high rank to the Middle Ages. But he did, and if this was naïve, even silly, it also took a kind of grand, reckless purity of spirit to fancy that he could be, or need be, up to the game. And a game, indeed, is what it surely was, a further incursion into the sphere of the make-believe.

The artist regularly returned to Switzerland, revisiting the scenes of his childhood, as to a source of essential refreshment and renewal, and there in Bern in 1933 he made the acquaintance of a young woman of twenty-one named Antoinette de Watteville. Now, of the few ancient, aristocratic families which for six or seven centuries had lorded it over the canton of Bern, none was more grand or more proud of its past than the Wattevilles. Their ancestral mansion, built in a style splendidly reminiscent of Versailles, was, and remains, one of the finest buildings in the city, a symbol of power, prestige, and privilege. Antoinette was blond, beautiful, wide-eyed, voluptuous, serene in the self-assurance of her physical and social distinction. Balthus fell madly in love with her. The Wattevilles received the intense, romantic—and penniless—young painter with painstaking politesse. He pressed his suit as best he could, pretending all the while to be a person entirely familiar with the way of life of people like the Wattevilles, one to whom every little reflex of aristocratic *savoir vivre* was second nature. It didn't work. Even he was unconvinced, and he was the one who most seriously needed convincing; in the *Wuthering Heights* drawings, where he is represented as the morose but idealistic Heathcliff, the features of Cathy are unmistakably those of Antoinette.

The Wattevilles may have been polite, but they were condescending. They smirked behind the artist's back, and he was far too sensitive and vulnerable not to sense it. The experience was desperately humiliating for a youth whose instincts and intelligence told him that the nobility of his calling far outclassed the lineage of these people who looked askance because he couldn't ride horseback like a gentleman. But his passion for Antoinette drove him to struggle against all odds to overmaster a situation in which the very odds against him were of his own making. That, perhaps, is the inevitable course for an artist. Antoinette, however, didn't care two straws whether her suitor was an artist or not. She found him unacceptable and after a while sent him packing.

This rejection had a shattering effect. It came, ironically enough, in the same year as the artist's first one-man exhibition, but there seems to have been no consolation in the prospect that his name might presently bring honor in the province of art. Fleeing from Bern in a rage of romantic agony, Balthus went back to his poor studio in Paris and there undertook to assert the supreme sovereignty of the creative personality by doing away with himself. It was only a gesture, necessary no doubt but essentially artistic, as a response to the shattering rejection. The would-be suicide was discovered in plenty of time by his friend Antonin Artaud, the semidemented, near-genius actor and writer, and the doctor said that the dose of poison swallowed had not been nearly lethal.

To an artist prepared to scorn contemporary taste, ready to flaunt his disregard for the aesthetic temper of his times, a sentimental and social setback, however upsetting at the moment, is unlikely to seem insurmountable. In fact, it may provide grist for his creative mill, and that seems to have been just what happened with Balthus. Antoinette did not disappear either from his life or from his work. In 1935 she came to Paris, where he was better able to press his suit personally and artistically. Meanwhile, in both realms he was making significant strides. He executed striking portraits of his friend Derain and his colleague Miró, and in 1936 an important breakthrough came when he was commissioned to paint Marie-Laure de Noailles. Though unmistakably a work of its era, the portrait also has the timeless quality so characteristic of Balthus, and there are the familiar reminiscences of past masters—not so much Courbet this time as Velázquez—which make no secret of the artist's ambition to paint masterpieces. The viscountess was delighted, especially as the painter had made her look a bit like one of his little girls, and she introduced Balthus to her fashionable friends. In the next year he painted a picture entitled *The Children*, based directly on a sketch of Heathcliff and Cathy, which was acquired by no less a connoisseur and celebrity than Pablo Picasso, with whom the young painter also became friendly.

His closest friend among other artists was a man seven years older than he who had already achieved some reputation as a Surrealist sculptor. Their friendship, which survived numerous contradictions and quirks for thirty years, had begun in the late winter of 1934, just before the Pierre Loeb exhibition, when André Breton and Paul Eluard came to call one day at Balthus's studio, bringing with them Alberto Giacometti. The painter showed a selection of his recent works, all much admired by the visitors, with the exception of one small painting which the sculptor criticized insistently, saying that he found the tonal relationships all wrong. The criticism brought a coolness, and when the callers had come out into the street again, Breton said to Giacometti, "Well, you've just made an enemy." The following summer, having traveled to Bern to make the acquaintance of Paul Klee, Giacometti went beforehand to visit the famous bear pits, where the municipal mascots spend hours on their hind legs waiting for visitors to toss them carrots. And who should he find also rapt in contemplation of the bears' ungainly acrobatics but Balthus, who was then in the throes of his frustrating courtship of

Antoinette. The two artists fell into conversation, and though Alberto was in a hurry because of his appointment with Klee, they went to have a drink together on the terrace of the Kursaal. The conversation grew heated, calling for close attention and careful thought, since both men were exceptional conversationalists—the one self-conscious and precise, like his painting, the other visionary and impulsive, like his sculpture—and as it evolved the two found that they were in agreement about almost nothing. With most men that would have seemed good reason for leaving acquaintance slight, but with artists of the caliber of Giacometti and Balthus, who were searching for compatible relations entirely in terms of a personal vision, the challenge of a peer was irresistibly exhilarating. By the time they finished talking that summer day, it was seven o'clock, Alberto had forgotten all about his appointment with Klee, and a historic encounter was missed. A dialogue was begun, however, which by its strange, almost perverse polarity gave each artist occasion to take stock of himself from a point of view virtually opposite yet profoundly concordant.

Alberto was interested in the art of the past as a means of seeking his way to the future, and this was just the period when he was abandoning Surrealist fantasy in order to devote himself entirely to rigorous representation of what he saw before him. Balthus was interested in the past as a means of reaffirming past values. Alberto was preeminently a man of his own time, responsive to its philosophical, political, and cultural climate, while Balthus had little use for the present. Alberto was the frankest of men and made candor the cornerstone of his ethical concept of human relationships. Balthus loved make-believe and secrecy. Alberto revered his mother. Balthus was ashamed of Baladine. Alberto lived like a pauper because he knew that riches and possessions can compromise one of life's greatest luxuries: spiritual freedom. Balthus yearned for grandeur, pomp, and things that money can buy. An enumeration of differences could be made much longer. But the two were united in their uncompromising commitment to representational art and to the indispensable continuity of a tradition which many believed extinct. They never saw eye to eye about the best means of continuing it, and if the truth be known, they didn't much admire each other's work. The more severe was the elder, the less critical the younger.

They were bound together by their passionate care, if not for one another then for what they both represented—perhaps, too, by a community of interest in somewhat perverse erotic adventure—and by an awareness, which must have been almost as clear to them as it is to us, that they were to represent the final flowering of the school of Paris.

In 1937 Balthus completed an enormous painting, eight feet by twelve, in which half a dozen figures are shown in various poses amid a landscape of jutting and precipitous mountain peaks. The evocation of Courbet is overt, insistent, serving notice once again that for this artist, as for his nineteenth-century forebear, the concern with painting well went along with a dogged resolve to paint masterpieces. Indeed, it is difficult to think of any other painter of our era whose guiding preoccupation has so clearly been the periodic production of works conceived precisely to define themselves as masterpieces, and in this, as in so much else, Balthus proudly stands apart from his time. *The Mountain*, whether masterpiece or not, is a stunning achievement for a man of twenty-nine. The haunting, otherworldly Balthusian world is conjured up in the golden clarity and unearthly stillness of high mountain air, and right in the center of the picture—the largest, brightest figure present, her arms upraised in a gesture both ambiguous and fetching—stands Antoinette de Watteville. However he may have worked his wiles upon her, whether as a suitor or as an artist, charming both the woman and the aristocrat, Balthus and Antoinette were married in 1937. Seen in the perspective of his previous humiliation, this must have appeared the definitive realization of the youthful dream. In fact, it was only the beginning.

The couple had two sons. The father kept on painting, while his work found an appreciative and prodigiously long-suffering dealer in New York in the person of Pierre Matisse, who held a first exhibition in 1938. Little sold. War came, but Balthus was demobilized before the fighting grew serious. He took refuge first in a tiny village in Savoy called Champrovent, then in Switzerland at Fribourg, and in both places peacefully went on painting pictures into which not the slightest hint of contemporary turmoil or anguish was permitted to intrude. When the hostilities were finished, and life in France had been revived in a style tolerably approximate to normalcy, Balthus returned to Paris. The postwar trend in taste was less than ever favorable to figurative art, but nothing so deplorably transitory could have altered the way in which Balthus saw things, and he went right on painting as before. A change, however, had come over him, which began to manifest itself in a rather peculiar way.

Marriage to an accredited noblewoman had not, it seems, turned out to be as thrillingly aristocratic as the imaginative young artist had expected. The grand luster, to be sure, of Antoinette's maiden name had been sacrificed at the altar, and the husband on his own account had little to offer by way of prestigious compensation. This was galling. There was his art, yes, but that didn't seem to promise anything very opulent or even impressive for the time being. Resources were scant because Pierre Loeb conformed to the contemporary taste, leaving Balthus dealerless in Paris, while Pierre Matisse, though prepared to buy pictures that did not sell, paid accordingly. Then there was another problem, which might have been foreseen, considering prospects from the outset, by anyone but those concerned. Nobody was growing any younger. Madame Klossowski was a married woman well past thirty, the mother of two not-so-little boys. Balthus, though, by the still-beguiling arithmetic of birthdays, was barely more than a child, and he seems to have felt an overpowering need to find a real person with whom he could enter into the kind of fantasy relationship that he entertained with himself by means of his paintings, through their subject matter, their technical and conceptual references to a vanished world, and their haughty disdain for the opinion of anyone but the artist. Just such a person was provided at just the right moment by one of those miracles which the creative temperament ruthlessly conjures up and then proceeds to consider as commonplace as the morning sun. This person was the teenage daughter of Georges Bataille, the well-known writer on matters of erotic mystique, a lover of Dora before Picasso, incidentally, and former husband of Sylvia Lacan, wife of the soon-to-become-celebrated psychoanalyst Jacques Lacan, himself a man of highly esoteric disposition. These adults, all friends of Balthus, thought it fine for the artist to take an interest in young Laurence, for her to pose for him, and they presumably felt that whatever else might transpire between them would be all to the benefit of posterity. Besides, Antoinette did not seem to mind, and she presently returned to a life of luxury in Switzerland, taking her sons with her. As for Laurence, the benefit to her of these arrangements got rather lost in the shuffle, though the loss itself remained resentfully present as long as she did. Of course, it was merely the loss of innocence, which nonetheless remained as an image in the superb portraits Balthus had made of her.

It was shortly after the departure of Laurence Bataille from Balthus's life that I began to see more of him, mainly with Dora but also occasionally at the luncheon parties given daily by Marie-Laure in her mansion, where she skillfully mixed painters, musicians, writers, duchesses, and interior decorators. He often seemed morose during this period, talking rarely, contemptuously critical of his artist colleagues—Derain and Alberto the sole exceptions to his scorn. And Dora. He spoke admiringly of her work, predicting great prestige for her in the future. She was, moreover, one of the very few friends to whom he made a gift of one of his paintings. She had recently helped him clean up the jumbled, dusty disorder of his studio, and as a token of gratitude he gave her an oil sketch on cardboard of the head of a young girl. It was unsigned, however, which nettled the punctilious Dora, and she had to nag him for some years before he consented to sign it.

People noticed that a change had come over Balthus as he approached the statistical age of forty. Very tentatively at first, almost jokingly, casually, as if the truth were embarrassingly self-evident anyway, he started putting it about that, being of noble birth, he was privileged to use the title of count. Oh, he just let the revelation slip out. His rightful name, he said, was Count Balthazar Klossowski de Rola. He didn't insist on it in the beginning, he merely seemed to suggest that the aristocratic fact might, after all, be allowed to speak, if not to whisper, for itself. To those who were listening, however, the utterance sounded strident beyond belief, and they happened to include Derain, Giacometti, Picasso, Artaud, Albert Camus, the viscount and viscountess de Noailles, Princess Caetani, and others. Some laughed, some sneered, some smiled indulgently, and everyone took it for granted that the artist had no legitimate claim whatsoever to a title. In that, for once, everyone was right. Titles in historic Poland were nonexistent before the partitions, save for the handful of princes descended from sovereign princes of the Grand Duchy of Lithuania and counts originally designated in the sixteenth century by the Holy Roman Emperor. After the partitions a few titles were accepted, or bought, from the Austrian emperor or the Russian czar. There was, however, a genuine aristocracy, defined by relationship to senatorial office, and its members had often assumed titles suited to their style of life while traveling abroad in the nineteenth century, a time when titles still designated economic, social, and, one might almost say, spiritual realities. But that time and practice were far in the past in the wake of the Second World War, which only made Balthus's presumption seem more fantastical. As for the name Rola, it was a heraldic appellation applicable to numerous families other than the Klossowskis, like a clan name in Scotland, and it rather insisted on modest provincial origins, as in Polish the word refers to arable land. It conferred no title whatsoever. To this fact members of the artist's own family were embarrassingly ready to testify, and as if that were not enough, documentary evidence was, and remains, readily available.* In view of all this, one might have thought that Balthus would have dropped his ongoing dalliance with the make-believe. He did nothing of the kind. He began ever so slightly to dwell on it. His self-deprecating smile and mocking drawl when mentioning it began to harden, so that those who heard him were given fair warning of serious intentions and of potential consequences equally serious. Many were appalled, denouncing the affectation as a lamentable lapse into the crudest kind of snobbery. Derain wanted to break off relations with his disciple, but his mistress tactfully recalled him to reality, telling him that the only artist friends of consequence he had left, he who had known them all, were Giacometti and Balthus. So he relented. Balthus didn't. He kept on allowing it to be understood that he was a count. If people laughed behind his back, he could not be bothered to notice. Besides, he had always been proud. People did laugh, and they said that the painter was an unconscionable snob whose noble pretensions made him look like a fool. Had they looked more closely,

* See Adam Boniecki, *Herbaz Polski* (Warsaw: Gebethner and Wolff, 1907), vol. 10, p. 185; and Simon Konarski, *O Heraldyce i "Heraldycznym" Snobizmie* (a work dealing specifically with pretenders to nonexistent Polish titles) (Paris: Ksiegarnia Polska, 1967), p. 43.

they might have seen that neither foolishness nor snobbery could account for an idiosyncrasy so overt on the part of an artist as secretive, subtle, and refined as Balthus.

The issue of the title per se was in a strange way irrelevant, though it pointed precisely to what was central, because every artist's responsibility as well as his license is to forge a self capable of creating the art necessary for the sustenance of that self. In Balthus's case the aristocratic pose did not signify a vulgarity of spirit. On the contrary. Aristocracy clearly represented for him a distinction of personal bearing that reflected the integrity of his commitment to standards and values which had prevailed when titles still meant something. Moreover, it was a way of emphasizing not only his detachment from the aesthetic fashions of the day but his positive loathing of them. And, further, it was a way of asserting that childhood dreams can come true, since the man who painted the portrait of the Vicomtess de Noailles knew very well that by doing so he had made a more vital contribution to the spirit and tradition of aristocracy than ever that lady had by bearing her title and name.

But even all this was neither all nor enough. Balthus had already before the war secured as a studio in Paris a couple of splendid rooms in a grand old building that had once been part of the residence of Diane de Poitiers, mistress to Henry II, King of France. He wearied of it. He wearied, in fact, of the bustle of Paris, where it became increasingly difficult after 1950—even in the ancient neighborhoods Balthus favored—to sustain a credible and fruitful identification with the past. The artist felt due for a change, while the nobleman hungered for it. What was wanted was a castle, a place both secure and imposing, where Balthus could live in peace with all the dreams and ambitions—both obvious and obscure—befitting his vocation. If, as it has been said, the hallmark of a true aristocrat is to have grand aspirations, Balthus had them to burn, and he made no bones about it. He roundly asserted, "I have a greater need for a château than a laborer for a loaf of bread." It was a bon mot, of course, but most people thought it in pretty bad taste. Besides, it was not a joke. And who are common mortals, after all, to evaluate the legitimate needs of the creator? So the Count de Rola traveled around the provinces searching for a suitable residence. Châteaus in those days were a dime a dozen. There was one

called Meyrargues, a superb fortress perched above a valley near
Aix-en-Provence, but the price was also high, and a new roof was
needed. It later became a hotel. The search was made difficult by
two things: the searcher didn't have a dime to his name, and the
genuine artist had requirements just as exacting as the make-believe
count. Dora proposed a handsome alternative in the village where
she spent her summers, adding, in the hope of making it more
attractive, that the property traditionally brought with it a title. Balthus said, "Oh, titles? I've got a surplus of those." The place was
subsequently purchased by another painter, one who also bore a
prestigious name: Nicholas de Staël, who never laid claim to any
nobility other than that of his métier, which, alas, he did not find
sufficiently uplifting to keep him from suicide a few years later.

Sometime in 1953 Balthus found what he'd been searching for,
a château called Chassy in an out-of-the-way corner of the Nièvre,
somewhere between Avallon and Autun. Fortunately the place was
for rent, not sale, and the rate was low. But it was unfurnished and
in a very mediocre state of repair. Still, Balthus seemed pleased,
and we all wondered whether the château was the real thing or
merely another aristocratic fantasy. Fantasy or not, it was real
enough to require someone to do a bit of housekeeping while the
painter worked hard to finish one of his most persuasive productions
in the bid to create a masterpiece, an enormous canvas called *Le
Passage du Commerce Saint-André*, a view of a Parisian back alley
where neither Courbet nor Baudelaire would have noticed anything
incongruous. Finding a housekeeper for the finicky count did not
present itself as an easy task, and the person who found her was
the very last one anybody might have imagined fit for the job: Alberto
Giacometti, who was often heard to grumble, "We're fed up with
Balthus and his little girls." Having made the acquaintance on a
café terrace of a young woman from the provinces named Léna
Leclercq, Alberto thought that maybe she would fill the bill for
Balthus, because she was a highly unconventional individual. The
illegitimate daughter of freethinking farmers, who were also idealists
and Communists, she longed to make her mark in life as a poet.
Since she was already in her mid-twenties, Alberto may have supposed that she would be a little old for Balthus's taste. So he introduced the two, suggesting that while the artist painted, the poetess

could do a bit of writing while at the same time dusting and cooking. It was an exceptionally bad idea, but all concerned thought it splendid.

By the spring of 1954 I had become so friendly with Dora that she invited me to accompany her south to Provence to spend some weeks in the house given her by Picasso in the little town of Ménerbes. I was delighted to accept, so we set out in my small black Renault on April 5. While having lunch in a bistro somewhere along the way, Dora suggested that we make a slight detour to say hello to Balthus in his château, located, she knew, near a hamlet called Blismes. I agreed. But how were we to find this remote spot, I wondered. Blismes was not even on the map. Unconcerned, Dora said that we need only ask directions en route and that one always found what one was looking for if sufficiently persistent. A chill rain was falling, and the prospect of searching the rather desolate countryside for a remote château held little appeal. Maybe, I suggested, it would be best to telephone first. Dora laughed. Balthus could barely afford electricity, let alone a telephone. She dismissed my hesitations, said that we'd only stay for a cup of tea and that Balthus would be overjoyed to receive callers in his lonely retreat. So we set out after lunch, leaving the main road at Avallon, stopping here and there to ask directions. Nobody had ever heard of Blismes, not to mention Chassy, but we kept on in the direction of Autun, and in the dreary town of Château-Chinon luckily chanced upon an ancient geezer who contemptuously informed us that we'd come too far, gone right through Blismes without even knowing it, passing in full view of Chassy—recognizable as a château, he added, only because it had round towers at its corners, and uninhabited till lately, he said, by some Parisian lunatic and his slut. Dora thanked this person very politely, and we went back the way we'd come.

Chassy, indeed, was by no means what one looked for as the archetype of a château, being merely a big, bare-faced house with bulky, round towers at each corner, standing on the down slope of a small hill, overlooking a perfectly ordinary little valley. The approach along a muddy track led through the yard of a nondescript farm. A red-faced woman stared at us with suspicion from beneath the dripping eaves of a shed. Dora put down her window and asked whether this was Chassy. The woman dourly nodded. Then Dora inquired whether Balthus was to be found at home. The woman said, "You mean *monsieur le comte?* Yes, you'll find him in there somewhere." So we went through the gate onto the unkempt lawn and parked by the front door. There was no garden, no park, no statuary, not a single fountain, urn, or vista, and under the cold rain the place looked singularly desolate. Knocking, we received no response; finding the door unlocked, we went inside. The interior was no more imposing than the exterior, and there was next to no furniture. Vast, unheated rooms, freezing as January. After wandering about for a few minutes, opening several doors, we found Balthus and Léna seated at a small table in a cavernous kitchen. A single light bulb hung on a wire from the high ceiling, and several buckets and caldrons were set here and there to catch the drops of water that fell with plunking regularity from leaks in the ceiling. The artist and his housekeeper did not seem a bit pleased to be found by uninvited visitors in this bleak setting, drinking tea from chipped cups. Dora obviously sensed, as I did, that our impromptu intrusion might, after all, be a gaffe and said that we had merely stopped en route to Lyons to say hello and would immediately be once more on our way. But Balthus insisted with some hauteur that we must also have a cup of tea, and Léna halfheartedly reiterated the invitation. It took a bit of doing to find two more cups and chairs; still we did have some tea, while Balthus with his well-practiced charm soon made it seem that we had been impatiently expected.

Presently the artist proposed to show us his studio, and we quickly accepted, aware that the offer constituted a singular privilege. It was on the floor above, to the left of the wide staircase, and on entering we immediately saw on the left wall a huge painting—the view of the Parisian alley occupied by six or seven quizzical figures and a white dog—since become famous as the artist's masterpiece. It was then nearly finished, having been worked on continuously for almost two years, first in Paris, then at Chassy; but there were some elements, the postures of certain figures, which still did not satisfy the painter, and he explained these in some detail—principally to Dora—while I studied the painting with admiration in silence. The studio was rather a mess, the floor littered with scraps of paper, some of them drawings. Other pictures, most of them turned to the wall, were posed at random here and there.

The visit was not prolonged, as Balthus pronounced himself very dissatisfied with the big painting, both reluctant and eager to hand it over to the collectors who had already bought and paid for it, of whom he spoke with contempt. He escorted us to the car, insisting that on our way back to Paris in a few weeks' time we must stop at Chassy for the night, as by then he would be well equipped to receive guests. Dora said that that was an excellent idea, with which I could only concur, whereupon we departed in the rain.

En route to Lyons we talked about the possibility of creating contemporary masterpieces, Dora understandably maintaining that none had been painted since *Guernica* and probably would not be. We also talked about Chassy and Balthus, very much amused that the neighboring farmers were willing, perhaps even pleased, to call him *monsieur le comte*. We agreed, however, that to settle for Chassy as the setting of his grand ambitions took exceptional force of character and an inflexible determination to make the workaday routine of life obey the dictates of high imaginative purpose. Amenities meant nothing, viewed in the perspective of a dedication which dismissed mere happiness as an uncouth irrelevance insofar as it had any bearing at all on the pursuit of man's noblest fulfillment. That pursuit had taken Balthus to Chassy. There were people who said that the itinerary was absurdly circuitous, but nobody could say that it failed to take into account the potential grandeur of the destination. What Chassy had to offer was space, both actual and ideal. There were those vast, high-ceilinged, well-lighted rooms, in which it was possible to see and to conceive works of art free from the constraint of twentieth-century confusions and preconceptions. Balthus believed that he was richly entitled to such space by virtue of his resolve to make good in his own time standards which nobody else had the stamina or the distinction to save from present-day frivolity, mediocrity, and anarchy. On the basis of evidence put forward in good time by this view, the judgment of hindsight seems to be very much on the side of the artist. In the meantime, given Balthus's inclination to seek romantic parallels in unexpected settings, the Château de Chassy could easily have been taken for a Gallic version of Wuthering Heights. The place was quite as bleak as the one imagined by the melancholy Emily Brontë.

My stay in Ménerbes that spring lasted for only twenty days. I had expected and hoped that it would be longer, but my hostess proved to be flighty, unpredictable, at times even irascible. I had to leave with her when she said the time had come. Regretful to be departing so soon, I thought maybe I could have delayed our departure, but I wasn't sure enough of myself to try. We stopped at Chassy on the way back to Paris, and Balthus had, indeed, arranged a couple of spartan guest rooms and an austere bath, all three heated only by tiny electric radiators. The château had not otherwise become much more imposing as the residence of a self-assured nobleman, though the rudiments of a dining room were being gotten together adjacent to the gloomy kitchen. I had a camera with me and mentioned that I'd be pleased to take a few photographs of the château and of Balthus. He acidly rejoined that he never, *never* allowed himself to be photographed. Of Chassy I could take all the pictures I pleased. I took one. Léna served the dinner, a good and plentiful meal with excellent wine, but both Dora and I thought she appeared sullen, ill at ease in her role as housekeeper. Balthus paid little attention to her, talking merrily to us about the death of civilization. Shortly after dinner Léna said good-night, but the three of us sat up till late in front of a feeble fire in the dining-room fireplace.

We were not sorry to leave the next morning. Balthus, we felt, had seemed buoyant and optimistic, although common sense might have argued that he had little cause to be. As a contemporary artist, he was for the moment far from successful. Sales were rare, prices low, collectors still the happy few, and the fastidious far between. He persisted with some difficulty and much resentment on the dole provided by a consortium of half a dozen dealers and connoisseurs who were willing to take a flier on the chance that a nostalgia for masterpieces would produce some. These prescient gamblers were Pierre Matisse and Henriette Gomes, both dealers, she having before the war been Pierre Loeb's secretary; a businessman named Claude Hersent and his wife, Hélène; the Baroness Alix de Rothschild; and Maurice Rheims, an auctioneer and connoisseur of keen discernment. In exchange for a monthly stipend, they expected to receive the painter's entire output. But Balthus worked very slowly. It's true that he always seemed to have all the time in the world, and never appeared to doubt for a moment that posterity would make time for

him. Meanwhile, the château needed to be filled with suitable furniture and appointments, for which works of art had to be offered
in exchange, and some members of the consortium were aggrieved
to learn that canvases were being traded for curtains and couches.
A Parisian decorator named Henri Samuel provided splendid draperies, couches, and some armchairs for one of the finest pictures
painted at Chassy.

With the passage of time the poetess had become increasingly
dissatisfied with her lot. As the château gradually acquired furnishings to the count's taste, it grew more and more difficult for a single
person to keep up an appearance of well-cared-for refinement. Between bouts of cooking, washing, dusting, and mopping, nonetheless, Léna managed to produce a volume of poems, sadly—because
so inappropriately—entitled *Unvanquished Verse*. Balthus once
asked her what historical personage she might have liked to be.
"Trotsky," she said. He tartly rejoined, "You might have chosen
Lenin. He, at least, succeeded." However, a couple of severe portraits of Léna were painted; in both one may discern her pride as
well as her disillusion.

Then the artist conveniently recalled that the wife of his older
brother had a very pretty teenage daughter by a previous marriage
named Frédérique Tison, in whom he had already taken a somewhat
more than avuncular interest, and it seemed to him that she might
do beautifully to preside over the Château de Chassy. And by another
of those opportune miracles that ease the creative life, all parties
found the plan quite pleasing. Except Léna. The count was unconcerned about the opinion of his housekeeper. There were scenes.
The poetess made an effort to end her suffering by ending her life;
it was unsuccessful, for an ambulance was summoned in good time
to take her to the hospital in Nevers, and the keen eye of the artist
observed with sardonic merriment as the vehicle departed that its
owner's name, painted on the door, was Sépulchre.

The Château de Chassy brought out the best in Balthus, especially after the arrival of his "niece," whose girlish charm and
commendable adaptability lent the place an aura of enchantment it
would never otherwise have attained. Of course, an artist's vision
was required to make all this believable. During his years at
Chassy—less than ten, unfortunately—Balthus reached the climax

of his career, painted many of his finest works, and executed scores of superb drawings. He made numerous portraits of Frédérique, who considerately remained an adolescent in pigtails till long after her twenty-first birthday. Of the ordinary little valley where the château stood, and of the vulgar farmyard in front of it, he created a remarkable series of radiant images. The Count de Rola felt that a castle was required to house his self-esteem, and Balthus thought it was the least he owed to the invaluable continuity of artistic tradition. Together they did very well at Chassy, and by it. The nobleman, the painter, the artist, and the château, not to mention Frédérique, made a beautifully composed and perfectly congruous tableau vivant. To be sure, it was not everybody's cup of tea, but precious few were invited to frame an opinion. It's a pity that things couldn't have gone on forever as they were then, in a state of exquisite equilibrium between artistry and aristocracy.

The public had gradually begun to notice that a painter of extraordinary powers was hidden away in that oddly nondescript neck of the woods. People started buying. Critics and collectors began arriving at Chassy to pay their respects and, if possible, acquire a Balthus or two. They were greeted by an Italian majordomo in a white jacket with gold braid who informed them that the count was in his studio and could under no circumstances be disturbed. The Museum of Modern Art in New York put on a retrospective exhibition in 1956. It did not create anything near a sensation, although perceptive connoisseurs paid suitable attention. The catalog was a thin brochure not at all pleasing to the painter. Creative trends on the far side of the Atlantic were, in any event, so far from congenial as to be virtually repellent. What interested Balthus most about America was that one of his earliest and most ardent collectors there happened to be an eccentric clergyman, the Reverend James L. McLean of Los Angeles, California, where nude nymphets on the wall of the manse may very well have looked right at home.

Despite the self-righteous and vindictive letter I had sent to Dora in November 1954, when she failed to visit me in the hospital, and the violently vituperative one I sent to Picasso and published in the press two years later, when he did not speak out against Soviet repression of the Hungarian uprising, she and I did not become altogether estranged. This was the beginning of her withdrawal from

the world, which would lead eventually to a life of proud and obdurate solitude. Still, in 1957 she continued to go out occasionally,
and it was to Marie-Laure's luncheon parties that she went most
frequently. When we met there, as we inevitably did, she was
friendly, talkative, vivacious, but there was no longer between us
that sense of some exceptional, even extraordinary, rapport that had
held us so close three years before. And how could I presume? The
relationship was simpler now, pleasant but less enthralling.

My friend Bernard Minoret and Dora had with time become
amicable, and an enduring souvenir of their friendship was presently
forthcoming as a consequence of Dora's irrepressible acquisitive-
ness, especially when something could be had for next to nothing.
Bernard's family owned a château, a real one, in the country fifty
miles east of Paris. Neither he nor his parents cared for the place,
which by 1957 had fallen into considerable disrepair but still contained some furnishings and household appointments. How Dora
learned of the château and its neglected contents I did not record,
but her acquisitive instinct and flair for a bargain were aroused.
Would there by any chance, she inquired of Bernard, be such items
as lace curtains, linen tablecloths, napkins, and sheets? Oh, yes,
Bernard felt sure there were hampers of such things in the attic.
Well, said Dora, if any of them were to her liking, she would be
prepared to give a picture in exchange. She had always been keen
on trading, she said. Bernard gladly agreed. So we drove out of Paris
one springlike morning in March and after about an hour came to
the Château de Monglat in the crocus-yellow sunshine. Bernard had
been right about the linens. There were trunks and wicker hampers
filled with them. Dora could barely control her excitement. We made
several trips downstairs to the car, our arms filled with lace curtains
and fragile fabrics, some of which had never been unwrapped from
tissue paper a century old. When we got back to Paris and heaped
on Dora's bed the piles of linens, there came the moment for her
part of the bargain to be kept. She proposed that Bernard choose
one of her paintings or a couple of gouaches from a portfolio. There
was no mention of a sketch by Picasso, of which she possessed
dozens, any one of which would have constituted a fair trade. But
she added that if Bernard did not want either a painting or the
gouaches, she would be happy to paint his portrait. This prospect

did appeal to him. She painted him in profile in her pointillist manner, a tolerably good likeness but a mediocre work of art. Bernard
was delighted, caring no more about Monglat and its contents than
his parents did, and never felt that Dora had taken advantage of
him.

Maybe it was this felicitous experience of barter that put Dora
in mind of my grandmother's carpet. She must have already known
about it, anyway. In 1956, when my parents and grandmother had
moved out of the large house where I had grown up, there were
quite a few things which were too large or for which there was no
room in the smaller residence. These were stored in the attic. I saw
an opportunity to acquire a bit of patrimony in advance and asked
what I might take back with me by ship to Paris. I had just then
occupied an apartment in the rue de Lille, where I sit today writing
these words, thirty-eight years later. I was allowed to make off with
almost anything I wanted, and one of the items I selected was an
enormous Persian carpet which had been the pride of my grandmother's living room in faraway Indianapolis, Indiana. Granny had
had an eye for carpets, if not for much else, and bought a lot of
them when she married in 1890. I still have several; they are exceptionally fine and much admired. But the big one could never
have fitted into any apartment I have ever occupied or aspire to
occupy. It was made for a grand space. Why I took it I can't imagine.
It was there for the taking, that's all, so I took it. Not knowing what
on earth to do with it once I arrived in Paris, I kept it stored in a
spare room adjacent to the apartment of Bernard's parents in
Neuilly. And there it lay, waiting in all likelihood, I suppose, for
moths or mice.

Balthus came occasionally to Paris. Dora and I sometimes had
dinner with him, usually at La Reine Christine. And it was during
one of these dinners that Dora mentioned my grandmother's dor-
mant carpet. Being so large, she said, might it not be just the thing
for the grand salon at Chassy? Never would such an eventuality have
occurred to me, nor, I think, would I have had the temerity to suggest
it. But Dora was fearless when confronted with anything businesslike. Well, murmured the artist, that might be, that might be. And
then, added Dora, no money need change hands, for she felt certain
I would be happy to accept in exchange some little sketch, water-

color, or drawing from the artist's hand. To be sure, said Balthus, but of course he would have to inspect the carpet first. Nothing could have been simpler to arrange. A day or two later, Balthus and I drove to Neuilly. With Bernard's help the three of us carried the very heavy carpet outside onto a lawn opposite the Minorets' apartment building and there unrolled it in the sunshine. Though worn, it was still quite splendid and, indeed, very large. Balthus walked round and round the carpet on the grass several times, trod upon it, and inspected it, I thought, with the skeptical eye of an Armenian merchant. Finally he said, "It will do. Not for a caliph's desert encampment, mind you, but it will do." I, however, would have the responsibility of delivering it to Chassy. That would be easy, I said, promising to make delivery within a couple of weeks. So the bargain was struck, and I felt very satisfied at the prospect of possessing some little sketch by Balthus.

On April 3 I drove alone to Chassy, with the carpet occupying the entire rear seat of my car. Balthus, Frédérique, and the Italian majordomo were on hand to help carry it inside and smooth it out on the floor of the grand salon, where I thought it looked quite fine enough for the count's rustic encampment, transforming the room by the subtle hues of its antique rose-and-azure coloring and adding an appearance of warmth to an otherwise chilly, half-empty space. Balthus strode back and forth across it, pronounced himself tolerably satisfied, and added that an undermat would have to be provided. Not by me, I thought. Frédérique in her appealing, girlish way was plainly happy with the addition of anything that would help make the huge house seem somewhat more cheerful as a home. I had automatically assumed, having promptly kept my part of our bargain, that Balthus would be prepared to do likewise. That only shows how little I had as yet understood the perverse and wily nobleman. He announced that it was time for a hurried tea, after which I would naturally wish to take again to the road for my return to Paris. We went into the dining room, where tea was quickly served by the majordomo. I awaited with rising surprise and some impatience a mention of the little work from the artist's hand that had been promised. It came at the last minute and only to defer the promise. He had no small sketches, watercolors, or suitable drawings, Balthus said, escorting me toward the door, that he could in all conscience offer as an exchange. But he assured me that I was losing nothing by waiting. Something good and satisfying enough for me would presently come along. All I had to do was wait.

Driving back to Paris empty-handed, I felt that I had been somewhat put upon. To wait was all very well, but I felt no certainty that the artist, known to be crafty and difficult, would ever keep his promise. The carpet meant nothing to me. I would never have had any use for it and probably could not have sold it for much. But a bargain was a bargain. When I vented my feelings to Dora, she laughed. It was pure Balthus, she said, to compel people to submit to his whims. That proved he was an authentic aristocrat. I would simply have to wait, though she generously offered to do all she could to prod the bargain toward a happy outcome.

So the weeks and months, the winter slipped by. Balthus appeared now and then in Paris. We had dinner with him. I felt shy about mentioning my expectation and, moreover, believed that it was up to the artist to keep his word. He mentioned our bargain now and then, inevitably adding that I had nothing to lose by waiting. Well, I was prepared to wait, but it began to seem that nothing was precisely what I might ultimately receive. And that thought irritated, but I did not want to be considered rude over anything so commonplace as a rug, no matter how large.

A year had passed since delivery of the carpet. Bernard and I decided to spend the spring somewhere in northern Italy—it turned out to be on the shore of Lake Como—and conclude our stay with a visit to Venice. Discussion of these plans took place one day in Dora's presence, whereupon she declared that she had always longed to visit the ineffable constellation of palaces and masterpieces afloat upon the Adriatic and would be very pleased to join us in Venice if her presence should represent no inconvenience. Both of us were happy to agree. Then, Dora said, we could return via Milan, visit the Brera, travel on to Zürich and Basel, and drop in on Balthus at Chassy as the last stop on our homeward journey. It sounded altogether delightful, and it was.

Having lingered long over dinner at an excellent restaurant in a small village on our return trip, it was nearly midnight by the time we reached Chassy. Not a glimmer came to greet us from the windows of the château. Dora and Bernard were loath to intrude upon this unwelcoming darkness, insisting that I should take it upon myself to waken our host. Finding the front door luckily unlocked, I went inside, turning on lights, going upstairs, and calling out the artist's name. He appeared after a few minutes from Frédérique's bedroom, shrugging into a dressing gown, and irritably showed us to our rooms, remarking that any polite hour for the arrival of guests had long since passed. There was nothing we could say. In the morning he was more affable, insisting that we stay for lunch, but we were not invited to visit the studio. Indeed, I never saw it again after that first visit four years before. Frédérique was quiet but self-possessed and quite as beautiful as she appears in the many portraits Balthus painted and drew of her during this period, perhaps his finest. It was at the luncheon table that Dora showed her mettle as a friend and as an enthusiast for bargaining by remarking that I had as yet received nothing in return for the fine carpet that lay on the floor of the grand salon. Balthus replied, predictably, that by waiting I was losing nothing, adding that in the studio upstairs there was not a single thing that would be suitable. Such being the case, Dora said, wouldn't it be simpler and more pleasing for all if Balthus were to make a portrait drawing of me. Why on earth not? replied the artist. I could come some day to Chassy to pose and that would be that. The date could be set at a future time convenient for all. I was delighted. And that would be one more portrait, Dora observed, added to those I already possessed by Picasso, herself, Lucian, Giacometti, and Cocteau. Not bad company to keep, said Balthus. So the understanding was reached. We drove back to Paris in the afternoon, Dora and I both very pleased by this unexpected turn she had given to the original bargain.

Bernard had been but slightly concerned by my dealings with Balthus. Contemporary art appealed to him hardly at all. He preferred decorative paintings of an earlier era or pictures that had some historical or literary content. As if stung by a wasp, he became insistently interested in the bargain with Balthus now that it promised a portrait rather than some little sketch, and he thought at once to insinuate himself into the arrangement. Perhaps he felt a piercing nostalgia at the recollection of his supercilious disinclination to pose for a portrait by Cocteau four years before. In any case, he proposed that I should ask Balthus to expand our bargain so that it might include a portrait of him as well as myself. I was very reluctant to do this. Bernard, after all, had had no part in the original negotiation. The carpet had not belonged to him, and he had never till now evinced any concern for the entire business. But Balthus had begun to be an artist who conferred aristocratic prestige, which Cocteau did not. Having painted Lady Abdy in 1935 and Marie-Laure in 1956, he was known to be at work even now on a large portrait of the Baroness Alain de Rothschild. To have one's portrait drawn by him would consequently constitute the sort of fashionable glamour to which Bernard was anything but indifferent. So he insisted that I present the case to Balthus. And he knew how to insist to such effect that, despite my reluctance, I consented. To my great relief, and somewhat to my surprise, Balthus immediately agreed. He seemed, in fact, quite pleased by the prospect of portraying Bernard. This was in late June, shortly before our departure for a summer on the Cape of Sorrento.

That autumn and winter I did quite a lot of traveling around France and Western Europe, visiting Amsterdam, London, Munich, Salzburg, and Vienna. In the spring I rented a small house about twenty miles north of Paris in a hamlet called Baillon, where I spent the better part of each week writing yet another novel. Nonetheless I saw Balthus several times here and there. No mention was made of the promised portraits. Bernard insisted that I should insist, but I fought shy of making an issue. That summer was the first I spent on Skyros, the Greek isle where I met Errieta Perdikidi, one of the most exceptional women it's been my luck to know.

Returning to Paris toward the end of September, I planned to fly to America six weeks later to spend a few months with my family and friends. Now it did at last seem to me that Balthus was overstepping the courteous bounds of our bargain. He had been in possession of the carpet for two and a half years. There had been a lot of talk, but nothing had come of it. Meeting Dora one day at Marie-Laure's, I asked her advice. She told me to present Balthus with an ultimatum, adding that he was by nature fond of ultimatums and would probably respond positively. So I sat down on October 10, Alberto's birthday, and wrote Balthus a letter protesting against his long delay in keeping his part of our bargain and stating that if he were not prepared to execute the promised portraits some time before my departure on November 12, I would come to Chassy and recuperate the carpet—embarrassed, I must admit, at taking such a peremptory tone and not knowing what in the world I'd do with the wretched thing if compelled to make good my rude threat.

The following Tuesday I received a telegram reading, "Expect you Thursday. Friendly regards. Balthus." Bernard was exultant.

The weather was radiant, Indian summer, golden light cascading along the roadside, which ran by glittering streams and ruined sawmills. We stopped somewhere for lunch. It was time for tea when we arrived at our destination, which now, in the perspective of desires at long last satisfied, began to look in reality like the castle of a romantic nobleman. Balthus was all smiles and Frédérique clearly pleased to have some company in their remote stronghold. After tea we were shown to our rooms and informed that drinks would be served at seven-thirty in the grand salon, which had now, indeed, been made approximately grand. To the yellow curtains, couches, and armchairs supplied by Henri Samuel had been added a grand piano, Louis XVI chairs and side tables, and oddments of elegant bric-a-brac. The only incongruous item was a very ugly bamboo coffee table that stood before the couch in front of the fireplace. When we were gathered for drinks, which were set out upon this exceedingly bourgeois table, I impulsively remarked that it was the only thing in the room that seemed out of place in the château. To which Balthus immediately rejoined, "Well, at least it's better than the rug." That brought an instant chill, which was dispelled only after a very specific intermittence by Balthus's snide chuckle. It didn't seem to bode very well for satisfaction of the purpose of our journey. Conversation resumed, however, consisting largely of a discussion of Byzantine history by Bernard and our host. The dinner was excellent, and while we were still at table Balthus announced that we must drive to Autun the next morning to admire the splendid sculptures adorning the tympanum of the cathedral. Also we must not miss the museum, which contained several fine Flemish paintings. And there was a very pleasant restaurant called Le Vieux Moulin where we could have lunch outside beside a pretty stream. We would be back at Chassy just in time for a bath, drinks, and dinner. No mention of portraits. Now, I had already told Balthus that we must leave on Saturday afternoon no later than four o'clock, as we had agreed to dine that evening with Marie-Laure and could hardly cancel the engagement at short notice.

Retiring to our rooms soon after dinner, Bernard and I wondered with a certain misgiving whether Balthus had brought us here only to make a mockery of the bargain, having no intention after all this time to honor it. Bernard was even more concerned than I was and asked me to suggest, should the time for us to pose ever come, that he be the first to be portrayed. I weakly agreed to do that.

The next morning Balthus had already retired to his studio before we had breakfast. Frédérique said he could not be disturbed. There was nothing to be done but set off for Autun, where we spent a very agreeable day, admired the justly famous tympanum, and had an expensive lunch at Le Vieux Moulin. That evening at dinner, having waited twenty-four hours without mention of the purpose of our visit, I braced myself to make bold with an inquiry as to the time when we might expect to be portrayed. Balthus threw up his hands, exclaiming that time was the very, very least of considerations. He must prepare himself psychologically for the ordeal of a portrait, he said. A drawing didn't take long, but the mental stress of preparation could last in some cases almost a lifetime. It sounded like Alberto talking. Anyway, the artist added, we had all day Saturday before us. I reminded him that we must leave at the very latest by four o'clock. Well, he said, nobody need worry, because the right frame of mind could make a quarter of an hour virtually equivalent to a lifetime. Then the dinner was over, and Balthus bid us a courtly good night.

In the morning Balthus once again had finished his breakfast and disappeared before we reached the dining room. He was in his studio, Frédérique told us, and must not be disturbed. But when, I inquired, might he be expected to return downstairs? Frédérique said that his schedule of work was subject to no imperative save its own. He might come down in ten minutes or in two hours, just in time for lunch. There was nothing for us to do but pack our small suitcases and sit in the salon, waiting. Balthus's studio was immediately overhead and we could hear his footsteps as he paced back and forth, presumably judging his work in progress between every two or three strokes of the paintbrush. This made our wait only the more exasperating, and it was already made irritating enough by the rhythmic rattle of Frédérique's knitting machine. This appliance, a recent gift from Balthus, produced finished lengths of knitted fabric far more rapidly than hand knitting would have made possible. I wasn't interested to learn how the mechanism functioned. All I knew was that its use required the operation of a metal arm that had to be yanked back and forth, producing a gnashing clatter that grated very disagreeably upon nerves already taut. So we sat there, waiting, while Balthus paced invisibly overhead and Frédérique sat imperturbably operating her noisy machine. The weather was again gorgeous. Shafts of pure October gold streamed through the high windows. How long we waited I didn't note. All of the morning. It seemed, in any case, far longer than the best frame of mind in the world would have cared to make equivalent to a lifetime, and our frame of mind was not by any means of the best.

It was past noon, anyway, when Balthus finally came downstairs. He brought with him, though, a large sketchbook and a handful of pencils. This seemed a promising sign, and it was, for he languidly remarked, "Well, now we have our little session of posing, do we not?"

Bernard darted a quite unnecessary glance at me, and I said, "Why don't you do Bernard first?"

"Impossible," Balthus replied. "His head presents a much more difficult challenge than yours, my dear Jim, so I'll do you first. Just sit in that armchair and face me. Good. Like that. And lower your head a bit."

He sat in a chair facing me, opened the sketchbook on his knees, and began to draw. Alberto had accustomed me to lengthy sessions of absolute immobility, so I had no difficulty holding the pose. It took fifteen or twenty minutes, no more. Balthus announced that the drawing was finished and tore the page from his sketchbook. From the first instant I saw the drawing, I didn't like it. I was depicted looking downward, not quite full face, the left ear prominent, my lips pressed shut. My open shirt and right shoulder were sketchily indicated. I thought the drawing made me look like a thug. But a bargain was a bargain, so I admired it, and in fact as a drawing qua drawing it is quite good. Only as an image of myself did I find it

disappointing. However, I was not going to quibble. "And now," I consequently said, "you can do Bernard."

But it was time for lunch. With a laugh Balthus remarked, "I couldn't possibly attack Bernard on an empty stomach."

My drawing was set down on the closed lid of the grand piano and we went to the dining room. By the time we returned to the salon and finished our coffee, it was after two. I said that I'd go for a walk while Balthus drew Bernard. But no, declared the artist, his hand wasn't yet quite ready. He would make another drawing of me first, a profile this time. So again I sat. This one was of the head only, far more satisfying to me than the first, executed more rapidly and with greater finesse. When it, too, had been placed on the piano, I said that now Bernard's turn had come. Not yet, Balthus protested. He would have to make still another drawing of me. I'm happy today that he insisted, for the third portrait turned out to be very decidedly the best. I am depicted once more in profile but from a slightly further remove, my shoulders and part of the chair on which I was seated also shown. Of Balthus's portrait drawings, I know of few finer. It was placed on the piano beside the two others, and I hoped that when the time came to conclude the bargain I would be allowed to take this one.

Then Balthus said that he was ready to take on Bernard. But they would work in another room. Gathering his pencils and sketch-book, he went across the hall to a smaller salon and Bernard followed. I put our suitcases into the car, then went off along the warm autumnal fields for a lengthy, leisurely stroll. I lay down beside a scarlet bush in the faded cushion of grass, content in the loveliness of the afternoon and the happy outcome at long last of the bargain. I didn't doze, because, by nature obsessively punctual, I hadn't forgotten that we must leave by four o'clock. So it was three-forty-five when I returned to the château, expecting to find Bernard in possession of his portrait and Balthus ready to tell us good-bye. But Frédérique was alone in the salon, banging away at her knitting machine. "Where are they?" I asked. She replied that they were still in the other room. It had been almost an hour. I said that I must go and find out what could be taking so long, since we must soon leave. Frédérique shrugged. Crossing the downstairs landing

of the staircase, I opened the door to the salon beyond. Balthus sat on a low chair with his back toward me, the sketchbook on his knees, Bernard on a couch five or six feet away, his head turned in profile. Over the artist's shoulder I could see the drawing on which he was working. It was superb, very detailed and strongly executed, head and shoulders an excellent likeness, far more powerful and finer than the portraits of me. Balthus waved me back, protesting the interruption, saying that he had not yet finished. Thus, I had no choice but to return to the salon and wait. Frédérique remarked that there was no limit to the time that Balthus might devote to a drawing once he became committed to its interest. However, it was now four o'clock. Fortunately, or unfortunately, the wait was not long. Bernard came into the salon alone, his head hanging, in appearance plainly dejected. I asked what was the matter. "He tore it up," Bernard replied.

"But it was superb," I protested.

"That's what I thought, but he said it was no good and tore it up and threw the pieces in the fireplace."

Balthus then came into the room. "I overworked it," he said. "But it was a good exercise. My dear Bernard, you mustn't fret. You lose nothing by waiting. We'll have another session and you need not even come to Chassy. I'm often in Paris. I'll come to you."

Bernard put as good a face as he could manage on the fait accompli. What could he do but accept it?

It was past time for us to leave, and I asked Balthus which one of the three portraits of myself I might have to fulfill our bargain. All three, he said, I must have all three. But the understanding from the first had been for a single portrait only, I protested, and I'd be perfectly content to take but one. No, no, Balthus insisted, I should have all three. And I must truthfully acknowledge that he did not have to insist very strenuously to secure my agreement. So we rolled up the three drawings and went out to the car. Balthus and Frédérique came along to wave us on our way. That was the last time I saw the Château de Chassy.

Driving back to Paris, naturally Bernard and I discussed the fate of his portrait. It seemed exceedingly bizarre that an artist as painstaking and accomplished as Balthus should have destroyed the finest drawing executed on that day while nonchalantly allowing me

to go away with three of lesser quality. Neither of us could understand it. But an artist sees his work, and judges it, with eyes that we
neither possess nor comprehend. Alberto was a perfect example of
that truism, implacable destroyer of his own work that he was. Balthus, however, unlike Alberto in almost every way one can think of,
was never very given to destruction of his creations. I felt a little
abashed to be returning to Paris with three drawings when Bernard,
who had been so eager to acquire one, had nothing. Still, I tried to
console us both with the assurance that Balthus would live up to his
promise that one loses nothing by waiting. After all, he had done
so for me. And whenever we ran into him during the next few years,
he conscientiously reiterated that promise.

Frédérique Tison had a brother named Jean-Charles, an exceptionally handsome, good-natured young fellow with whom we
became casually friendly and who through his sister was well acquainted with Balthus. A few years after our last visit to Chassy, he
told a close friend of ours, who inevitably repeated this to us, that
one of the artist's favorite stories was the tale of the torn-up portrait
of Bernard, which he related with great mirth as an instance of
punishment he had enjoyed inflicting on someone who had brashly
intruded upon a bargain in which he had had no rightful part. That
this may, indeed, have been the truth of the matter casts a strange
but credible illumination upon the character of the artist. An aristocrat, to be sure, can derive enjoyment from the mortification of a
person judged unduly presumptuous. An artist, however, proud and
vigilant in veneration of his calling, who destroys purely for malicious satisfaction a work upon which he has expended a maximum
of talent, seems peculiarly at odds with himself. The case is interesting, because as time wore on, the conflict between Balthus and
the Count de Rola became more and more open, its cost more
and more perceptible. Bernard, of course, chooses not to believe
the explanation provided by Jean-Charles, preferring to think that
Balthus was sincerely dissatisfied with the drawing he destroyed. I
am not of that opinion. But by waiting, to be sure, Bernard did
lose something in this case, because Balthus never again drew his
portrait.

In 1961 Balthus was given a boost by one of his old cronies,
André Malraux, a creator also dedicated to concepts of personal

glory and exalted spiritual purpose which many deemed passé, and some, in fact, outré. But in his own time he had become an almost legendary figure, and, as the favorite of General Charles de Gaulle, to whom the idea of grandeur was the stuff of life itself, he was now enjoying a kind of mythic consecration as minister of cultural affairs. Malraux believed that art exists virtually as an autonomous reality, and is thus more an outgrowth of past art than a response to contemporary stimuli. He and Balthus were made for discriminating mutual esteem. Malraux appointed his friend director of the French Academy in Rome, an institution established by Louis XIV in the seventeenth century, when the Roman sojourn and initiation had been a prestigious sine qua non for any artist who hoped to make a name for himself. The Prix de Rome was coveted as evidence of outstanding promise until at least the mid-nineteenth century, and the appointment was happily accepted by great and mediocre alike. Ingres was a promising winner at age twenty-one, later spending many contented and industrious years as director of the academy. So the post came in the gratifying context of glorious antecedents and precedents. These, it's true, may not have looked like much when considered from the viewpoint of young artists overseas who regarded Picasso as effete and elevated to the rank of contemporary icon a clumsy and garish portrait of Marilyn Monroe. But such a viewpoint was precisely what Balthus considered beneath his notice, and a better refuge for his abhorrence could hardly have been found than the French Academy. Besides, Chassy had begun to seem a bit cramped. The count complained that he had barely enough space in which to contemplate his achievements with decent impartiality. And he cannot have failed to observe that his "niece" had definitely reached marriageable age. She was left behind at Chassy. Removal to Rome must have appeared to offer the best of imaginable worlds, and to the Count de Rola it indubitably did. Balthus, on the other hand, forfeited a significant degree of distinction.

Standing at the brow of the Pincian Hill, the French Academy is housed in the Villa Medici, one of the noblest landmarks of the Eternal City, erected in the sixteenth century with a helping hand, so it's said, of Michelangelo himself. Its public rooms are of awe-inspiring dimensions, the private apartments hardly less palatial.

But when the new director arrived in 1961, he found that the villa had fallen on hard times and showed distressingly little evidence of erstwhile splendor, though it was not in the least like Wuthering Heights. The overwhelming relevance of that novel, in any event, was by this time evidently a closed chapter. To restore the Villa Medici to a viable degree of magnificence, and make it into a fitting residence for one who did not balk at the dictates of nobility, became the new director's first priority, one which he pursued in person with exemplary elegance and attention to detail. He even found time to take a passing interest in the young winners of the Prix de Rome, whose aesthetic fortunes were temporarily entrusted to his super- vision, though none of them gave signs of great promise and only a couple had the good taste to paint pictures that resembled his. As for his own pictures, very few were produced during these years, because the director was too busy looking after palatial renovations to paint, while the count had a very crowded schedule of official and social engagements. He also had a countess to pay attention to. A year or two after taking up residence at the villa, Balthus traveled to the Far East and in Japan made the acquaintance of a young woman named Setsuko. She accompanied him back to Rome, be- coming bride and countess all at once.

Balthus's craving for grandeur and nostalgia for the standards and style of a bygone age got all the satisfaction at the Villa Medici that anybody could have dreamt of, and more. Princes and prin- cesses, cardinals, ambassadors dined at the count's table, where exquisite foods and wines were served on plates and in goblets em- blazoned with golden crowns. If the count had been cautious, almost apologetic about using his title in Paris, and even during the early years at Chassy, no circumspection prevailed in Rome. Protocol was the inflexible rule. Invitations to official functions at the villa were sent out in the names of the Count and Countess Klossowski de Rola. The French ambassador was made to understand that the director of the French Academy and his wife were unlikely to appear at receptions and dinners in the Palazzo Farnese should they fail to be received, presented, and seated with all the deference due their rank, which made things a bit ticklish for the diplomat, because there were plenty of noblemen in Rome whose ancestors had for a millennium or so been keeping an implacable eye on their places in relation to the salt. Still, the Rolas were much in demand, a great social success in Rome. Balthus was suave, witty, sardonic, an excellent teller of entertaining stories, trenchant in his judgments of art, literature, music, and manners. Setsuko was exquisitely gracious, attired in gorgeous kimonos of silk so heavy and richly embroidered that they looked as though they would stand up by themselves. The guests and friends were not all nobility, diplomats, and churchmen, either. There were also a few artists and writers, congenial spirits, and one of the closest of these, in fact, was a latter-day virtuoso of personal fantasy and erotic make-believe named Federico Fellini.

If anybody wondered what was going on in the artist's secluded studio in the villa's gardens while the count and countess were busy being sociable and aristocratic, such curiosity was neither well received nor well rewarded. Visitors were greeted with impeccable politesse, but even the painter's dealer, Pierre Matisse—now compelled to advance enormous sums against the promise of pictures that existed only in the artist's imagination—frequently found the studio doors denied him. It was Balthus, and Balthus only, it seems, who was in the artist's own view entitled to any reward. He had awaited it with unbending determination for forty long years, and he was resolved to have it on his own terms, since it was on those terms that he seems from the beginning to have staked his belief that the reward due to great achievement must be but another aspect of the deference due to great aspiration. And certainly no one could contend that Balthus was undeserving of high esteem. But somehow or other in Rome the fragile equilibrium between aspiration and achievement went awry. Perhaps it was because while there Balthus at last came completely into his own as a self-creation commensurate with his ambition to personify and perpetuate traditions of an erstwhile order. The Count de Rola had become a real person, not a fiction, not a storybook character, and in the process he had somehow lost the old power to create a convincing world for the inhabitants of his imagination. Compared with the pictures painted at Chassy, the few executed in Rome look stilted and artificial. They are works of exceptional formal skill and refinement, needless to say—Balthus has never known how to be vulgar—but the onetime passions and life-giving fantasies are gone, leaving behind only self-indulgent, decorative reminders of a simpler day, signed with the same name though not by the same man.

Balthus lingered on in Rome. The original term of his appointment expired, but he managed to get it renewed. The villa hadn't yet been restored entirely to his taste. And then there were the gardens, which were also grandly entitled to attention. Hadn't Velázquez painted here? The count lingered on. Something about the Eternal City held him. Maybe it was in part the memory of one of his ancestors, Jacob Maximilian Klossowski, sent by King Wladyslaw IV in 1643 to administer the Polish Church of Santo Stanislav, a charge he tenaciously held, despite havoc at home, until his death thirty years later. Rome is the city in the Western world richest and most imposing in a continuous accumulation of art and history, of cultural, intellectual, and spiritual associations. The artist and the nobleman felt comfortably at one with it and with each other in it. The time would fatally come, however, when directorship of the academy must pass into other, less illustrious hands, and against the anomaly of that day Balthus looked around for an alternative residence. He found something north of Rome, not far from Viterbo, called the Castello di Monte Calvello. It was a very large, ancient, and patrician pile, more in need of repairs and appointments than Chassy had ever been. This time, though, there was no want of money. At the very moment when the artist's powers had begun to flag, the prices of his works took a leap and have never since ceased climbing. The old consortium of dealers and connoisseurs had long since been disbanded, but their flier had turned out to be really meteoric. When at last a new director was named to the Villa Medici, Balthus blandly informed him that the place couldn't be vacated overnight, owing to urgent creative commitments already undertaken. This urgency lasted a couple of years or so, while the count and countess kept on entertaining and the artist painted a few more pictures and made a lot of drawings that looked like things done long before by Balthus. Even the countess got to work with brushes and paints, and her things, too, looked wonderfully like Balthuses. So the dominion of the make-believe made itself in its own image.

And then the couple had a child. A little girl. That, perhaps, was all that was needed to close the magic circle in which Balthus had lived since his own childhood.

The infrequency of birthdays, however conducive to visions of youth, had failed to avert the audit of years, and one day the Count de Rola found that he was well past retirement age. After a decade and a half, he was compelled to relinquish the Villa Medici. A sense of deprivation seems to have ensued, and the alternate castle didn't prove satisfying as a substitute for the grandeur of the Eternal City. Moreover, with old age staring him in the face, the artist found that he might yet want to take his chances on the advent of a masterpiece or two by getting down to some hard work. To the surprise of all except those who knew him intimately, he went back to Switzerland. It was in Switzerland that he had spent the better part of his childhood, and his first great infatuation with the aristocratic principle had taken place in Switzerland. And there was even a creative association, for his most important artist friend, though unlike him in almost every way, had nonetheless been Swiss; and while director of the Villa Medici, Balthus had been able to pay homage to the memory of that friendship by organizing in 1970 a retrospective exhibition of works by Alberto Giacometti. So the final return to Switzerland was in many ways a reaffirmation. Balthus had long ago created an otherworldly world, and now the Count de Rola retreated into it and reigned over it, closing off the frontiers to others and insisting upon prerogatives that nobody had ever wanted to argue about in the first place. He established himself, his wife, and his daughter in an immense eighteenth-century chalet, reputed to be the largest in Switzerland, at Rossinière in the Canton of Vaud. It was very grand, but the atmosphere was said to be rather cheerless and lonely. Exhibitions of his work were organized, but the artist, as usual, loftily declined to appear, leaving the workaday arrangements of fame and honor to others, brusquely rebuffing the solicitations of journalists and the inquiries of art historians. In 1977, when Pierre Matisse held a large exhibition in New York, the catalog preface was penned by the count's Roman colleague, Federico Fellini, who concluded his panegyric with the assertion that to understand Balthus is to understand the times we live in; the lesson is made plainer, he says, quoting Michelangelo, "if at the end of the day, we look inside ourselves so that we can finally distinguish the only reality possible from all that seemed real to us—invented reality." To search inside himself for a reality of his own invention was precisely what Michel Balthazar Klossowski had been doing for more than half a century.

Then the curators of the French National Museums and of the Metropolitan Museum of Art in New York decided jointly to mount a great retrospective exhibition intended to establish and consecrate once and for all Balthus's stature as a modern master descended directly and legitimately from those great predecessors chosen long ago by the aspiring youth as his rightful forebears. This exhibition was shown in Paris at the Pompidou Center from November 4, 1983, until January 23, 1984, and at the Metropolitan Museum in New York, whither Balthus could not be bothered to travel, from February 29, 1984, the artist's birthday, until May 13. It was viewed by large crowds and greatly admired. I was asked by a review devoted to literature and art to write an article about Balthus on this occasion. I did so, relating everything that I knew about the artist, his work, formation, and family background, leaving out almost nothing except the story of my grandmother's Persian carpet, which still lies in tatters on the floor at Chassy, so I'm told by Frédérique. I didn't expect that Balthus, whose obsession with secrecy was well known to me, would be pleased by my article, which appeared in December of 1983. But I was surprised to receive a letter from my old friend Lucian, who loathed my piece and ended his denunciation by stating that it was "the work of a poisonous cunt." His bitterness must have been grievously aggravated ten years later when Balthus remarked in an interview with the British rock star David Bowie, "I have a horror of dear little Freud . . . I was really shocked by the last thing I saw."

I was really shocked that Balthus might ever have made such a statement about a fellow artist, even one who might not have been his admirer and friend or shared with him strong convictions as to the proper role and conceptual aspirations of a painter. Between 1984 and 1994, however, a profound and astonishing change had come over the Count de Rola. He no longer wished to be a painter of whom *nothing is known*. On the contrary. Little by little it began to seem that he had acquired a taste for celebrity, allowing for the surmise that artist and aristocrat had always had in common a hidden hankering for the inelegant commotion of popular apotheosis. Even to the best of men the desire for glory clings longer than any other passion. When fame is the spur, however, all prerogatives of privacy, not to mention those of secrecy, are arbitrarily set aside. The first photographs of the painter began to appear in newspapers and magazines in the mid-eighties. It was surprising, perplexing, intriguing. The man who had never, *never* wished to be photographed now gazed imperturbably back at the viewer with serene hauteur from the glossy pages of publications destined to pass through the hands of a million readers, most of whom knew nothing about art but cared a lot about the doings and sayings of famous men and women. Beneath one such photograph appears the phrase "The voluptuous and peaceful style of an aristocrat weary of the world." What had come over him? He had always refused to be interviewed, but now the more and more frequent interviews often begin with the artist's statement that he invariably refuses to be interviewed. "The most mysterious of living painters," asserts one interviewer. But the mystery is the interview itself. "Balthus Speaks!" cries one headline. *"Monsieur le Comte,"* says another. Why? It is a well-known fact that the surest way to attract attention is to flee from it. Balthus thus fled for a long time, but his stamina apparently flagged at last. In the autumn of 1992 an entire issue of the Swiss art review *DU* was devoted to Balthus and his work. And he even consented to become a member of the jury of the Venice Film Festival. Some people say that the pursuit of fame is principally the work of the Countess de Rola and that she exacts a fee for interviews and photographs. If so, more's the pity, for it is Balthus, not Setsuko, who poses and talks. To be sure, he talks almost exclusively about art and artists, expressing acerbic opinions about all his contemporaries except Giacometti. He has recently agreed to appear and talk about himself and his work in a film currently in production. But he does not mention his past as a man. Antoinette, Laurence, Léna, Frédérique, and all the pubescent young models exist only as images, never as people with real—not invented—lives. However, the man who freely talks and talks about the matter which has been central to his existence, and which has absorbed his entire physical, intellectual, and spiritual resources from the beginning, is talking willy-nilly about his private life, inviting anyone interested to lift the transparent veil of secrecy. It is better so, and one likes to think that Balthus recognized that fact as the evening of his life grew late.

An artist who stands haughtily aloof from his own time, basing his whole aesthetic posture upon that stance, is exposing himself to the danger that the future may pass him by. The history of art is pitiless, more pitiless even than the rest of history, because the kind of immortality it offers is the truest kind, and the offer is for all or for nothing. Phidias and Rembrandt stand head and shoulders above Alexander and Napoléon. Great creators have usually looked into the future for the prospect of great fulfillment, seldom into the past, because the past proposes mainly the ground of criteria, which are, after all, fruitless to cultivate, having been harvested already, and duplication, where possible, is by definition pointless. Looking to the future, though, is a daunting business, which does not sit well with an appetite for emulation, anachronistic honors, and titles. The most, and least, an artist can do for posterity is to acknowledge that his demise will in no way differ from that of a billion other men, and prove that he has been able to take great creative account of that grim, miraculous fact. If he can do that, then maybe his creations will live up to the one dream which appears to set man apart from other creatures on earth, and by doing so he can provide his fellow men with a few noble instants of surcease from the contemplation of their own nonentity. This, perhaps, is too somber and idealistic a view of the artist's option, in which case it would leave ample room for the possibility that the future may do well by a bid for its attention by one who showed little confidence in its discrimination. Admirers of Balthus will hope so, and it is true that their hopes are not based on bluff. The nobleman may be bogus, though indispensable, but the artist is real. His reality is even greater than his identity, and he is bound to an involvement with it so passionate that the outcome goes beyond the personal. Greatness always starts that way. How far it can go, only time, and death, will tell.

4

46, rue Hippolyte

and After

[T H E   G I A C O M E T T I

B R O T H E R S]

1

Paris. Mid-February 1952, toward ten in the evening. Lonely, having dined alone in the neighborhood's cheapest restaurant, I sauntered rather disconsolately along the boulevard Saint-Germain, hoping to encounter in one of the cafés where we all used to meet some acquaintance with whom to while away a few hours. Finding no familiar face at the Flore, I went on to the Deux Magots, and there on the banquette facing the entrance sat an Englishman I knew almost well enough to call a friend. His name: Peter Watson.

Peter was a paragon. Everyone liked him. With good reason. He was courtesy personified, generous to a fault, intelligent, handsome, very rich, humorous, entirely lacking in pretension, and passionately interested in art, literature, and music. Not creative himself or hankering to be, he craved the stimulating and easygoing company of people who were, having early wearied of the fashionable society to which his wealth and cultivation provided access. Besides, it was far easier to live openly as a homosexual in the bohemian world of artists and writers. Before the war, he spent most of his time in Paris, where he had a luxurious flat in the rue du Bac filled with works of art, some of them masterpieces, by contemporary painters and sculptors, many of whom became his friends. He was kept company there by an American youth of exceptional beauty named Denham Fouts, a notorious hustler and incorrigible drug addict who had run away from home in Florida at the age of sixteen and been supported by a succession of rich admirers, including the future King of Greece, before meeting Peter, the first man to sincerely befriend him rather than exploit him sexually. Nineteen thirty-nine put an end to all this. Denham returned to America, and Peter to England, leaving behind most of his splendid collection, which was sold without compunction during the Occupation by the Romanian dilettante to whom he had entrusted it.

At loose ends in London, Peter was persuaded by Cyril Connolly, a brilliant young man of letters, to subsidize the publication of *Horizon*, a review devoted to contemporary literature and art. It was a sensational success, survived the war against all odds, and became the most distinguished, prestigious periodical of its sort on either side of the Atlantic. Little magazines seldom have long lives. *Horizon* lasted a decade, though its memory has remained impressive till today. In the very last issue, published in January 1950, appeared a short story entitled "The Boy Who Wrote NO" by an unknown author called James Lord. That was how I met Connolly, who introduced me to Peter, Lucian Freud, Sonia Orwell, and a quantity of other people. It was at a soirée in Cyril's apartment in October 1949 that for the first time I saw a sculpture by Alberto Giacometti. This was the *City Square*, a piece representing several spindly, emaciated men striding in various directions on a low pedestal, with one slender, hieratical woman standing motionless apart from them. This sculpture immediately appeared to me the most extraordinary work by a contemporary sculptor that I'd seen, deeply moving and utterly original. Fortunately I was able to see many more, some of them even more impressive, at a large exhibition at Pierre Matisse's gallery in New York in November 1950. By that time I was acquainted with the work of Brancusi, Lipchitz, Laurens, Arp, Marini, Moore, and even third-raters like Zadkine and Bourdelle. None of them for me came close to the aesthetic finesse and originality, the profound human empathy and simple spiritual grandeur, of Giacometti. I knew that he lived somewhere in Paris, but it never occurred to me to try to seek him out. The brash audacity that had led me to ring Picasso's doorbell seven years before had by that time been tempered with reasonable discretion, and I had plenty of friends, some of them artists, with whom to spend the hours when I was not trying to become a writer.

So I had been surprised not to find Bernard, Olivier, Jean, or Ned at the Flore that evening in February 1952, but the compensation for their absence was more than satisfied when I found Peter, whose visits to Paris were, alas, infrequent, at the Deux Magots. Though he was not alone, I went directly to his table. He greeted me with warmth and indicated the chair opposite. Beside him on the banquette sat a stocky man of about fifty, tousle-haired, his face deeply lined, dark-eyed, with exceptionally large hands and clothes none too clean. Peter introduced us. The name was Alberto Giacometti.

It may seem, I fear, at best banal to say that I was instantly mesmerized by the presence of this person, but that is the truth. From my journal:

February 15, 1952

Dinner alone at Raffy's in the rue du Dragon. Made notes for short story about identical twins (male) who fall in love with each other and are destroyed by jealousy. Narcissus as a sort of suicide.

After dinner looked in at Flore. Nobody. Surprising for a Saturday. At Deux Magots found Peter Watson, whom I hadn't seen since we met again by chance—in front of the Hôtel de Talleyrand at the corner of the rue de Rivoli and the rue St.-Florentin and he told me that it was in that house that he'd been to his first ball. He always seems a bit melancholy, Peter, but smiling gamely. That's his charm. He once said that the place on earth he most liked was high in the Atlas Mountains because it was so lonely. However, he wasn't alone last night, asked me to sit down and introduced me to . . . Alberto Giacometti! We shook hands and he said something polite. I was immediately conscious of the concentration of his sizing me up, as if he were making a decisive judgment, scrutinizing me for some sort of personal characteristic that might or might not appear satisfactory. Very intimidating. But at the same time perfectly open and attractive. Of course I was thrilled to meet this man whose work I had admired so much. The thrill tied my tongue in knots, though. Peter and Giacometti were talking about a mutual acquaintance named Isabel. Giacometti said, "She's a man eater." Peter said, "She's a woman eater, too." Giacometti very intrigued by suggestion this Isabel might be lesbian, and Peter said she was having an affair with some lady who was a Buddhist. They talked about Giacometti's present work, concerning which he expressed great dissatisfaction. I ventured to say that I had found the New York exhibition admirable. Giacometti shrugged and said, "That just shows that you see only with your eyes." But he laughed. He has very small teeth set widely apart and stained dark from tobacco—he smokes incessantly—so that when he laughs he looks like a peculiar jack-o-lantern. "Well, that's better than seeing with your feet," he said. He asked me a number of personal questions: where I come from, what I'm doing in Paris, etc., and I was surprised by the feeling that he seemed honestly interested in my answers. Still, I felt intimidated by him even when it was clear that he meant to be friendly. The only other person with whom I've ever felt intimidated in the same way is Picasso, and he and Giacometti don't seem at all alike, G. much more warm and open. Then Peter and Giacometti had a long conversation about politics, mostly Communism. Peter said there must be something to it in spite of everything because there are people of integrity who believe in it. Giacometti said that Torquemada had also been a man of integrity, and he hated Communism because it turned the truth to derision. I didn't have much to say, though I hated Communism not only for making dogma of a lie but also for killing millions of people in its name. We were drinking whisky and after a couple of hours I had had more than enough. Peter and Giacometti seemed ready to go on all night. I said that I'd have to leave. Being so attracted to Giacometti, though, and feeling that he had responded with kindliness to my presence, I got up my courage to ask whether I might someday come to see him in his studio. He immediately said yes and that he'd give me the address, because he didn't have a telephone. He tore a page out of a magazine that he had in his jacket pocket and wrote down his name and address: Alberto Giacometti, 46, rue Hippolyte-Maindron, Paris 14. I said that I'd come someday soon. In the afternoon, he specified. So I told them both goodbye. Peter was returning to London on Monday.

Walking home, I felt elated. I'd met someone who mattered, different from anybody else I'd ever encountered. Well, it

probably won't make much of a difference to me personally,
but one feels somehow more right with the world to know that
there are people like Giacometti in it. And if it makes one feel
more right with the world, doesn't that mean that even in spite
of Hitler the world can be right with itself? Mozart. Cézanne. I
certainly hope so. My whole life is based on that assumption.

I didn't want to seem presumptuous, though I knew that I was
preparing to be. On the other hand, neither did I want to wait so
long that Giacometti might forget who I was. A week would probably
suit both cases, I felt. While waiting, I frequently thought about the
artist I'd met with Peter, and the more I thought about him the
more I began to feel that knowing him might, after all, make a
difference. There was a powerful attraction, anyway, and from the
very first there was not the slightest doubt in my mind that he was
a great artist. Giacometti was not yet famous in 1952; many people
might have assumed that at the age of fifty he was not destined for
enduring greatness. Prices for his works were low. Pierre Loeb had
a portfolio of superb drawings that anyone could pick through at
twenty dollars apiece, and they didn't go like hotcakes, though my
pocketbook, alas, was then too pinched to afford one. But Giacometti
had created masterpieces. I knew that, because I'd seen them, beginning with the one on the table behind the couch in Cyril Connolly's apartment, and I was absolutely convinced that they were
masterpieces. I believed that as firmly as I believed that one could
see the world in a grain of sand, heaven in a wildflower, hold infinity
in the palm of your hand and eternity in an hour. Not simply because
these masterpieces were entirely original and unlike any other works
of art I'd ever seen, but because they were so mysteriously, wonderfully, and feelingly what they were. Not an infinitesimal trace of
trickery or technical sleight of hand marred their human integrity.
And, yes, I must admit that my boundless admiration for his work
allowed me to feel that I had a decent excuse for intruding upon
Alberto Giacometti. The outcome seemed peculiarly irrelevant. I
didn't expect the sun suddenly to set in the east. To wait a full week,
however, exceeded my patience, so I went the following Thursday.

The rue Hippolyte-Maindron forty years ago was a short and
nondescript thoroughfare bordered by small houses—some with

scraps of garden—several shops, a café, a lumberyard, and a few artists' studios. At the far end were the grimy, rather grim walls of a primary school. Number 46 adjoined the recreation yard of this establishment. Double doors opening from the street led into an open passageway about fifty feet long and six feet wide with habitations and studios on both sides. Giacometti's was the first on the left, with a high window and skylight, his name painted in white letters on one of the glass panes of the door. I knocked. A hoarse voice promptly shouted, "Come in." Even after all these decades, my surprise of that first visit to Giacometti's studio remains instant and unforgettable. During my lifetime I've visited scores of artists' studios. None could compare with his in its picturesque, humble, and disorderly but sovereign spiritual power. Instead of attending to descriptive or evocative efforts by the elderly memoirist, however, I believe there may be more matter for thought in the impulsive, naïve account of the twenty-nine-year-old visitor:

> *February 19, 1952*
>
> *Just now come back from spending half the afternoon with Giacometti. Hardly know where to begin to try to describe what it's like to be with him. I mean not only in his company but in his world. Because he makes it his to such an exciting extent. Maybe it's the excitement plus the extraordinary extent that are so intimidating. Better begin at the beginning.*
>
> *He'd said the other day to come in the afternoon, so I arrived at a little before three. Rue Hippolyte-Maindron out of the way and notable for nothing. Giacometti's studio is at the corner of the rue du Moulin-Vert in a sort of complex, some parts only one story, others two or three, the whole place looking as if it had been thrown together with a few old sticks and a lot of chewing gum. No romantic* La Bohème *atmosphere. In short, a dump. And that's part of the surprise, of course, as if he deliberately wants to impress you by the quasi-squalor of the decor. Or impress himself. Who knows? There may be something to that. Anyway, he said to come in when I knocked, and if the outside is surprising, the inside is amazing. Giacometti was working on a female figure in clay about two feet high.*

He turned and glanced at me, holding out his hand which was covered in clay, so I shook his wrist, which I understood to be what he intended. He immediately resumed work on his sculpture, running his fingers up and down the figure, pinching and gouging the clay so fiercely that lumps sometimes fell onto the floor, while at the same time he regularly took puffs from a cigarette that lay on the edge of the sculpture stand. After a minute he said, "I was sure you'd show up sooner or later. People sometimes say they want to have a look, then you never see them again. All to the good. But I said to myself, 'That one will give it a try.'"

"What made you so sure?" I asked.

"Peter told me that you're a writer. Words are always in search of images, aren't they? And images can profit from words. So artists and writers take to one another. Always have. Long before Vasari. Musicians are different. Why don't you sit down?"

There were a couple of chairs, both of the café kind. I took the one that looked least rickety. The studio is small and cluttered. Hard to imagine some of the life-size sculptures coming out of such a limited space. A broad window with a curtain sagging across the lower third fills the north wall and below it is a long table littered with empty bottles, dozens of old paintbrushes, several palettes, and a few broken plaster sculptures. There is one large easel with a couple of low wooden stools near it. A yellow wooden cupboard against the wall, its broken door hanging in pieces. Beside it some shelves and several portfolios stacked against them. In the corner an old bed heaped with newspapers, books, drawings, and a few paintings propped against the wall. Another set of shelves with a lot of tiny sculptures on top and canvases on the floor in front. A pot-bellied heating stove and high, black pipe. Under steep stairs that lead up to a narrow balcony a battered chest of drawers. Three sculpture stands with a couple of high stools. A large map of Europe tacked to the wall by the foot of the stairs. Here and there heads and figures are painted or drawn directly onto the walls. Cigarette butts and burned-out matches litter the ce-

*ment floor. Everything is covered with a film of dust. Even the
light was dusty. The place, as a matter of fact, is such a mess
that you couldn't hope to do the messiness justice except by sitting there and breathing it in. Then it becomes amazing, being
Giacometti's mess with him contained in it, creating it, created
by it, and adding his creations to it. No words or photographs
could convey that sense of a kind of miraculous birthplace. And
everybody knows that being born is a messy business. Especially when it happens every day in the same place to the same
person in the same way. I can't tell quite what that means, but
I felt then and there that the explanation must be like explaining the function of knowledge.*

*Giacometti appeared to have forgotten all about me as he
kept constantly fingering his sculpture—not changing it very
much as far as I could see—at the same time lighting another
cigarette. I was content simply to sit there, being a believable
part of the place, and I closed my eyes, wondering what my
believing would be like if seeing wasn't the proof of it. More
wonderful in a way.*

"Asleep already?" said Giacometti.

*"Not at all," I answered, opening my eyes. "I was just
trying to find out what this place would look like if I couldn't
see it."*

"And what did it look like?"

*"I can't say. But I think that if I was able to say, then
maybe I could actually create the place somehow. I mean
make it real in my own way."*

Giacometti laughed. "So we're playing the same game."

"How's that?"

*"You were seeing the studio with your eyes closed in order
to create it for yourself by the means most suited to you. I'm
working on this sculpture with my eyes open but I'm blind to
the origin of it. That is, I'm trying to show what I see when I
have a woman's figure before me without having the woman's
figure before me. It's impossible, but there is a possibility in it.
That's why I keep on relentlessly working, when there's no
hope except to fail." He laughed again and lit another ciga-*

rette, although the previous one was still smoldering on the edge of the sculpture stand. "Failure is my best friend," he said. "If I succeeded, it would be like dying. Maybe worse."

What could I say? The way he takes you into his confidence is breathtaking. So natural. As if you'd known each other for years. And yet I still felt intimidated. I sat there in silence for a time while Giacometti kept on tweaking his sculpture and puffing on his cigarette. The daylight outside began to dwindle. I felt I ought to leave but didn't know quite how to go about it, which was strange, because it should have been simpler than coming in. Giacometti seemed almost to be unaware that he was not alone. After a while he took some rags from a battered metal tub on the floor and very carefully wrapped them around his sculpture. Then he said, "We go to the café now." Obviously he took it for granted that I would accompany him, as if my presence were as natural as leaves on trees. That was amazing, too: the way he accepted you. So we went to the café. It wasn't far. At the corner of the rue d'Alésia and the rue Didot, a workaday place with an old-fashioned zinc bar and a few tables. The barman called Giacometti by his first name, which startled me. He had coffee, I Coca-Cola. He talked about his work, the impossibility of it, the despair he felt sometimes about ever achieving anything worthwhile but at the same time the exhilaration of this despair. I didn't try to remember his exact words. What impressed me—aside from the fact that it seemed extremely curious for anyone who has accomplished so much to feel as he said he does (and there was not the slightest question of his sincerity)—what impressed me was his way of talking about his work and his relation to it as if he were talking about something that had no relation to him personally. And that completely eliminated from his talk any trace of self-importance or egotism. He could have been discussing the composition of the solar system, and in a funny way you felt that he was. That made it truly enthralling to listen to. I should have made myself remember more. But I was too excited and still intimidated. After about half an hour I said I'd have to leave. Giacometti said, "Now that you know

*where to find me . . ." What a thrill! He leaves one without
any doubt as to being in the presence of a great man. Picasso
seems like a miraculous trickster by comparison.*

My friends weren't much impressed by the fact that I'd made
the acquaintance of Giacometti. They all had heard of him, though.
A large exhibition of his work had been shown seven or eight months
before at the Galerie Maeght on the Right Bank. Marie-Laure de
Noailles said that he had both sculpted and painted her portrait
shortly after the war, but when I asked to see the results she flightily
replied, "I suppose he still has them. I didn't want to live with things
that would oblige me to think I looked like a Giacometti." True, all
the portraits of her that hung in her house were flattering. Giacometti
never flattered, though he always caught an intense likeness. Still,
Marie-Laure owned two of his early sculptures, bought from Jeanne
Bucher and Pierre Loeb before anyone had heard of him, and she
and her husband had commissioned a large stone sculpture for the
garden of their Riviera château in 1932. Vain, she nonetheless had
an eye for what was first-rate. Later, alas, when she herself began
to paint, she lost it.

After that first visit to the rue Hippolyte-Maindron, I inevitably
looked forward to another. Nobody, I think, having met Giacometti
once, would willingly have let the opportunity for a second meeting
slip by. And I don't mean only people interested in art. The attraction
that came spontaneously from him was felt just as powerfully—and
I learned this for a fact from their testimony—by barmen and taxi
drivers as by art collectors and museum curators. The only question
in my mind was one of very relative courtesy. That my reappearance
would probably constitute a nuisance I took for granted, and I willingly, not to say gladly, accepted the discredit, but at the same time
I was anxious not to constitute such a nuisance that I would no
longer be welcome. So it was a question of time. How long ought
I to wait before returning to that awe-inspiring studio? And the
question of time was made ticklishly specific by my knowledge even
before the end of February that I was to leave for America on
April 9 and would very likely be gone for at least a year. Thus, I
had a month before me during which I could try to find out whether
between Giacometti and myself there existed a chance of anything

more than casual acquaintance. My uncertainty showed what lack of discernment prevailed. Even after two meetings I should have understood that by the very nature of the man an acquaintance with Giacometti could under no circumstances be casual, however intimidating he might be.

During the month of March I went five times to the rue Hippolyte-Maindron. Only on one occasion did I fail to find him at work in the studio. His brother Diego, to whom I had been briefly introduced in passing, told me that Alberto had gone that afternoon to see his dealer. Diego occupied a narrow, cramped studio on the other side of the passageway from Alberto's. What he did there I didn't know and stupidly imagined to be of no importance. In fairness it must be said that Diego did nothing whatsoever to make himself appear in any way important. He was reticent and withdrawn to a fault. A fool could easily assume, as I did, that he was a useless dependent who profited to no good end from his brother's accomplishments. And Diego, to be sure, might very well have been satisfied on the whole to allow such a preposterous misconception to prevail. It took a long time—say twenty or thirty years—for me to glimpse the truth.

So I saw Giacometti again only four times before sailing to America. Our meetings were all more or less identical. I would drive to the rue Hippolyte-Maindron, park in front—it was possible in those halcyon days to park anywhere in Paris—and knock on the studio door. The artist would shout, "Come in." And when I'd done so, he would be likely to murmur, "Ah, it's Lord." He never called me by my first name, but once apologized for this seeming lack of cordiality by explaining that he called only his wife and brothers by their first names. Through the years, it's true, I observed that close friends like Sartre, Genet, Michel Leiris, Beckett, and even schoolboy chums like Christoph Bernoulli were invariably referred to by their surnames. I would sit down, but Giacometti, while working on a sculpture, always remained standing or half-perched on the edge of a high stool, and it was only sculpture that occupied him during my first visits to the studio, spindly figures of women's or men's heads. We talked. I thought that he was glad to have someone to talk to while working and that, indeed, my visits were not unwelcome. And yet I continued to feel quite as intimidated by him as at

first. Perhaps more so. In fact, each time I went to the rue Hippolyte-
Maindron I had to get up my courage, as it were, in order to present
myself at the artist's door, despite the easygoing welcome that I
invariably received. It wasn't that I feared he might suddenly turn
brusque and ill-tempered, as I knew very well that Picasso, who also
intimidated me, could. There was something more serious. All my
life I had dreamed of men who were truly great. Beethoven. Balzac.
Byron. Rembrandt. I believed that creative achievement of the first
order was the only access to a truly heroic life. That was the great
adventure compared to which the exploits of an Alexander were the
wild, brave doings of a brilliant rascal. About the heroism of the
great creative life, I had learned enough to know that it was usually
beset by severe travail and demanded unique spiritual fortitude. And
by the time I met Giacometti, I had also learned enough to know
that I possessed neither the heroism nor the fortitude necessary to
sustain it. That he possessed both I felt certain from the first. What
is more exhilarating than to encounter a person one can admire
without reserve to the very limit of admiration, and beyond? When
I first knew Picasso, I fancied that maybe genius was contagious.
With Giacometti I learned that it was not, and the lesson was most
welcome, for by then I understood that a great man is unlikely to
lead a very jolly life. I was prepared to work hard, and I have, but
I also wanted to enjoy myself, and I have. Giacometti provided a lot
of the enjoyment one way or another. Certainly nothing was ever
the same for me after I met him.

We talked principally about art and artists. There appeared to
be few of his colleagues for whom he had much esteem. Picasso,
he declared, should be put in prison. When I said that I had two
drawings of myself by him, Giacometti replied that then I must
understand why he was a danger to the public. I think there was an
element of jest in such statements, but at the same time Giacometti
was also prepared to argue his opinions with forceful ingenuity.
About Picasso, anyway, though they had once been friends, he was
consistently censorious to the end. But if he belittled the work of
most of his contemporaries, his most severe criticism was invariably
directed toward his own efforts. While fingering the damp clay,
running his fingers up and down a figurine, or working at the eyes
of a head with his penknife, he would repeatedly exclaim that what

he was doing was worthless, that there was no hope of ever producing anything acceptable, and that he would be better off sweeping the streets. Virtually in the same breath, of course, he could state that nobody else was attempting to do what he attempted anew each day, which meant quite simply that nobody could equal the power and purity of his vision. I certainly believed that, and still do. Balthus once remarked that Giacometti was the only man he'd ever known who could look at a perfectly ordinary teacup, for example, and see it as if he had never before beheld such an object. Not that he seemed in the least vain. When Giacometti said that he found more aesthetic satisfaction in looking at the tin soldiers in toy-shop windows than in studying the works of his contemporaries, he was expressing nostalgia and regret, not vainglory. Besides, there was very often the twitch of a smile at the corners of his mouth. It was the most enchanting hint of a smile I've ever seen. His lips remained closed, but their extremities lifted ever so slightly while his eyelids quivered and an ambiguous glint came from beneath them.

I never tired of his company, especially as I knew that all too soon I would be deprived of it. We usually went to the café at the corner of the rue Didot toward the end of the afternoon. I noticed that the expressions of dissatisfaction with his work were usually more vehement and morose when he was outside the studio than when he was actually at work, although I never felt that he was actually unhappy or truly despondent. And it was at the café that I usually left him. The last farewell was cheerless for me because I realized perfectly well that I had not made a friend of someone whose company was incomparably uplifting, who both entertained and inspired me, and with whom I had no good reason to believe I might ever become better acquainted. I said that I hoped we'd meet again someday.

"I'm not planning to croak just yet," said Giacometti, "so we're sure to run into each other. I'd like that. And you can write me a letter. I won't answer it, because I never write letters except to my mother. But I like to receive them."

So we said good-bye, and one week later I was in the middle of the Atlantic Ocean. That spring and early summer, at the expense of the Rockefeller Foundation I made a prolonged tour of the United States in the company of an obscure French author called André

Fraigneau. It was supposed to have a serious purpose, but Fraigneau
was not a serious man; consequently we just traveled about spending
Rockefeller money without scruple, going even to Canada and to
Taos, New Mexico, where in one day we met the three exceptional
women of that locality, Frieda Lawrence, Mabel Dodge Luhan, and
the Honorable Dorothy Brett. After Fraigneau returned to France,
I went to live with my parents, an arrangement which I found somewhat oppressive as I approached the age of thirty. However, I was
perfectly comfortable, provided with a decent allowance, and permitted to do exactly as I pleased, which was to set about writing still
another bad novel. I frequently thought of Giacometti but did not
presume to send him a letter. The following spring I undertook to
solicit from wealthy collectors and art dealers sufficient funds to
purchase Cézanne's studio at Aix-en-Provence and transform it into
a memorial museum. The money poured in. I was invited to Washington to receive the polite commendation of the French ambassador, who said that his government would be pleased to invite me
to sail for France on June 11 in order to attend later that month the
inauguration of the first Cézanne exhibition ever to be held in his
birthplace, forty-seven years too late to compensate for the ridicule
with which his fellow citizens had treated the great and lonely
painter.

I went to Aix, spent the summer on the Riviera at Villefranche,
in the fall visited Italy, Greece, and Egypt, and returned to Paris
only toward the end of October. So it had been eighteen months
since I'd said good-bye to Giacometti in that homely café at the
corner of the rue Didot. I didn't think that he would have forgotten
me, but I had good reason to wonder whether someone whom he
had seen half a dozen times and who had no outstanding achievements or distinction of any kind to recommend him might expect
to be greeted with warmth, not to say enthusiasm, by a man of
genius twenty years his senior. But this uncertainty didn't stand a
chance against my passionate desire to evolve somehow and somewhere in the orbit of a creator whose powers possessed for me all
the vitality and truth to be seen in the stars. It *was* a passion, and
passions don't plead to be pardoned for their excesses. Having waited
a couple of weeks for a semblance of self-possession to collect itself,
I went late one afternoon to the rue Hippolyte-Maindron. The day

happened to be unseasonably warm, and the studio door stood open. I could see Giacometti inside working on a sculpture, but I knocked anyway. He glanced round, raised his head, and exclaimed, "You! I was telling myself that you'd given up on me. It's been weeks since you last showed up."

"I'm not a quitter," I said, surprised by his assumption. "And in fact it's been a year and a half since we saw each other last."

"Already," Giacometti murmured, shaking his head. "I don't suppose you'd lie about it. A lie is the only sort of betrayal that I seriously disapprove of. But it seems like the day before yesterday. Sometimes I wake up in the morning and think my mother is about to haul me out of bed to go to school."

"Well," I said, "it really is too bad that time can't be imaginary."

"For Hamlet it can," said Giacometti. "And didn't you promise to write me a letter? I never received it."

"It wouldn't have been interesting," I protested.

Giacometti said nothing, continued to work on his sculpture, and I sat down. After a time he said, "I sold a batch of drawings yesterday, so we have quite a bit of money for a change. What's more, today is Diego's birthday. We thought we'd go to the brasserie in the rue d'Alésia and drink some Champagne. Why don't you come along?"

"I'd not like to intrude," I said. "It's a family celebration, after all, and to Diego I'm practically a stranger."

"To Annette you're a complete stranger," said Giacometti. "She's my wife. Of course, if it wouldn't appeal to you, don't worry."

"Oh, but I'd be happy to come," I truthfully insisted.

"We won't have to talk about Cézanne," Giacometti said, smiling. But then we did talk about Cézanne for some time and I related my efforts to save his studio.

Before long it was dark. The artist turned on the electric light, a bare bulb with a saucer-shaped shade suspended on a wire from the overhead balcony, one more poor detail adding to the stark austerity of the studio. He wrapped damp rags round the sculpture he'd been working on, applying them with the graceful solicitude, I thought, of an ancient Egyptian embalmer.

I was delighted but startled, almost embarrassed, to have been invited to join the birthday party. It was an intimate occasion, and

I was anything but intimate with those to be present. I couldn't imagine why Giacometti had invited me, one more instance of my obtuseness and naïveté. But maybe I can claim a crumb of absolution by acknowledging that even today there are aspects of his nature and conduct that I cannot fathom.

Annette came into the studio. My instant impression was of a pretty young woman, simply dressed, demure. Smiling when introduced to me, her handclasp firm, she said she'd heard about me from her husband. He told her that I was to join them for dinner, whereupon she smiled again and said that that would be very agreeable. I had a surprising sense that she was more pleased than Giacometti by the prospect of my presence. As for Diego, when he appeared a few minutes afterward, surprisingly well dressed in a blue blazer and gray trousers, he was, as usual, amiable but withdrawn, and my addition to the party seemed neither here nor there to him.

The brasserie where we went for dinner was called Les Tamaris, an unpretentious but garish place where the Giacomettis obviously were regular clients, greeted with effusion by the proprietor and his talkative wife. We sat by the window at a table which I gathered was habitually theirs. They knew all the waiters, and I was surprised to hear Giacometti called by his first name by everyone. He evidently sensed this, because he remarked that he, who used the first name of almost no one, was called Alberto by taxi drivers, barmen, and almost all the people in the neighborhood. Such being the case, he added, I might as well do as the others did, so from that day—it was November 15, 1953—I called him Alberto, hesitantly at first but very soon with the feeling that to do otherwise would have been an affectation.

We drank three bottles of Champagne. The dinner wasn't very good, but the company was wonderful. As the evening progressed we became quite jolly—even Diego, who told a few funny stories of his adventures during the Occupation. Annette observed that living conditions in wartime Geneva had been difficult, too. Alberto said that she was an idiot and that Geneva had, comparatively speaking, been like the cavern of Ali Baba. Annette seemed not in the least disconcerted by her husband's reproof, giggled, and said, "Oh, Alberto." He took a pencil out of his pocket and made a number of wonderful drawings on the paper table cover. By the end of the evening I felt almost—but only almost—at ease. Giacometti continued to intimidate me, the other two not at all. I was greatly pleased, though, to have been allowed to think that I was welcome in their midst, and when we got up to go I had an extraordinary feeling—perhaps due in part to the Champagne—that the moment might prove to have brought about a difference in my relations with all three. I was sad to see the wonderful drawings left indifferently behind on the table cover. As we walked away on the sidewalk outside, I could see through the window the waiter carelessly crumpling the paper into a ball, obviously preparing to throw it away.

It did bring about a lasting difference, that evening of unprecedented laughter and Champagne. Although I continued to be intimidated by Alberto—this was an effect of the natural malaise arising from the abyss which separates those possessed by genius from the rest of us—I no longer felt timid about presenting myself at the rue Hippolyte-Maindron. And I was welcomed there with unaffected good humor not only by Alberto but also by his wife and brother. Of the three, Alberto was by far the most interesting, friendly, responsive, candid, and easy to talk to. And it was principally to see him, of course, that I began to visit the studio with moderate regularity. Annette I considered pleasant, eager to please, but not very interesting, intelligent, or sensitive to art. Diego, I felt, was very different from the two others, shy but strong and resourceful, keeping very much to himself, devoted to his brother, whose sculpture, I soon observed, owed much to the manual dexterity of the modest sibling. The three of them, each so unlike the other two, seemed to dwell in a world apart, a sort of magic domain, ruled by the sovereign creator, whose girlish consort assisted his creativity and was ennobled by it and whose silent, deferential brother in the shadow of the throne was invaluable to its stability. Outsiders could look in upon this little state but never, I thought, become part of it, because its territorial integrity seemed to depend upon the exclusive interdependence of the triumvirate. That's how the rue Hippolyte, as they called it, appeared to me at the time.

I need not, after all, have been unduly sad to see the drawings on the table cover at Les Tamaris destroyed by the waiter. The hand that had made them was literally indefatigable and turned out to

be exceptionally liberal as well—with me, anyway. Alberto sometimes lined up recent drawings against the wall at the back of the
broken-down bed in the corner in order to study them and try to
see, as he said, where he'd gotten to. One chilly afternoon that winter
when I arrived at the studio, I found him standing by the bed scrutinizing a group of about ten drawings. They were all on large sheets
and of various subjects: heads, figures, still lifes, interiors. After a
prolonged pause, shaking his head, Alberto murmured, "Pitiful."

I thought them all superb and said so.

"If I had any self-respect, I'd burn the lot," Alberto said. "And
I think I will," he added, nodding at the nearby stove.

"Please don't!" I exclaimed. "There must be at least one that
you'd regret."

"Well," he sighed, "one, perhaps, but only one. Tell me which
it is."

I studied them all for several minutes and decided that the finest
drawing was not the most spectacular, which was a large head, very
dark and heavily worked, but a careful, subtle study of a single plain
chair in a room before an open window. Pointing to it, I said, "That's
the one."

"If there is one," said Alberto, "yes, that would be it. I did
it in my mother's home." He picked it up and held it out toward
me. "Here. Take it. You saw it was worth saving, so you should
have it."

I made some token protest, asserting that this was excessive
generosity, to which Alberto replied that it would be hypocritical to
refuse. He was right. So I took the drawing from his hand and the
thrill of possession flooded my veins like electricity.

"And for your sake," Alberto added, "since you are so discerning, I'll spare the others." He gathered them carelessly together
and dropped them into one of the portfolios beside the bed.

It was a miracle, that vision of the very ordinary chair standing
somewhere in perfect isolation, wreathed in solitude, the one surviving relic which could testify to the sometime existence of an
otherwise-unknown civilization. I had it framed and hung it in my
bedroom.

From my journal:

March 16, 1954

*Dora [Maar] and Alberto being the two people of conse-
quence that I've seen most frequently this winter, it's natural
that I talked to each about the other. They knew one another
quite well, of course, while Dora was with Picasso, because
that was the time when Alberto used to go regularly to the rue
des Grands-Augustins. Neither of them see him now, and both
criticize him severely in conversation. Alberto likes gossip, is
amused to hear about my relations with Dora. When I told
him that she had invited me to spend the month of April with
her in Provence in the house that Picasso gave her, he said that
I'd better be ready for anything, because Dora might not be
easy to get along with if I didn't turn out to be an acceptable
replacement for Picasso. I said, "Who would want to be?" We
both had a good laugh, but I'm not a bit sure Alberto meant to
be funny.*

*Conversation with him is a kind of pleasure that I've never
known with anyone else. It not only makes you feel that you've
got to be at your best but even allows you to imagine that you
are at your best and that your best is almost good enough to be
adequate for him. He possesses the most prodigious agility with
ideas, opinions, judgments, always prepared to turn something
on its head, quick to contradict himself and keep half a dozen
possibilities in the air like a one-man team of jugglers. But this
in a way is only the fun of it, and as he talks he occasionally
smiles with that charming quiver at the corners of the lips. The
seriousness comes from an absolute conviction that he is in profound possession of the truth. He possesses it just as I might
possess, say, a pocket handkerchief or a fountain pen. And one
is grateful to him for this, because it is a delight to feel that the
truth is your friend. Not that he would hesitate to assert that he
might very well be wrong. But that only makes him all the
more right. And as for candor, I've never known anything even
to begin to compare with it. Fred [a professor with whom I had
an affair while in college] used to pride himself on his frank-
ness. But I learned to see how he fooled himself. Alberto is as
free as the breeze with everything concerning himself and his*

*relations with all the world. Sex and money are two topics
most people are skittish about. Alberto is perfectly prepared to
talk about what he does in bed and with whom (difficulty in
satisfactory consummation with Annette, but easygoing on the
whole with prostitutes—sex as a sort of mechanical function—
liking an extra partner now and then, boy or girl ad lib). He
says he's afraid of money, though he irritably acknowledges the
need to have enough. Just enough for whores and taxis, he
said. But he's beginning to have more than enough, and it
worries him because both Annette and Diego set store by
money. Annette wants him to open a bank account, but he's
reluctant, prefers hiding cash in the studio and bedroom next
door. Then he can easily put his hand on it when he needs
quick cash to help some prostitute in trouble.*

*Talked about the probable débâcle in Indochina after the
Viet Minh attack of a few days ago. Alberto said that it would
be to everybody's advantage for the French to surrender now
and get out, but because politicians are scoundrels and moun-
tebanks, they will wait until it's too late for any decent accommodation. Alberto becomes quite heated when talking about
politics, especially when denouncing the unscrupulous doings of
politicians. He says that General de Gaulle is certainly as unscrupulous as the rest but that all the same he is a man one
can admire. I agree. We go to the café.*

Before I went south with Dora I saw Alberto again. Sometimes,
I felt, he went out of his way to puzzle me, to compel me, perhaps,
to give more thought to circumstances concerning myself than I was
quite capable of. For example, during that last visit, March 30, he
pointed to a good-sized pearl-gray painting of a nude female figure
and said, "That one is for you."

"Is it?" I exclaimed. To possess that painting would, of course,
have satisfied an overwhelming desire, but I was too much in awe
of the opportunity to feel I was entitled to it. "Why?" I asked.

"Well," Alberto said, smiling, "if you can't tell me why it ought
to be yours, then maybe I'd better keep it."

Perplexed, I said, "I have no right to it, but perhaps it has a right to me in some way, because I think it's very beautiful and would be happy to possess it."

"That's superficial," Alberto said. "Still, it could be an acceptable approach to the question. I suppose it will have to do. Your happiness, however, is neither here nor there. Even so, you can carry off the painting."

"I don't know how to thank you," I said.

"I should hope not," Alberto grumbled. "That would really be the limit."

The limit to what I didn't know. Not the limit to my presumption, in any case, for when I took the canvas from the floor I noticed that it wasn't signed. Like Picasso, Alberto never signed a work unless it was to leave his possession once and for all. Without embarrassment I pointed out to the artist the absence of his signature. It was he who seemed embarrassed. But that, perhaps, was his perverse side. He said that he couldn't sign it in oil paint because this would take days to dry and might become smudged. Ink would do. He took out his fountain pen and very carefully signed his name in the lower righthand corner. Then to my astonishment he said, "If Annette comes in, you mustn't let her realize that I've given you a painting." What this warning might signify I didn't begin to guess until years later. Fortunately Annette did not come in, and I went off with the painting when Alberto set out for his late afternoon visit to the café.

The peril of keeping a journal is that one may drown in it. The temptation to plunge into the pool that contains one's image can betray the commitment a writer must make to the priority of other people's passions. I repeatedly needed to reprove myself for excessive attention to myself at the expense of more exhaustive and specific descriptions of others, their mannerisms, behavior, opinions, and exact words. With Picasso, Dora, Alberto, Cocteau, Braque, Balthus, and others, I was haphazardly conscientious, hit-or-miss most of the time, although attentive to the importance of those I believed to be important. Alberto was the most difficult to do justice to, and he was in every way the one by whom I aspired to do best. His conversation was richer than Cocteau's, albeit without the clever cadenza orchestration. He was the most unusual, the most intelligent, the most inexplicable, the most lovable. Yes, there was a romantic element in my attraction to him, but I didn't realize what it was until long, long afterward. I'm talking once again about myself, and yet the romantic aura emanated very much from him, too.

I spent the spring and summer with Dora in Provence, and saw little, if anything, of Alberto.

And then something surprising happened. In July and September Alberto executed from life a series of some two dozen drawings of Henri Matisse, having agreed to sculpt in low relief for the French National Mint a commemorative medallion of the aged painter, whom he admired more than any other living artist. He was very interested in these drawings, which were superb, kept them in a separate portfolio, and showed them to visitors and friends almost with pride, an unprecedented attitude for him. It so happened that one of these portraits of Matisse was, by common consent, including that of the model, very clearly the best. It was the only one to show the old man full face and full length, seated in his wheelchair, and obviously the one to which Alberto, who readily conceded the point, had devoted the fullest concentration and the longest session.

During the previous year Alberto had become friendly with Jean Genet, the celebrated author whose works glorified treachery, lawlessness, a perverse practice of homosexuality, and a devastating contempt for the whole structure of organized social and moral affairs. Vain, mendacious, imperiously unprincipled, he was at the same time a masterful commander of language, a charismatic conversationalist, and an eloquent champion of ideals in which he did not believe. Alberto was fascinated and painted two portraits of him. So Genet in 1954 was very often in the studio.

I was also very often there just then, because that autumn Alberto had asked me one day to pose for a drawing. I had no idea why he selected me as a model. Usually he chose persons who were very close to him—Diego, Annette, his mother, or friends close enough to be deemed intimate, of whom I certainly was not one. At all events, I was anything but averse. After one drawing had been completed, he asked to do another. And when that was done, he asked me to come back the next afternoon to pose again, a request my heart leapt up to grant. I must have posed off and on over a period of a fortnight, during which Alberto produced at least fifteen portrait drawings. When he decided that, as he put it, I'd helped him as much as I could for the time being, we spread all the drawings out on the bed in the corner of the studio and he said, "I'll sign them now and then you can take them home."

"What?" I exclaimed. "All of them?"

"All those you like," he said. "It's normal, because you made it possible for me to do them."

"But there are too many," I protested, meaning to appear modest when in fact I felt only craving. But the Puritan ethic of foolish self-denial and hypocritical seemliness was strong, so I took only six. I didn't know Alberto very well then.

So I was more often at the studio during those weeks than customarily. Arriving one afternoon—unannounced, as usual, in the absence of a telephone—I found Annette and Genet by themselves, with one of Genet's portraits propped on the bed. Annette introduced us, then left us alone together. Genet gazed at his portrait but did not speak. As the silence became embarrassingly protracted, I made some banal remark about the power and fine likeness of the portrait, whereupon Genet exclaimed, "Get out! I want to be alone with my portrait."

Startled, humiliated, I withdrew in furious silence, too weak-willed to stand up to the famous novelist. Later I complained to Alberto of my treatment by his friend. He laughed and said I should have told Genet to go fuck himself and stood my ground, as I had every reason to do; then I'd have had nothing to complain about. I was compelled to agree that, as always, he was right. Nothing further was said. I didn't see Genet again for sixteen years. He stopped posing for Alberto not long afterward, but a decade later published a short book of unparalleled brilliance and psychological insight about the artist and his work, a masterpiece of intuition and understanding.

And then the surprising thing happened. Arriving one afternoon at the studio, I found Alberto in a state of evident agitation. "I'm very upset," he said. When I asked why, he told me that the finest of the Matisse drawings had disappeared, the one most prized and praised by everyone. He and Annette and Diego had repeatedly searched both studio and bedroom, to no effect. So there was no possible explanation for the drawing's disappearance save that it had been stolen. But by whom? That disagreeable question was made but more so by a logical sequence of others. How was it that a thief had happened to select that particular item? Careful inspection showed that nothing else in the studio had been taken or even tampered with. Moreover, the drawing was unsigned, and the identity of the model would not necessarily be evident to everyone. Therefore the missing item represented a far less valuable and negotiable asset than sculptures and/or paintings which had been spurned. What then could have been the motive of the thief? Common sense argued that he must have recognized the drawing's special significance and that this special significance must accordingly be assumed to attach to its disappearance. On both counts the one for whom the significance was most special could be none other than the artist. Might this suggest that the thief had had a purpose of which the drawing was merely a symbol? All questions without answers, lest the thief himself be inspired to explain.

Alberto was neither incensed nor outraged by his loss. "I'm not opposed to theft," he said. He was saddened by the disappearance of a work he particularly prized and by the peculiar circumstances involved. What mainly concerned him was the hope of recovering the drawing. He would, he said, be happy to pay ten times its commercial worth in order to get it back. For this to be possible, however, he would have to discover the identity of the thief. That person obviously had to be someone familiar with the artist, with his work, and with his studio, so familiar, indeed, as to be able to come and go at will, for it was ridiculous to suppose that the theft of a drawing on heavy paper measuring some twenty by twelve inches might have been perpetrated in Alberto's presence. And there were at that time only four people who came and went freely in the studio, whether the artist was present or not. They were Annette, Diego, Genet, and myself, the first two by definition above suspicion. And so Alberto said to me, "It had to be either Genet or you. Was it you?"

I told him that it was not I. His question did not offend me. Alberto was too tolerant, sensitive, and fastidious ever to offend anyone. But I was curious and surprised. The only suspect other than I, after all, was famed as a thief, had often done time in prison for theft, had glorified stealing in his writings, and had made an artistic celebration of his contempt for honesty and trust. Was it not plausible, I asked Alberto, that these well-known facts might point to the whereabouts of the missing drawing? He smiled. Did my supposition, he inquired, by any chance stem from continued resentment over Genet's rudeness? I smiled in turn and said he knew better. He did, he conceded. But it was precisely because Genet had made such a literary exaltation of thievery and proclaimed the sovereign right to steal that it was unthinkable in this instance to suspect him; because the bond of friendship, sympathy, and understanding forged between artist and model precluded the symbolic significance and satisfaction of stealing; because Genet was, in any case, too subtle to be so obvious; and because to steal from Alberto, himself unfettered by bourgeois conventions or scruples, would have been contrary to the logic, not to mention the compulsion, of ritual theft. All this was very well, I said, but what I wanted to know was whether Alberto had asked Genet the same question he'd asked me. He had not. Genet knew that the drawing was missing and had said nothing. To ask him whether he had taken it, given his renowned proclivities, would be to accuse him, and an accusation would appear to take his guilt for granted, a standpoint repellent to any person of decent feeling. In short, considering Genet's past, the injustices he had endured, and the life of guilt he had led since the age of ten, the question would have constituted an irreparable offense, and Alberto said he would rather lose the entire contents of his studio than risk offending a friend.

As for me, he added, he knew there had been no risk of offending me by asking the question, because I was a young man of good family, saved from misfortune by the precedence of polite society and spared indignity by the conviction that good manners always prevail. If I had taken the drawing, that would have been merely a weakness, if not a misdirected gesture of admiration, and there were few things in human relations more beneficial to happiness than forgiving the weakness of a friend. (A preachment, incidentally, which Alberto did not invariably practice.) "I'm rather sorry you didn't take it," he said, "because then I would not only have gotten it back but would have had confirmed my agreeable feeling that you have the backbone of a reprobate behind the bourgeois façade."

"Behind the bourgeois façade," I said, "don't forget that as a homosexual I'm no stranger myself to the life of guilt."

"Only enough to ensure the enjoyment of three meals a day," Alberto replied.

As I've said, argumentation with him was no joke, though always entertaining and often funny.

Alberto never again in my presence mentioned the missing portrait of Matisse. So the mystery of its disappearance would have seemed to remain entire. But in time it deepened, and in the depths a rather repellent but logical clarity eventually appeared.

Genet before long told Alberto that he had wearied of posing and would do no more of it. He felt, he explained, that prolonged submission to the portraitist's scrutiny was transforming him into an object. Alberto, though annoyed at the loss of his model, made him a gift of the finer of the two portraits. He said he thought Genet's attitude very literary, which may suggest that he did not want to understand his friend's reasons. To say that they were literary was to say that for Genet they were vital, and in time the writer provided literary evidence which proved that the model had seen the artist with a perspicacity so profound as to defy the laws of likelihood. Luckily, before long Alberto found two other models, who occupied him more obsessively than Genet ever had.

In June of that year, 1954, a brief article by me praising Alberto's work had appeared in an obscure, short-lived review called *La Parisienne.* In the autumn I was asked to write a much longer piece for the first issue of a new art review edited by my friends Georges and Peggy Bernier, to be called *L'Oeil.* This was a serious challenge. Alberto had till then been relatively little written about, and principally by distinguished critics like Georges Duthuit, Carola Giedion-Welcker, Michel Leiris, Francis Ponge, and Jean-Paul Sartre. *L'Oeil* promised to be an important publication, and my article would be accompanied by numerous photographs. I was no less intimidated by the challenge than by the artist himself, though we could by then, I suppose, have been taken for friends. So I spoke to Alberto about the proposed article and told him of my misgivings. He brushed them aside. "Don't worry," he said. "Think in terms of centuries. A hundred years from now it won't matter what you write. I think you appreciate my things. They don't deserve it, but no matter. You're a writer, so it's your fate to write. A hopeless situation. Just like mine. There's your article: an artist is a charlatan without hope. You can say I said so. Don't worry. Nobody will blame you."

But I did worry and was fearful of blame if I failed to do justice to the things which, in fact, I did appreciate or to the artist who had made them, the man I admired more than any other. So I talked about my worry to my friends, who listened charitably but without concern, and one evening at the Café de Flore, while I was dwelling on my difficulty, a man at the adjoining table leaned across and said in English, "Forgive me if I'm indiscreet, but did I hear you talking about Giacometti?"

I said yes, then he added that he was a friend of the sculptor and wondered what my connection might be. I explained that I, too, was acquainted with Alberto and just then happened to be much worried over an article I'd been asked to write about him. The stranger, who was fat, going bald, about my age, and English, introduced himself with some solemnity, as if the name David Sylvester were one that well-informed persons would recognize automatically. To me it was not. Not yet. Much interested in my article, Sylvester said he wished to read it immediately. That would be impossible, I replied, as I had completed only a first draft, which was handwritten and would be illegible to anyone else. This did not deter the portly Englishman. And where, he inquired, was this draft? In the room I occupied in a small hotel nearby. Then I must go and fetch it at once, he declared with imperious nonchalance, and then we could go together to his hotel room in the rue de Seine, where I would read the text aloud to him and he could give me the benefit of his criticisms, which would probably be of much assistance. It was close to one o'clock in the morning. I had no desire to sit up half the night submitting my labored efforts to the judgment of an unknown, autocratic, self-important critic. But the unexpected opportunity to receive help was tempting. I agreed. Leaving my friends, I went to fetch the manuscript. Sylvester was waiting for me alone at the corner of the rue Saint-Benoît. We spoke little while walking to his hotel, and I wondered whether I was naïvely exposing myself to the danger of a very undesirable pounce on the part of this overweight and almost-ugly stranger. Whether he was homosexual or not I couldn't guess, but there was something disagreeably epicene about him. I need not, however, have worried.

His hotel room was even smaller than mine. He reclined on the bed, while I sat on the single, uncomfortable chair and read my text with embarrassment to the ostentatiously pensive Sylvester. When I finished, he pursed his elastic lips and sighed portentously before speaking. At length he said that he hadn't believed me when he overheard me babbling about Giacometti at the Flore. But I could excuse the error because I had accomplished something. Nothing altogether new or vitally important. No first-rate perceptions. But I had a grasp, an authentic grasp, of what Alberto was about. That was what mattered. As it happened, he was writing about Alberto just then, because he was organizing a highly important exhibition of Giacometti's work for the Arts Council in London. It would open in the spring. "Perhaps you will come to see it," he concluded.

"I'll be in America then," I said.

"Too bad," said Sylvester. "Now I must go to sleep. Alberto will approve of your article. You have no cause to worry. Good-bye. No doubt we'll meet again one day."

That day, to be sure, did come, though not until 1970, when everything between us would henceforth evolve gradually toward a lamentable dénouement, which might have been foreseen when I meekly consented to read aloud my first serious effort to write about Alberto in Sylvester's hotel room in the middle of the night. Meanwhile, David had posed for a memorable painting and had organized in London a retrospective exhibition even more important than the first, his status as an authority on Giacometti's works therefore incontestable.

I was scheduled to sail for America in mid-November, the date of my return highly uncertain. So I was taking with me everything I owned, which I always did in those years, entailing quite a lot of fuss, packing of trunks (not wanted on the voyage) and filling metal suitcases with books. And inevitably I contrived to get my friends involved in the fuss of my imminent departure. Marie-Laure issued invitations to a going-away party. Bernard promised a soirée. Even Dora suggested a good-bye dinner *tête-à-tête*. And Alberto, too, wished to make a farewell gesture. It was princely. When I arrived at the rue Hippolyte-Maindron that November afternoon, I found the sculptor industriously tweaking a large bust of his brother. His hands were covered with clay, so I shook his wrist, a form of salutation that had become customary. He nodded toward the long table beneath the studio window. Amid the litter of dusty turpentine bottles, dried-out paintbrushes, and discarded palettes stood three bronze busts of Diego. "I want you to have a souvenir to take back to America," he said. "These three things were in our storage room, and Diego brought them along this morning. If there's one that you like, take it."

The choice was easy. I selected the sculpture I thought most characteristic of Alberto at his best, a striking likeness of his brother and also the largest, about twelve inches high with a dark brown patina.* Holding it in both hands, I said, "How can I thank you?"

"Maybe when I've read your article in *L'Oeil* I'll want to take it back," Alberto said. "In the meantime, I have a feeling that you rather liked the little still life of apples that's over there on the floor by the foot of the bed."

He was uncannily perceptive. I had never spoken of that still life of several apples in a bowl, but two or three times had picked it up from the floor to admire it close at hand. The painting was not large but exceptionally intense and strong, rendered in a Rembrandtesque chiaroscuro of dark browns, black, and gray. No subject matter could have been simpler, but no other artist of that era could have rendered it with such immediacy and power. "You're right," I said. "It's a wonderful picture."

"Then take it as well," said Alberto. "It's not an easy picture. I like it, too, because it's a failure that grazed the danger of success. So it's a good riddance."

"You're too generous," I said, but I didn't refuse the painting. Alberto was a difficult person to thank, because his concept of generosity was moral, not material. I told him that I would write to him from America and that I hoped he would approve of my article when it had been translated into French and published in *L'Oeil* a couple of months later. Our parting was cordial but not emotional.

I went to say good-bye to Diego in his studio across the passageway, and he was, as usual, amiable but withdrawn, almost gruff. He took no note of the sculpture and painting I had in my hands.

---

* *Tête de Diego*, reproduced in *Alberto Giacometti*, by Reinhold Hohl (New York: Harry N. Abrams, 1971), no. 195 (photograph of another cast).

As I came out from the passageway into the street, I encountered Annette, just then returning home. Unlike Diego, she stared with conspicuous astonishment at the sculpture and painting. "What are you doing with those things?" she demanded, in voice and manner clearly doubtful of my right to carry them off.

"Alberto just gave them to me," I explained, "as good-bye presents. I'm leaving for America in a few days."

"Well, you don't know how lucky you are," she said in a tone of unmistakable vexation. "I can't guess what got into him. And he gave you all those drawings of yourself as well. You must understand that he's not in the habit of passing out his things to the first person who knocks on the door. Quite the contrary, as a matter of fact. Of course they're his and he can do as he pleases. I congratulate you, anyway. Have a good voyage." And she went inside without offering her hand for me to shake.

I didn't depart as scheduled, however, because two days prior to the sailing I fell on the stairway in the Café de Flore and broke my left ankle, an accident which required surgery and a stay of ten days at the American Hospital, in the farthest reaches of suburban Neuilly. While there, I asked my friend Bernard to bring to the hospital the sculpture and painting Alberto had given me, and I put them on the table beside my bed to keep me company as I impatiently awaited recovery. And what was my amazement one afternoon when I awakened from a drowse to find the artist himself seated at my bedside! I knew perfectly well by then that it was only with the most extreme reluctance that Alberto interrupted his obsessive schedule of work for any reason whatsoever. That he had taken a taxi from the distant fourteenth arrondissement all the way to the depths of Neuilly to visit a sick acquaintance seemed almost a contradiction of his character. I didn't even know how he had learned of my accident, for the rue Hippolyte was then still without a telephone. But there he was. Many years later I told Diego of his visit, and the younger brother at first refused to believe in such a departure from usual practice. When I insisted, he shook his head and said that it was unprecedented. Alberto stayed for almost an hour. We talked and laughed. He was surprised to see the sculpture and painting on my bedside table, picked up the bronze, turning it round and round in his hands, and murmured, "I should be ashamed to have given

you something so miserable." I chided him for seeming disingenuous, but he insisted that he had no hope of ever being able to
reproduce what appeared to him to be reality. Nonetheless he fooled
himself along, he said, with the notion that another day might bring
him half a step closer to the unattainable destination. It was impossible to doubt his sincerity.

Convalescence kept me in France eight weeks longer than
planned. I saw Alberto two or three times. He told me the story of
the injury to his right foot caused when a woman lost control of her
car and ran him down in the place des Pyramides. As a consequence
he still limped slightly. It had been one of the most important and
propitious experiences of his lifetime, he said. I later wondered,
when talking with Diego, whether it was the nature of my accident
that had brought Alberto to my bedside, but by that time it was too
late to inquire. Not that, in any case, I would have presumed.

By the time my article appeared in *L'Oeil*, I was in America.
Alberto wrote to tell me how well he liked what I'd written, saying,
in fact, that it was the best article anyone had yet published about
him and his work. This was not so. I came to realize in time that
he habitually considered the most recent article the best. Perhaps
he forgot the others. He kept none and, unlike Picasso, did not
subscribe to a newspaper clipping agency. What was written about
him or about his work meant next to nothing to him compared to
the paramount importance of what he aspired without much hope
to accomplish in the unpredictable future.

My article crossed the ocean and brought me the acquaintance
of a man called James Johnson Sweeney, director of the Solomon R.
Guggenheim Museum, an institution then housed in an old Fifth
Avenue mansion and not yet condemned to the incompatible confines of the structure designed by Frank Lloyd Wright, an architect
who cared nothing for either works of art or their pleasing display.
Sweeney was a large, bluff man, a rare connoisseur, and gentleman
of the old school, unprepared to compromise taste or conviction. In
the winter of 1955 he was preparing a retrospective exhibition of
works by Alberto, the first to take place in New York and, in my
judgment, the most beautifully installed that has ever been shown
anywhere. Learning that I owned examples of Alberto's work, Sweeney asked to borrow some for his exhibition. He immediately se-

lected the little painting of apples and one of the drawings of me. The entire museum was freshly painted white for the occasion, while sculptures, paintings, and drawings were placed with unerring appreciation of the most striking aesthetic character of each. Suitable attention was paid in the press, the cognoscenti came to admire, and Pierre Matisse, Alberto's dealer in New York, sold a few works—reluctantly, as was his wont. But the general public did not crowd those elegant galleries, so soon to be destroyed. New York, absorbed in the self-importance of the abstract expressionists, was not yet prepared for Alberto. That would take another decade.

I stayed fourteen months in America, an arduous experiment in learning whether I could adapt myself to life in my homeland. When the answer appeared to be no, I once more packed up everything I owned and booked passage aboard the same liner on which I had sailed away from France. Needing money, I reluctantly sold a number of works of art, including the bronze bust of Diego that Alberto had given me as a going-away present. It brought two thousand dollars, the same amount I got from a large, early Cézanne drawing of a nude youth—a goodly sum in those days.

When I reached Paris, Alberto, Diego, and Annette were among the first people I sought out. I told Alberto that I had sold his gift, and he said, "Well, it was yours."

"I was sorry to let it go, but I needed the money to come back here. You're not angry?"

"What you do with your property is none of my business. But I'm glad you had the heart to tell me, because I knew about it anyway. The person you sold it to offered it to Pierre, and he told me. The art world is a very small one, you know, and everybody learns everything sooner or later. I made a good investment by giving you that head of Diego because it brought you back here, and I'm glad to see you again. It feels a little odd, though, to be your sugar daddy. But then . . . I *am* old enough to be your father."

We both laughed, and of course it was funny, although I'm confident that neither of us understood it then.

Alberto and Diego, I thought, were just as I had always known them—"always," in this instance, amounting to a mere four years, during which I'd often been absent. But I had thought and thought about Alberto in particular, had written much about him in my journal, and placed him at the head of my spiritual family. About Annette I had never thought as hard or as often, because I'd felt from the first that there wasn't a very great deal to be gained by it. She was likable, easy to get along with, stood up to Alberto's teasing with commendable élan, and was indispensable to him as a model. But she didn't know much about art in general or appear to care deeply for Alberto's work in particular. I often wondered what in the world they found to talk about when alone together, because the importance of the shirt front in Cézanne's portrait of Vollard was as remote from her ken as Aldebaran. Nor did she ever seem interested in acquiring knowledge that would enrich her understanding of the remarkable situation which chance, aided by her stubborn resolve, had offered her.

In that spring of 1956, however, it seemed to me that Annette had changed, that she was no longer the girlish, giggly, rather silly but good-natured young woman I had known before. I found instead an individual often peevish and sullen, who no longer made light of her husband's jests and occasionally gave vent to waspish, sarcastic bursts of petulance. Surprised by this metamorphosis, I did not feel entitled to mention it to Alberto so long as he said nothing, but I saw no reason to be reticent with Diego. When I mentioned the change I thought I'd observed in Annette, he snorted, shrugged, and said, "She only knows how to do two things: sweep the courtyard and go to the dentist. But now she wants to live like a grande dame, now that Alberto's making a lot of money. She wants to move out of here, and install herself and Alberto in luxury. Imagine it! Her right as a wife, she says. Oh, she must have worked him over hard to get him to marry her. And now it's not enough. Yes, she's changed. It's too bad. When she was just a petite bourgeoise from the suburbs of Geneva, things were all right. Now they'll only get worse. You'll see, poor Lord. Alberto's very naïve, you know."

That was the last thing I'd have said about him, and yet the absolute nature of his integrity may, it's true, have entailed a certain naïveté. Diego would have known, and a decade later I had reason to think so. However, there were still occasional outings as carefree and jolly as those I'd known with all three since that unexpected birthday party at Les Tamaris. The four of us now and then went late to dine at La Palette or La Coupole, sometimes to a movie, which always prompted the brothers to insist that films had been better before they learned to talk. Alberto caressed Annette's hair and called her "my little girl." In fact, she, too, could have been his child. I thought, and hoped, that maybe Diego's gloomy forebodings for the future might prove mistaken.

In the absence of Genet, somebody even more exotic had entered the life at 46, rue Hippolyte: a Japanese professor of philosophy named Isaku Yanaihara, aged thirty-eight, on temporary leave from his university in Japan to study at the Sorbonne. He had arranged to meet Alberto at the urging of a friend from home, had been duly impressed by an artist who could talk to him about Hegel, and had soon fallen into the usual habit of dropping by the studio in the afternoon to chat. It wasn't long before the artist invited the professor to pose. And soon afterward Annette's ill humor was erased as if by magic when she became Yanaihara's mistress—a situation, so Alberto maintained, which he wholeheartedly welcomed.

I didn't like Yanaihara, finding him arrogant and aloof, lacking entirely in the formal politesse traditional, if insincere, among the Japanese. Besides, I didn't think he much liked me. As an American, maybe I reminded him of his nation's humiliating defeat. At all events, I did not endeavor to make myself ingratiating when I encountered Yanaihara at the studio. Whether Alberto ever noticed this, I don't know. If he did, he probably didn't care, for on the whole he liked to keep his friends and/or acquaintances in separate compartments, preferring tête-à-tête meetings. He never introduced me to anyone. I met a few of his friends, like Balthus, Michel Leiris, and Olivier Larronde, through the fusion of creative environments peculiar to Paris.

When Alberto was busy or absent, I had gradually taken to spending some time with Diego, who was always present, always busy with some painstaking chore for his brother, but always prepared to talk while continuing his work. Once his natural reserve had been overcome, I found him a far more easygoing conversationalist than Alberto. He did not oblige one to think, for he was not in love with ideas. He liked gossip and ludicrous stories. So did Alberto, as a matter of fact, but with him there was always the underpinning of theoretical speculation. It came out that Diego, too, disliked the Japanese professor, considering him rude and sneaky. When they encountered each other in the studio, Yanaihara didn't bother to greet Diego and Diego took no trouble to conceal his contempt for his brother's model and his sister-in-law's lover. And whenever Diego's countenance clouded over with displeasure, there was no mistaking the dark vexation or threat of outburst. The Giacomettis had impetuous tempers, never hesitating to be obstreperous when angered. The turmoil was usually brief and hurriedly concluded.

Alberto scolded me once and lost his temper with me once, which doesn't seem a bad record for fourteen years of off-and-on acquaintance, considering that my insouciance and intellectual inadequacy must have frequently been trying. The scolding came as an ice-cold surprise in November 1956. I had written and published in the press a long, moralizing letter to Picasso, denouncing his failure as a committed member of the Communist Party to condemn the brutal Soviet oppression during the Hungarian uprising. When I next visited the studio after publication of this letter, Alberto glared at me in pursed silence by way of greeting. When I said hello, he didn't answer. Plainly, much was amiss. Aware I would not be spared knowledge of what this was, I kept silent. After a moment, which seemed itself as long as a crime, Alberto said, "You did wrong."

"I suppose you mean the letter to Picasso," I said.

"To write it was possible. To publish it should have been impossible."

"Why?" I asked. "Is Picasso above criticism? You yourself are constantly saying how much you disapprove of him personally and dislike his art."

"That may be so," Alberto acknowledged. "I have a right to opinions. But I have no right to pass judgment in public, given the fact that I myself am a menace to public welfare. Like you. And like Picasso. You see, Plato was right about artists, and I don't want to argue the point. You did wrong. Whether Picasso is right is irrelevant. Do you take issue with the logic of irrelevance?"

"No, of course not," I admitted sheepishly. "But I've written about you, too, and published it. Was that wrong?"

Alberto smiled. "Maybe one of us is a bit of a Jesuit," he said, and we never again spoke of the letter to Picasso, though he inevitably came into our conversations like the Abominable Snowman or General de Gaulle.

In April of the following year, while staying with Marie-Laure in Hyères, I came down with a case of the mumps, an affliction innocuous for children but liable to provoke painful and disabling consequences for those past the age of puberty. Such was my case. Whether or not the swelling of my testicles caused sterility, I will never know; the only advantage to me of having had to endure this illness was to learn from Alberto afterward that he also had been infected after the age of puberty and had, as a consequence, been left sterile. But maybe this was just as well, he said, because children would have been a great nuisance to him and as a parent he would have been woefully incompetent. But of course Annette, having known from the first that her husband was incapable of begetting children, now longed to be a mother. Alberto advised her to find a surrogate father. Anybody would do, he insisted. But Yanaihara, who for several years flew back and forth between Tokyo and Paris, was already a father and did not sympathize with Annette's maternal longings. Frustrated, feeling unloved and misunderstood, she became still more petulant and short-tempered. Alberto felt guilty, which did not help his temper, and there were scenes. Diego observed with dismay the evolution of the marital imbroglio, knowing that it was principally his brother's fault, since he was a thinking person, whereas his wife was prey solely to her emotions. But he would never blame Alberto for anything, because he understood that genius deprives its possessor of even the supposition of free will.

Now there were no more carefree dinners at Les Tamaris. Diego seemed to have determined to stay aloof from the trouble between Alberto and Annette. He had friends of his own, of whom I gradually became one. Now and then we would have dinner together, almost always at an Italian restaurant in the rue des Canettes. Afterward we usually went to the Flore for a nightcap or two, having already had more than enough to drink. And it was there one night that, to my stupefaction, he bitterly denounced Alberto's work, exclaiming that those emaciated figurines were not true sculpture at all, that any Beaux-Arts student could do as well, if not better, and that he was in a position to know, because every sculpture made by Alberto passed through his hands and he could make them just as well as his brother could—all this accompanied by pounding on the table and gasps of exasperation. Fortunately this outburst was short-lived and never repeated in my hearing. Sometimes, though, Diego would sigh and say, "Oh, Alberto can be very difficult. God knows he can be very, very difficult." But after he was gone, the bereaved brother sometimes said, "Alberto was my luck." To be sure, he was, but Diego, being also a Giacometti, knew how to make the very best of it.

Balthus and his so-called niece, Frédérique, came occasionally from their rural château for a few days' distraction in Paris, where I sometimes ran into him. As he knew that I was seeing Alberto regularly, he suggested—in the continued absence of a telephone —that I arrange a date when all of us could have dinner together. Happy to comply, I spoke to Alberto and a date was set. This was one of the very rare occasions when I would have an opportunity to observe the interaction between Alberto and a close friend, a fellow artist, moreover, so I looked forward to it eagerly without any pre-sentiment that a drama might ensue. Arriving at the studio on the appointed evening at about eight, I found Balthus and Frédérique already there, and Annette also, all of them dressed and ready for the evening. I had reserved a table for five at La Palette. Alberto was the only one not ready. He was still working on a large female figure in clay, muttering to himself, as he habitually did, that it was worthless, impossible, and that he would never be able to accomplish anything to his satisfaction. Annette said, "Alberto, we're all ready and waiting. Wash your hands and come along."

Suddenly Alberto turned away from his sculpture and glared at me. "You!" he cried. "I've been waiting for you to show up. If you dared. The pretension of it. And the insolence. Lower than the low. You don't deserve anything but . . . but . . ." He stuttered, gasped, and abruptly turned back to his sculpture, seizing it with both hands and hurling it onto the floor. "There! That's what you deserve. Nothing and less than nothing."

"Oh, Alberto!" exclaimed Annette.

Appalled, frightened, I didn't know what to do or say but had to say something, as Alberto was still sputtering with rage and crimson in the face. "What's the matter?" I whispered. "I don't understand. What have I done. I thought you were . . ."

"You thought, you thought," Alberto shouted. "You didn't think at all. It was you who arranged this evening, and you didn't think to ask Diego, did you? And Diego is worth more than all the rest of us put together. Did you think of his feelings?"

"But Diego never has dinner with us anymore," I protested. "And when I asked you to fix the day, you said nothing about Diego, so I didn't think . . ."

"You didn't think," Alberto furiously repeated. "You didn't think, because you don't know how to think. That's all there is to say. And look at my figurine. I've been working on it for months."

"I'm sorry," I said. "That's all I can say. It would be rude to ask Diego now, so all I can do is say I'm sorry." Having said that, feeling unhappily abashed but at the same time wrongfully put upon, I walked to the door and left the studio, went through the passageway and out into the dark street. Before I could reach my car, however, Balthus hurriedly came after me. I should pay no heed to Alberto's tantrum, he said. They always passed quickly. Besides, I was not in the wrong, because, in fact, he also was aware that Diego no longer spent evenings with Alberto and Annette. But a possible reason for the outburst, which I couldn't very well have known, was that Diego had recently been deserted by the woman he'd lived with for twenty years and Alberto feared that he might be lonely. Not that Diego would ever have complained. But I mustn't take offense, Balthus insisted. I must come back and act as if nothing had happened, and I'd see that the evening would be perfectly pleasant, after all. He took my arm, so I reluctantly went along. In the studio Alberto was brushing his jacket and straightening his tie.

"Ah, there you are," he said when I came in. "It's a lucky thing you thought better of running away like the village idiot. You'd have ruined our evening. Well, come along, you girls. Don't keep us waiting."

So we drove in my car to Montparnasse and had dinner at La Palette, a restaurant where the walls were covered with ugly paintings by failed artists, views of the seashore, gaudy still lifes of flowers, slick nudes, and cute dogs. "Exactly the sort of pictures I'd like to paint," Alberto said, "if only I could." This ironic equivocation led to a prolonged discussion with Balthus about the authenticity of representational painting as a viable mode of self-expression under contemporary circumstances. But was it expression of the self, indeed, that determined the nature of an aesthetic undertaking, Alberto mused, or was the spirit of the era a more powerful determinant of the creative impulse? This spirit of the era, Balthus suggested, was a pitfall, because it had no meaning except in the past tense, which was to say that only tradition could be depended upon to establish persuasive artistic criteria. And that, he added, was why Courbet and Seurat were the greatest painters of the twentieth century. I did not participate in this theoretical discussion and had very little to say, anyhow. Annette and Frédérique talked about clothing and the problems of furnishing a château. Still feeling the effect of Alberto's tongue-lashing, I did not enjoy the evening and was glad when, later than I would have liked, it came to an end.

I'm not in the least sure that Diego would have enjoyed the occasion any more than I did, or that he would have welcomed an invitation to be present. His name was not mentioned once while we were at the restaurant. In any case, I felt that I had been berated unfairly, and this was especially distressing because my grievance had been caused by the man I admired more than any other, the only one I felt could never be wrong, whose presence on earth made life nobler and more precious. So my resentment was keener than common sense should have allowed, and in order to emphasize it, I vainly and foolishly let several weeks go by without appearing at the rue Hippolyte.

I did reappear at the studio door eventually. Rather sheepishly. Alberto was working on a large painting of a man's head—Diego —very dark and powerful. "Look how this is going," he said by way of greeting, as if I'd last been in the studio the day before. "I think I'd better give up painting once and for all. And I would if I could find somebody else to do it for me."

"Good luck," I said.

Alberto turned on his stool to gaze at me intently. "It is not usually considered polite," he said, "to make fun of another's misery."

"I didn't mean it that way," I seriously replied.

"No, no, of course not," Alberto said. "But the joke is on me all the same, and it's a bad one. Well, sit down and tell me who was at Marie-Laure's for lunch the last time you were there."

"André and Rose Masson," I said.

"André was one of my first French friends in Paris. He painted some good pictures then. Now they're terrible and he's rotten with pride, and Rose is a bitter old goat. When all of us were young and poor, being an artist was almost fun, because one could practically consider it a joke. A bad joke, of course, but laughable all the same. Shall we go to the café?"

As we walked along the rue d'Alésia, Alberto began to sing one of the bawdy songs that he had learned in the whorehouses before the war and liked to remember.

> *Oui, je vais te faire un pompier,*
> *Mais d'abord il te faudra me piner.*
> *Oui, tu aimes te faire pomper.*
> *Hélas, il n'y a plus rien à sucer.*

In the café we chatted amicably about this and that. Never a word concerning Diego, Balthus, or the circumstances of our last meeting. Alberto said that he was concerned for Annette because she had nothing to do, was not deeply interested in anything except herself and her love life, which brought her slight satisfaction, and therefore was unhappily idle, which she blamed on him. She should have some occupation, no matter how pointless, he said, but she lacked the strength of character to endure monotony. So it was his lot to be blamed for her frustrations. He'd told her all this time after time, but she didn't know how to listen. "It's terrible," he murmured, "to think of all the harm I've done her."

"Such as?"

"Such as permitting her with premeditation to be exploited by me when she had no notion of what it would be like."

"What is it like?"

"Slavery. And now it's too late. She wouldn't know what to do with freedom. It would probably kill her."

I had no answer to that. Alberto finished his coffee and cigarette,

I my Coca-Cola, in pensive silence, then we strolled back toward the studio. On the way, Alberto looked at the trees lining the sidewalk and said, "A tree is much more useful than a human being."

When we reentered the studio, he said, "Look at this place. What a mess. All these paintings piled up everywhere. Why don't you take one? It's been a long time since I've given you anything. If there's a painting you like, take it."

I realized at once, or believed I did, why he chose this moment to offer me a gift. So I said, "There's no reason to give me a painting just because you got angry with me the last time we met."

"It's a gesture of gratitude," Alberto said. "You remember that other night when I dropped my sculpture on the floor? Well, it was a miracle, that accident, because when I came back from the restaurant and picked it up again, I found that it was completely transformed for me. It was as though I'd never seen it before, and suddenly I saw just what I had been looking for all those months. I worked on it for an hour and it was finished. Diego made a mold in the morning, and the day after, we sent a plaster cast to the foundry. But, of course, if there are no pictures here that you like, I won't be offended should you go away empty-handed, only sorry and understanding, because I realize that they're all such failures."

"It's not that," I protested. "Not at all. You know very well how much I admire your paintings."

"In that case, take your choice," said Alberto.

To choose wasn't easy. After looking at all the paintings with care, I selected a rather severe portrait of Annette in a rose-colored dress. Alberto signed it in oil paint, warning me to take care not to smudge the signature before it had time to dry. That was the third painting he had given me. Or was it the fourth? There was also a small but very powerful head of Diego on a green background. I can't remember, and foolishly neglected to note, the exact chronology of his gifts. The greatest, of course, was not a material thing but for that very reason more precious, one which even today I can gratefully appreciate.

It was a spring afternoon. We are now in 1958. The door to the studio stood open. Alberto was working on some piece of sculpture. Beside the stove a heap of drawing paper lay on the floor, and I immediately observed that there appeared to be drawings on each piece. "What are all these drawings doing on the floor?" I asked Alberto.

"I've been cleaning out my portfolios," he said. "And those drawings are not worth saving. So I put them down there to use for lighting the stove."

"But there must be at least fifty. Surely they can't all be bad. I'll just have a look."

"Waste of time," grumbled the artist.

Nonetheless, I sat down and started sorting through the pile of drawings. They were of all kinds. Many, I realized, were slight sketches that Alberto would never agree to preserve. Others, however—heads of Diego and Annette, still lifes and standing figures of women—were beautifully finished, and I couldn't understand why Alberto should want to destroy them unless for some murky reason their quality itself offended him. I selected twelve that I felt he couldn't deny. The most beautiful was a wonderfully precise and limpid bouquet of flowers, chrysanthemums, on a table with a single apple beside the vase. I told Alberto that I had found a number of drawings too fine to burn. Grumbling again, he took them from my hands and spread them out on the bed.

"Well," he said, "it's humiliating. But I grant you're in the right. They are worth saving. Except one," he cried. "You're not infallible. This one is too miserable." He snatched the bouquet of flowers, tore it up, and flung the pieces onto the floor. Then he sat down, took a pencil from his breast pocket, and signed the other drawings one by one. When finished, he handed them to me. "It's only right that you should have them. Without you, they would have gone up in smoke."

"But they're so many," I objected without conviction.

"Diego and Annette saw them there and didn't protest," Alberto said. "You saved them. So by rights they go with their savior."

"Well, thank you truly," I exclaimed, elated more than embarrassed.

"*They* are grateful," said Alberto, "and that's what matters."

I can't say why Alberto was so generous to me. In time I learned that he wasn't habitually very generous. Indeed, there was only one other person to whom he gave his works so willingly and prodigally and this was Louis Clayeux, director of the Galerie Maeght, his Parisian dealers; and it seemed quite in the nature of things that he should offer much to Clayeux, a sensitive and intelligent man who played an essential role in furthering Giacometti's career. Balthus, a long-standing friend, was given only a single small sculpture, later stolen from him by his son. To Leiris, he offered but a tiny drawing and made a series of etchings for a volume of poems composed after the writer's abortive suicide attempt. To Sartre he gave a couple of drawings; to Simone de Beauvoir, a bronze head of Diego, nothing more. To other friends and acquaintances he would give the occasional drawing or lithograph. Even to Yanaihara, who patiently posed for many paintings and drawings, he never gave a single painting, only a handful of prints and drawings. Then why so much to me? Did he have an imaginative purpose which he kept to himself? I'll never know. But I like to think that he did. And, later, Diego was also remarkably generous. And Bruno—the third brother, the brilliant architect, the only Giacometti still alive as I write this account—with his warm and subtle wife, Odette, gave me exceptional cause to be grateful. All my life I have received gifts from artists, many eminent, many obscure, and it is a fact that I have lived for, and by, art in my own way and as much as I could, which is to say that admiration as an art in itself has for fifty years been the touchstone of my raison d'être. Maybe all those artists were responsive to that. I hope Alberto surmised that something worthwhile might someday come of it. But I never felt deserving. Today, I am still astonished.

Annette's affair with Yanaihara, an impractical proposition from the first, came to nothing, and he returned to Japan for good. There is a clear distinction between Alberto's pre-Yanaihara and post-Yanaihara work. This, however, was of slight concern to Annette, who was beginning to feel that life had not done as well by her as she deserved. To be sure, she had wanted to be the wife of a remarkable man, not a run-of-the-mill bourgeois, and in this ambition her success had been outstanding, not to say triumphant. As Madame Alberto Giacometti, she was treated with courtesy, sometimes with deference, by people like Pierre Matisse, Miró, Stravinsky, even Malraux, who would never have given her the time of day had she been Madame Pierre Dupont. But there was a flaw in the fait accompli: Monsieur Alberto Giacometti did not invariably treat her with deference, sometimes not even with courtesy. He was now a rich man, but he persisted in living like a pauper and expected the person who lived with him to do likewise. If she made an inept or superficial remark, he was usually quick to jeer at it. Worst of all, he did not take her seriously as a woman of surpassing emotion. In the role of lover he was admittedly far from ideal, though he took no trouble to conceal frequent pleasures with prostitutes. She had known this, and had had to accept it, from the beginning, but as the years wore on and she was not yet forty, the situation grew galling. Alberto advised her to take lovers. She did. But they were not always prepared to be as overpowered by passion as she was. Disillusion ensued. There were unhappy scenes, several of which I witnessed at the studio. Annette was not abashed by a show of tears before a neutral party. While his wife wept, Alberto irritably advised her to hop into bed with the first man available. It wasn't ill-intentioned or bad advice, but Annette's intelligence was in her heart, not in her head, and she had mistaken herself for a femme fatale when in fact she was a romantic, rather innocent girl. Such confusion could only cause trouble. It came, indeed, with increasing bitterness and vengeance. Alberto accepted it because he was a man of honor and realized that responsibility for life's blunders cannot be assumed by a person incapable of understanding them.

Diego grew to despise his brother's wife, avoiding her whenever possible and speaking to her only when obligated. "She's a whore," he said, "and not even any good at that. If my mother knew what things have come to here, it would kill her." I never met Annetta Giacometti, to my enduring regret, but from all I had heard of her, I guessed that Diego's assumption might almost be accurate.

Diego, meanwhile, had begun to design and build the furniture for which he would later become famous. The two brothers had collaborated on decorative work in the thirties to earn their living, and the younger had never altogether ceased making the occasional candlestick, ashtray, vase, or lamp. But as the demand for sculpture by Alberto became more and more pressing, Diego, who made molds, plaster casts, and armatures as well as patinating every piece, had less time for work of his own. In addition, he was sometimes called upon to pose, as he had been doing since childhood. Few people in the fifties knew that Diego produced objects of his own design, and at first Alberto's friends and their friends bought Diego's work more or less with the idea of doing both brothers a favor. Alberto constantly praised Diego's productions, leading visitors to his studio to admire the latest object and exclaiming, "Diego has talent to burn. He's a monster. He knows how to do everything. Oh yes, he's got talent to burn."

The first time that Diego led me to his home, a one-room dwelling in a shabby lane giving off the rue d'Alésia, he remarked, "It's sort of a slum, isn't it?" It was, and he had been living there for more than twenty-five years. But in 1960 Alberto bought the small house at 54, rue du Moulin-Vert, just around the corner from the rue Hippolyte-Maindron. And who, incidentally, was Hippolyte Maindron? An obscure nineteenth-century sculptor entirely forgotten today. I wonder whether it will ever occur to anyone to rename that short and unimportant thoroughfare rue Alberto-Giacometti. Braque, after all, has his street, Picasso his grand museum. Anyway, Diego moved into the little house, which he made attractive for himself and his cats, though never very clean and always disorderly. Now he could walk to Alberto's studio in about two minutes.

Annette, whose well-justified complaining about the discomforts and inconvenience of life at 46, rue Hippolyte had grown more and more strident, was also offered by her husband a pleasant apartment adjacent to Montparnasse. It needed renovation and she devoted herself with excitable rigor to the job, soliciting assistance and advice from one and all. Why, even I was asked to come to the rue Léopold Robert and give my opinion concerning the tiles in the small kitchen. I said that they were in excellent taste, and to my astonishment they were. But Annette for some flighty reason took a dislike to this apartment when it was finished and never lived there. Another place was later found for her at 70, rue Mazarine.

Many people, I think, and myself in particular, felt that there was something almost abstract about Alberto's frequent insistence upon his admiration for prostitutes, his respect for their simplicity, and the easy satisfaction provided by their generosity. All this had been consistently reiterated for decades, but no prostitute was ever seen by Alberto's friends at the studio or anywhere else, unless one was invited—an occurrence of supernatural rarity—to accompany him on his nocturnal wanderings. Only once was I ever asked to go along to a rather sinister dive in the rue Vavin called Chez Adrien. It was there that Alberto met the prostitute who proved, he said, the truth of everything he had always maintained about the women who pursued her profession. And there was nothing in the least abstract about her. Alberto made her as concrete and durable as only an artist can. He made her immortal by portraying her again and again. She came to his studio—daily. She was introduced not only to Alberto's wife and brother, both of whom hated her, but also to his friends. She drove about in a scarlet roadster given her by her admirer. I met her on only two or three occasions and did not know what to make of her. She was called Caroline. Alberto was indefatigable in relating her extraordinary qualities of outlook and behavior. That she happened to be an occasional thief as well as a prostitute made not the slightest difference to him. On the contrary, he was delighted to hear tales of her doings in the underworld. Annette was enraged, the more so as she suspected that Caroline's price was far higher than the going rate. There were violent, acrimonious scenes. Diego kept his peace, but he was troubled.

During the sixties I had an affair with an American I'd met in Paris who wanted to live in New York. Desiring to make my life with him, I agreed to return to America, a move I had never anticipated. But I kept the small apartment in Paris purchased for me in 1958 by my parents (the very one I now use as a hideaway in which to do my writing), and almost every year I returned to France for a month or two, thus never losing touch with my friends there. This turned out to be prudent.

In the summer of 1964 I arrived in Paris in late July. Alberto had gone to Switzerland, while Annette was enjoying herself at the villa of Pierre and Patricia Matisse on Cap-Ferrat. I had dinner alone with Diego, who told me that Annette had more or less commandeered the Matisses' villa, asking to stay there alone while they went off on a cruise aboard their yacht, a request not easy to refuse but granted with reluctance. Nor was that all. Annette was having an affair with an art dealer from Los Angeles named Frank Perls, a resident in a hotel close by the villa, where both were royally waited upon by the Matisse servants. All of this Diego had learned from

Patricia, who was fond of him and fonder still of gossip, and used the telephone with abandon.

I had agreed to spend a few days at Saint Moritz with my old friend Bernard and his parents. That resort being not far from Stampa, I telephoned Alberto and asked whether I might spend a day or two with him en route from Saint Moritz to Lake Garda, where I was to visit some acquaintances. He said he'd be happy to see me. So I arrived in Stampa in the midafternoon of August 6 and found Alberto sitting in front of the inn, the Piz Duan, which had belonged to his grandfather. It was there that I was to sleep, in a small room above the flashing stream that courses down the center of the valley. We had a drink, then went to the Giacometti house just across the road. The family had occupied only the ground floor and a semibasement. I was surprised by the smallness of the rooms, but next door stood an ancient barn that had been converted into a studio by Giovanni, Alberto's father, a painter of distinction. There were numerous pictures by him in the house and studio, some of them very fine. And in the studio there were also paintings and sculptures by Alberto, early works executed when he was barely more than a child, and piles of drawings, many of these recent.

Alberto asked whether I'd like to visit a beautiful little town far up on the mountainside. Called Soglio, it had hardly changed since the Middle Ages. As a boy he and his mother had often climbed up through the fields and high forest of chestnut trees to take food to his father, who painted many landscapes there when the weather was fine. We drove up there, and indeed the place possessed an ineffable charm. Sitting outside the inn, which had been installed in an ancient house, we drank lemonade and chatted. I told him I'd had dinner with Diego in Paris but refrained from relating the principal subject of our talk. It was Alberto who brought up Annette. For both brothers she presented a grave problem. Now that husband and wife lived apart, she nevertheless had no intention of giving him up, despite the fact that she had other lovers. He remarked with some humor that there were three convictions to which Annette clung absolutely and which made life difficult not only for her but also for those close to her. The first was that even if she had five lovers all at once, she would feel intensely jealous and possessive toward all of them. The second was that people who work for their living are fools. The third was that nothing in life matters save passion. With a set of primary beliefs like that, Alberto observed, one is bound to have difficulties. And yet he seemed sincerely devoted to her, very aware that he had an enduring responsibility toward her.

Returning to Stampa, we went to the studio, and Alberto worked on a head of Diego in plasticine which he was doing from memory, while I looked through a pile of drawings. One of them was a large sketch in oil on paper of a man striding along. I remarked to Alberto that I thought it particularly fine. "It's a man who trots," he said, then added after a moment, "if you'd like to have it . . ."

"You know I would," I said. "I'd like it very much."

He took it out of my hand and wrote on it, "For James Lord, in memory of his visit to Stampa, 6 August 1964, very affectionately, Alberto Giacometti."

Delighted by the gift, I was even more happy with the inscription. I had known Alberto now for more than a decade, seen him often in a variety of circumstances, and had conversations with him which could only be called intimate, but I still felt intimidated by him as I have never felt with any other person. That he should express affection for me—in writing on a beautiful work from his hand—was profoundly gratifying. And yet I couldn't help asking myself how it was that he should feel affection for me, I who had so little to offer save my incommensurable admiration. I had done nothing for him aside from writing a couple of undistinguished articles. And what, indeed, could a person like myself aspire to offer a man of genius? A few moments of banal companionship. But genius, perhaps, grants glimpses of the future. If so, Alberto may have been swayed by them. I like to believe it. We talked at some length about the differences between an object of art and a work of art. Alberto said that he was glad to have designed decorative objects in the thirties for the Parisian decorator Jean-Michel Frank, because by expending as much care on the proportions and finish of a lamp or vase as he had expended on the execution of some of his Surrealist sculptures, he came to realize their limitations and was able to go on to other work in a way he might not have found had he not sincerely devoted himself to the creation of objects not intended to be works of art. "A vase," he said, "no matter how rare or beautiful, can never be a sculpture, and nothing can ever make it one." This led us to talk of abstract or semiabstract sculptors like Brancusi and Arp. Alberto remarked that during the last thirty years of his life Brancusi had had nothing left to do but polish works he'd executed long before. Rodin, on the other hand, at the end of his life was starting anew. "He could have gone on working for a thousand years," Alberto said. Arp, he recalled, had once come to see him and, speaking almost with despair, had said, "Don't ever do what I'm doing."

We had dinner at the inn. All the people there knew Alberto and spoke to him, I noticed, with respect, but invariably called him by his first name. Afterward we went back to the studio, where Alberto stretched out on a bed, I sat in an armchair, and we talked for a long time about Diego. Anybody acquainted with the two brothers could not help recognizing the compulsion of the elder to idolize, indeed to idealize, the younger. Diego once made a trip to Egypt and in his youth racketed around northern Italy, doing all sorts of jobs, including a bit of smuggling. When Alberto spoke of these adventures, one might have thought he imagined them nearly equivalent to the exploits of Lawrence of Arabia. In addition there was no restraint to the praise lavished upon Diego's furniture, lamps, vases, and other decorative objects, for which the demand was now gradually increasing. While we talked about Diego, it seemed to me that Alberto was very subtly appealing to me to agree with him, to confirm his high opinion of his younger brother. "Diego has imagination to burn, doesn't he?" Alberto said repeatedly. And I agreed, because it fortunately happened to be true. The fact is that Diego, once one got to know him, was far easier to like than Alberto. Both were extraordinarily companionable and entertaining, but with the younger the intimidation of genius was absent, and for friendship's sake that made all the difference. It had grown late. Alberto, I suspected, would want to work for a while before going to bed, and I hoped to make a reasonably early start in the morning for the drive to Lake Garda. So I went across the road to the inn and was sung to sleep by the Schubertian melody of the stream outside.

Alberto had asked me to come and say good-bye before departing in the morning. Hesitant because he usually slept very late,

I nevertheless went along about nine-thirty and found him wide awake, sitting up in bed, drinking coffee and smoking cigarettes. We chatted for an hour or so. I told him that after Lake Garda I was going to stay with Marie-Laure at Hyères, and Alberto recalled the good times they had had there in the thirties. He and Luis Buñuel had built a life-size wooden giraffe in the garden, but for some reason the Vicomte de Noailles had found it disfiguring and insisted that it be taken down. "I've always regretted that giraffe," Alberto said. "There's a big stone sculpture by me somewhere in the garden. As a matter of fact, it was Diego who made it, but don't tell anyone, because the Noailles paid for something by me." I promised to tell no one, and have more or less kept the promise till now. By the end of August, I said, I'd be back in Paris. Then we'd meet again, said Alberto, and he thanked me for coming to see him. I had the impression—it was only an impression—that he'd have liked me to stay a little longer, but I didn't want to impose. So *I* thanked *him* —perhaps too profusely—and went on my way.

The people with whom I stayed on Lake Garda were casual acquaintances living in an immense villa overlooking the lake. The wife was extremely rich, the husband an aspiring sculptor, very pretentious. What a contrast after Stampa and Alberto! I was pressed to accept one of the husband's works as a gift, a bulky, ugly bronze, a nuisance to cart around. I stayed only two nights. The wife told me she had a painting by Raphael in her bedroom in Milan. Could that be true?

It was a relief to arrive at Marie-Laure's eccentric château in Hyères, where I happily remained more than two weeks, then returned to Paris.

From my journal:

Paris, Friday, 28 August 1964

Yesterday was a Giacometti day.

At twelve-thirty I walked to the rue Mazarine, where Annette now lives, as she had invited me to lunch. Her apartment is in an old building, not at all handsome, but the apartment itself could be attractive if ever she managed to pull herself together and tidy up the clutter. There is a small bedroom at the rear (unmade bed) and a good-sized salon with tall windows overlooking the rue Mazarine. Not much furniture: a large armoire, a couch, a couple of tables, some side chairs, and an easy chair. The paintings, most of them by Alberto, are hung any odd way, there are drawings tacked on the walls, other paintings and books piled on the floor. Not a displeasing mess but a mess all the same. Annette is looking very well. In fact, I've never seen her looking so well, tanned, seemingly in excellent spirits, having just returned from a month spent on the Riviera at Pierre Matisse's villa. We had a drink. She told me that she has taken a job for four afternoons a week in the African Department at the Musée de l'Homme, where she will be cataloging wooden headrests. Not that she cares two straws about headrests, but she needs something to do, a specific occupation, away from Alberto and the studio. She's fed up with posing, and Alberto constantly criticizes her for doing nothing and being interested in nothing. The job at the Musée de l'Homme had been arranged for her by Michel Leiris, who is an ethnologist of repute as well as a distinguished writer, and the only friend of Alberto, she said, who had always been kind and attentive to her. Annette is a peculiarly girlish, kittenish sort of woman, never gives one the impression of being mature. She seems vulnerable, but Alberto maintains that she can be very stubborn and shrewd when it comes to getting what she wants. After a while we went downstairs to the restaurant which is immediately below her apartment, a simple but pleasant place called La Fourchette d'Or. We talked about one thing and another, rather impersonal conversation for the most part, because Annette is strangely "removed." One feels that she's trying to be sociable but doesn't know how, and I remembered Alberto saying there were only three or four people in the world she truly cares about, the rest being interchangeable. I asked her a number of personal questions about her relations with her family, and she was obviously startled that I should presume. She answered, however, but added, "I've always wanted to keep my life apart from my family." Is she ashamed of them? I didn't inquire.

After lunch I took a taxi to the studio, where I found Alberto in the bedroom, lying on the unmade bed fully dressed *with his shoes on the sheets. He was at his gloomiest and most pessimistic, immediately started talking about how impossible it is to accomplish anything either in painting or in sculpture that is at all satisfactory. A strange and seemingly unreal statement when considered in relation to the truly splendid work he showed me later. He is absolutely sincere when he says such things and, during the three hours I spent with him, kept coming back obsessively to his dissatisfaction. Yet he has a very mercurial temperament and is quite capable of feeling that, after all, he* has *accomplished something of value. In all the time I've known Alberto, though, never once have I heard him express anything like pride or true pleasure in anything he'd accomplished. He talked yesterday at some length about the essential part of* illusion *in the finished work of art. It is the necessity of illusion (the impossibility, that is, of creating anything which is really like a human head) that makes a Cycladic head, Alberto insisted, so much more alive and convincing than a Roman portrait bust. In some of his work he has gone to extremes in this pursuit of illusion, and he says that because it is impossible to make a sculpture lifelike, he can make it more like life by heightening its illusory quality.*

He talked about his illness and operation for cancer of the stomach, all of which occurred while I was away in the U.S., and said that since then he'd never felt better. He is going to London in a day or two, he said, to see the rooms in the Tate Gallery, where his large retrospective exhibition, organized by David Sylvester, is to take place next year. After his return he suggested that I pose for him. For a painting this time, but only a quick sketch on canvas, executed in a single session, since I had often urged him to leave an occasional picture in this initial state. It goes without saying that I agreed. We went into the studio. He always says, "There's nothing in the studio. I've done absolutely nothing." As usual, there were many new things, superb sculptures and paintings, especially the portraits of Caroline. After a time he suggested we go to the café at the corner of the rue Didot and have a drink. We did, and sat there for an hour and a half talking. I didn't even try to remember everything we talked about in order to record it here,

but I do recall that we discussed the contemporary impossibil-
ity, as Alberto felt it, of accomplishing anything genuinely sat-
isfactory in art. He mentioned Rauschenberg and said his work
represented an impasse. "His head is underwater," he re-
marked. We talked about literature, too, and in that domain as
well Alberto knew of nothing contemporary to admire. He re-
called that the sense of space and perspective in Gatsby *had*
deeply impressed him.

Annette eventually appeared, looking very pretty, being
very kittenish with Alberto. He was obviously pleased to see
her, smiled, and promptly began to tease her. I've witnessed
this routine of teasing any number of times. It always ends the
same way. Annette finally takes offense because Alberto seems
deliberately determined to make her seem ridiculous or stupid
(which I can't help suspecting to be his intent), and then Al-
berto himself becomes annoyed because he finds Annette's reac-
tion silly. So they have an argument. The pretext on this
occasion was an issue as banal and foolish as going to Cook's
to fetch the tickets for London. I wanted no part in this, and as
it was getting late anyway I left.

Sunday, 30 August 1964
When I got to the studio yesterday, I found a note from
Alberto on the door, saying that he was at the café. Walking
over there, I found him alone in the back room, reading an ar-
ticle in Match *on the First World War. We started at once to*
talk about Annette. After I left them at the café, she had a tan-
trum because Alberto had teased her about getting the tickets
for London. She maintained that he showed no consideration
*for her in front of other people—*ne lui montrait pas d'égards
—and added that he was (1) insane and (2) bloated with pride
and self-satisfaction, because he feels that as a consequence of
his work he is not an ordinary person. "About that, at least,"
he remarked, "she was right, regardless of the fact that my
work is a mountain of failure." The odd thing about their rela-
tionship is that Annette looks back with real nostalgia on the
days when Alberto was not yet famous and they had little
money. It irritates her particularly that there are people con-

stantly waiting to see him: journalists, collectors, museum cura-
tors, etc. They are rarely alone together. But when they are
alone, all Annette wants to talk about is the decoration of her
apartment. And she is enraged because Alberto refuses to spend
much money. Not, I suspect, that she might ever become a
spendthrift. She's too Calvinist-Geneva for that. But, at least,
she'd enjoy having fine clothes like Patricia Matisse and per-
haps a few pieces of jewelry.

Sunday, 6 September 1964
   Yesterday after lunch I decided to stop by the studio to see
Diego and find out just when Alberto would return from Lon-
don. Taking a taxi from St.-Germain-des-Prés, I thought to
myself on the way, Alberto being Alberto it wouldn't be at all
surprising if something unexpected had happened, if he'd de-
cided to stay longer in London. When I arrived at the studio
and went into the passageway, I saw the doors to the studio
itself and the bedroom were closed and assumed that Alberto
and Annette were still in London. One of the two studios at the
back of the passageway, the one with the telephone, was open.
I called out Diego's name. No answer. But then I heard the
sound of a door opening and saw Annette come out of the bed-
room in a bathrobe. "What are you doing here?" I exclaimed.
She told me that Alberto had fallen ill the day before they were
supposed to leave. So they hadn't gone, after all, to London. I
followed her into the bedroom. Alberto was lying on the un-
made bed, fully dressed, but with his shoes for once on a news-
paper instead of the sheets. He had been resting, and Annette
had been lying there with him. I sat on the wicker chair by the
table, while Annette lay down again beside Alberto and nestled
against his shoulder very affectionately, tenderly, and, as usual,
very girlishly. The father-daughter element of their relationship
is very pronounced. Alberto began to tell about his sickness,
how the fever had come on very suddenly. After a moment he
turned to Annette and said, "You can explain it, can't you?"
She said, "Of course not, do you think I'm that intelligent?" To
which he replied, "Not at all. I know you're crassly stupid. You
have no knowledge about anything whatever!" He laughed,

smiled at me, and Annette, lying against Alberto with her eyes
closed, giggled. He had his arm around her and was caressing
her throat and cheek. She began to talk about something—I
can't recall what—and suddenly Alberto pressed his hand over
her mouth. "You talk too much," he said. She pushed his hand
away and kept on talking. Alberto put his other hand over her
mouth, but smiling, joking, and she shared the joke. Then after
a moment he pressed his fingers lightly on her throat and said,
"Do you realize that you could be dead in five minutes?" I
said, "In two." Alberto said, "In one, if I wished." Annette
laughed. But Alberto insisted that it was possible. I objected
that Annette would undoubtedly resist and that people acquire
exceptional strength when they are attacked. But he was sure
he could kill her if he wanted to. Then, he said, he could plead
insanity and instead of being sent to prison he would be sent to
an asylum, where he'd have a pleasant, warm cell, be supplied
with canvas and clay, and could work in peace. The guards
and doctors, he said, would even pose for him. It would be an
ideal situation. Not only that, he said, but there would be tre-
mendous publicity and he could sell his work for higher prices.
That idea amused him greatly and is, in fact, very amusing
when one considers how indifferent he is to money. I pointed
out that there was a flaw in his scheme. "What is it?" he
asked. "Me!" I said. "Because I would have to do everything to
help Annette or become an accessory to the crime and as guilty
as you, or almost." That didn't give him a moment's pause. He
smiled and said, "Then I'd kill you, too!" But, I protested, then
he couldn't possibly claim insanity, because the motive for killing me would be so calculated. Oh, he said, he'd get away
with it by talking and talking and talking. That was the secret:
to keep talking. One mustn't, I said, seem too intelligent. On
the contrary, said Alberto, the more intelligent one seemed, the
better chance one had of convincing a court one was insane.
Besides, he went on, he could easily justify my murder by explaining that I was an undesirable element in society and that
he was ridding the community of it. That notion amused him
tremendously, and I thought it quite funny, too, but I didn't
ask him to explain, because I suppose in a way I agree with

him. We continued for a while to talk about Alberto's whimsical idea of a double murder. The idea of vast publicity seemed to appeal to him immensely, because he repeated several times that his picture would certainly be in all the papers. He asked me whether I thought it would. "Without doubt," I replied. "Of course," he said, "you'd get a lot of publicity, too." Not so much, I observed, being only one of the victims, and the less interesting of the two. Moreover, what would I care about the publicity, being dead? Well, it was true, Alberto conceded, that probably I wouldn't get so much publicity as he, because the murderer always gets more, but I would get some. The fact that I'd be dead didn't seem to trouble him in the least. For anyone who doesn't know Alberto, it's difficult to explain how conversations like this are both funny and interesting at the same time, because so much depends on his expression, far less on the tone of voice. Though the entire conversation was preposterous, both Annette and I and, above all, Alberto took it semiseriously as a credible eventuality. That didn't prevent me from laughing when Alberto said the whole business would make his prices go up. But Alberto himself only smiled, never laughed, and at any moment would, I'm sure, have been prepared to defend the plausibility of his ideas with an impressive display of ratiocination. Perhaps thinking of all that, Annette presently said that if she died before Alberto, she wanted him to have her buried in the Montparnasse Cemetery. "Certainly not," he said. "Why not?" she asked. "It's too expensive," Alberto replied, smiling. "I'll send you back to Geneva." Annette definitely did not want to be sent back to Geneva, and she insisted that the Montparnasse Cemetery was the place she wanted to be buried. Alberto presently mumbled some remark of which the exact phraseology was rather vague and the meaning as plain as a nail: that he would certainly die long before she would. And I remembered his remark of several days before: "Maybe there's a terrible death awaiting me."

I went to the studio a couple of days later to say good-bye to Alberto and Annette. He told me that he would be gone for three days only, while Annette would stay longer, visiting Isabel, the woman he had long ago loved, a real devourer of men. "And when I come back," he added, "we'll see about the famous portrait."

"We'll try to see," I said.

Alberto laughed and told me not to be impertinent to my elders.

To my surprise Alberto did return from London, as planned, on Friday the eleventh. I went to the studio the next day, and it was that afternoon at about four o'clock that he began to paint my portrait. I've already written a short book describing in detail what happened and what was said during those weeks of posing for Alberto, and it would be futile to repeat it here. I have wanted in this memoir to recount the details of my personal relations with the Giacometti family: Alberto, Diego, Annette, Bruno, Odette and Silvio.

While I was posing for Alberto, incidents and conversations naturally occurred which, for various reasons, I did not include in *A Giacometti Portrait*. As I still possess the pages written thirty-one years ago, I've found a few details it may be interesting or amusing to ventilate now.

On Thursday, September 17, for example, Alberto and I happened to speak of Matisse. A few days before, I had been in Diego's house and for some reason went upstairs to his bedroom, a very rare occurrence. Above Diego's bed I was astonished to see a good-sized painting by Matisse, a half-length portrait of a young blond woman, brilliantly rendered in orange and scarlet. Expressing my surprise to Diego, he replied, "It's a gift from Alberto." I mentioned this to him. "It's true," he said. "When I was in Basel not long ago, I went to Beyeler's gallery and I saw that painting. All of Matisse seemed to be in that one picture. It had been a very long time since I'd seen a work of art that I really longed to possess. So I proposed an exchange with Beyeler. He agreed and I took the painting. But I still haven't given him anything in return. When I got back here, I hung the Matisse in the studio. But after four days I could no longer stand to look at it."

"You could have hung it in the bedroom," I said.

"I couldn't stand it in there, either," Alberto said. "So I gave it to Diego and he's very happy with it."

Although my portrait had originally been meant to be finished in a single afternoon, Alberto had wanted to work on it longer, a desire I could hardly decline to accommodate. My original plan, however, had been to return to New York by mid-September. Still, I wanted to please Alberto, and the notion that I could at last be of some use to him gave me pleasure. But this did entail modification of my plans, which the two of us discussed. There was another consideration, too.

Not to have wondered whether Alberto would give me my portrait when finished, considering how prodigiously generous he had already been, would have been almost perverse. Of course I could not ask. And I knew that Alberto in his own way could be perverse. He was friendly with David Sylvester, had painted a fine portrait of him, but had not given it to him, selling it instead to Pierre Matisse. He had painted numerous portraits of Yanaihara but had given him none. What reason, then, had I to expect that my portrait might ever become my possession? Alberto, being nobody's fool, naturally assumed that I would long to own the portrait, and this assumption provided him with an excellent opportunity for teasing, one of his favorite diversions.

On September 19, when work on the painting had proceeded for a time, Alberto said, "You aren't going to leave for the Americas, are you?"

"No," I said.

"I'm going to make serious progress with the painting from now on, and I need you. But I'll pay you for posing."

"Are you crazy?" I exclaimed. "That's out of the question."

"Certainly I'll pay you," he insisted. "I have to pay you. I have to give you something, because the portrait will never be good enough to give you."

I said nothing.

He smiled slyly and after a moment added, "You must be thinking, 'What a dirty trick!' "

"No," I said, "that's not what I'm thinking at all. I'll tell you later what I'm thinking."

What I was thinking was that, no matter what became of the portrait, I had the rare, wonderful opportunity of expressing my admiration and affection for this great man by participating, however passively, in his creative struggle. And so in a very humble way I was able to make a token repayment for his generosity. But I knew that such sentiments were not of a kind that Alberto would like to hear openly expressed. He was truly modest to a fault. The teasing went on for some time, and I quite honestly had no idea whether the painting would one day be mine or not. Moreover, I was so caught up in the adventure of which it was a symbol that I came to care more about its satisfactory termination than about the question of its eventual owner.

On the score of gifts, in any case, I would have been more than churlish to feel malcontent, having received three small but beautiful sculptures since I'd begun to pose. Five or six years previously, Alberto had been invited to submit a design for sculpture for the plaza of the newly erected skyscraper housing the headquarters of the Chase Manhattan Bank in New York. He had first made three tiny sculptures as a maquette—a walking man, a standing woman, and a man's head. Later he made large versions of all three, but they were not accepted by the bank. The three tiny sculptures were in the studio, and one afternoon as I was admiring them while resting from the pose, Alberto said, "Do you want to do me a favor? Please take those things away. Looking at them is beginning to get on my nerves." I was happy to comply.

It should have been obvious that Alberto would never have teased me so much or so long if he had not intended from the first to make me a gift of the painting. On September 26, he said, "In any case, the picture will be yours. If it's bad, I'll give it to you with indifference. If it's good, I'll give it to you with pleasure."

Annette came in just as Alberto spoke those last sentences, and I said to her, "You heard that, Annette."

"Yes," said Alberto, "she's a witness."

"Yes, I heard it," she said. "But Yanaihara posed far more than James, and you never gave him a painting."

"If he wants a painting," said Alberto, "he can come back and pose some more."

I inquired about the condition of Caroline's leg, which she had injured and which was causing her considerable pain. Annette puffed out a breath of air and said, "It's nothing. She can walk, can't she?"

Laughing, I observed that that was a harsh criterion. Annette did not respond and shortly went into the bedroom to take a nap.

Alberto said, "She's indifferent to anything that doesn't concern her. If she had what Caroline has, she'd make an enormous fuss."

The next day when I arrived at the studio, Alberto was conferring with Pierre Matisse. I waited in the bedroom with Annette, who seemed in a peevish humor. So it was probably tactless to mention how pleased I was to receive my portrait as a gift. "You're very lucky," she said. "What are you going to do with it?"

"Well, I'm certainly not going to sell it."

"You'd better not," Annette said sourly. "Alberto would be very displeased if you did. It always makes him angry if people sell his gifts."

I didn't tell her that I had already done so and that Alberto knew it. At that moment, for the first time, it occurred to me that Annette must be jealous of my relationship—I couldn't call it friendship—with her husband. The thought stirred in me feelings of pity for her, which I'm sure would have been unwelcome if expressed.

Alberto came into the bedroom then. "Pierre's taking fifty-eight drawings," he said. "He's going to exhibit them in November. Drawings of all periods. I only had one Lord left, and he wanted it, but I held on to it. Maybe, I thought, Lord himself might like to have it."

"I'm embarrassed to confess that I would," I said.

Annette put on her raincoat and went out the door, saying, "I'm going to the Samaritaine to buy some towels."

Alberto sighed. "I often think of the old days when everything was serene, when Diego, Annette, and I used to eat together at Les Tamaris. You remember Les Tamaris. It was closed seven or eight years ago. Now everything is changed. It all began with Yanaihara. I didn't realize it at the time. But even foreknowledge doesn't necessarily alter the course of events. People can change things only by changing themselves. I can't say how much I regret that I no longer have the same sort of rapport with Diego and Annette. They both despise Caroline. We used to go to the Parc Montsouris for dinner, too. Come, let's work a little now."

Alberto had decided to send my portrait to the Carnegie Institute in Pittsburgh, because he'd been asked to exhibit a painting there and he wanted to show the very latest thing he'd done. It would have to be shipped, still wet, on October 2, and consequently the first, a Thursday, was the last day I posed. I was to leave the following afternoon. Alberto insisted on accompanying me to the airport. En route in the taxi he explained that when the Pittsburgh exhibition was finished in January, the painting would be sent to New York to Pierre Matisse, who would turn it over to me. And what, I asked, would he wish me ultimately to do with it, the most important gift he had ever made me? Why, just enjoy possessing it, he said, if possible. What I did with it, he added, concerned me alone, because it was my possession and my portrait. I could give it away or sell it or bequeath it to some museum. Anyway, he would be dead and would never know. However, he said that it would sadden him if the picture were to be destroyed, because he had enjoyed working on it, it had taught him something, and, above all, he liked the fact that the two of us would remain united on that canvas long after both were dead.

The very first thing I did when arriving in New York was to sit down and write up an account of all that had happened while I posed for Alberto. I had at that time a close friend named Wilder Green, a Giacometti enthusiast and collector, also a curator at the Museum of Modern Art, where, as it happened, a large Giacometti retrospective exhibition was even then being planned to open in June 1965. I showed Wilder my text about the portrait, which he found sufficiently interesting to show in turn to the director of publications at the museum, who proposed to publish it as a small booklet to be distributed along with the exhibition catalog. Not knowing what Alberto would think of this proposition, and aware that he could not read English, I turned for advice to Pierre Matisse.

For a quarter of a century after the war, I constantly visited the art galleries in New York, Paris, and London. Those I visited most frequently in New York were the galleries of Curt Valentin, Eugene Thaw, and Pierre Matisse, all three of whom became friends. Pierre was the least approachable, a cold, secretive, suspicious man, who in fact had no close friends at all. But I did become very friendly with his wife, Patricia, who also worked in the gallery, a lively, eccentric, entertaining woman, who gave very good parties and drank far too much. My friendship with her led me to see a good deal of Pierre. He also liked my text but felt that a few details had better be left out for discretion's sake. These he read in French to Alberto over the telephone, and they decided together what should be published and what deleted. Pierre at the same time was planning to exhibit in November the fifty-eight drawings he had bought from Alberto and asked me to write a preface for the catalog. I did.

The retrospective exhibition at the Museum of Modern Art in New York was an important one. One hundred and forty sculptures, paintings, and drawings of all periods were shown, including my portrait, which had been delivered to me as Alberto had planned. The public was impressed. Crowds were considerable. Critical comment in the press was enthusiastic. A second, and even larger, retrospective exhibition, arranged by David Sylvester, was taking place at the same time at the Tate Gallery in London. Alberto visited it twice. His aversion to travel and his refusal ever to go up in an airplane being well known, nobody expected him to come to New York. So surprise was considerable when he announced in September that he would arrive to see the exhibition exactly four days before it closed. Pierre Matisse made all the arrangements. He and Patricia would accompany Alberto and Annette on the outward voyage, aboard the *Queen Elizabeth*, arriving in New York on October 6, while the artist and his wife would sail homeward together just eight days later on the *France*. All this I learned from Patricia, telephoning from Cap-Ferrat.

On the evening of their arrival I went to the Matisses' apartment on East Ninety-fourth Street, where they were lavishly installed on the top three floors of a large townhouse. I had last seen Alberto exactly one year before. When he came into the library, I was shocked. He was haggard and gaunt, and his very uncharacteristic blue suit hung on him as if only a skeleton were beneath. Still, he was as lively as ever. His first words to me were, "From now on I'm going to have to watch what I say in your presence. If I'd known you were writing everything down, I might have been a little more reticent."

"But didn't you once tell me," I protested, "that writers are supposed to write? And if they are serious about it, they write down everything that seems important, plus a good deal that isn't. Besides, there are quite a lot of people who like the book."

"That's what Pierre says, so I guess it must be all right, after all."

"I hope you'll be able to read it someday."

"Oh, I'd be ashamed to see what idiotic things I'm capable of saying."

The next afternoon he, Annette, and I visited the exhibition, where the director and a number of curators were on hand to welcome him. He looked at every single sculpture, painting, and drawing with painstaking scrutiny, seeming surprised, as if he had never seen any of them before. There was a museum photographer present who took many photographs, including one, to my great pleasure, of Alberto and me standing in front of my portrait. After gazing at it for a number of minutes, he said, "We made an opening. But it could be larger. You'll come back and pose again, won't you?"

"Of course I will," I said.

"But all the rest is very disappointing," he sighed. "How could I have done so poorly? I was sincere, you know. Let's go and have a drink somewhere."

It was raining outside. We went to the St. Regis bar, which was almost empty at five o'clock, and had a drink while Alberto bemoaned the inadequacy of his work. However, he said, "I can do better. I know I can do better."

"Oh, Alberto," said Annette. "You know perfectly well how good it is."

"I don't even know my name," said Alberto. "And what does it matter? Pretty soon there won't be anybody to call by my name anyway."

Pierre Matisse did not seem eager to guide Alberto and Annette around New York. Patricia took Annette in hand with obvious reluctance, and I was left to visit the city, its monuments and museums, alone with Alberto. We went to the Metropolitan and the Frick, but he hurried through both like a man in a frantic race against the hour of closing. "I'm done with museums," he said. When I tried to have him pause before Rembrandt's great self-portrait at the Frick, one of mankind's supreme masterpieces, he said, "I'm on bad terms with Rembrandt for the moment." But Goya's great painting *The Forge* held his attention.

The only thing in the city to excite him was the Chase Manhattan Plaza, where as yet no sculpture had been selected to stand before the sheer precipice of the skyscraper. He was gripped by the notion that he might still produce something capable of holding its own before that overwhelming façade. We visited the plaza several times, once in the middle of the night, when not a soul was abroad in the Financial District, and Alberto directed Annette and me to stand here and there on the broad, empty plaza in order to try to gauge what proportions a sculpture might require in order to be most effective. As soon as he returned to Paris, he said, he would execute a large figure, larger than any he had ever produced before, and maybe it would do.

There were receptions and dinner parties. At the museum a group of contemporary artists was invited to meet him. It was an ironic occasion. All of those present seemed in awe of him, but none of them appeared to realize that he represented a tradition which they possessed neither the vision nor the character to perpetuate. Alberto understood only too well. Later he said, "It was a bit funereal, wasn't it?" After a week Alberto had obviously seen enough of the New World. Annette, on the other hand, was delighted by the city, its luxurious shops and restaurants, and, above all, by the warm, sincere deference paid to the wife of the great artist. She might have enjoyed a longer visit, but Alberto wanted to go home. Though he had brought with him a portfolio of drawing paper, he made only one drawing while in New York, a portrait of Pierre asleep sketched in the library one night as the three of us had lingered late over our brandy.

So Alberto and Annette departed aboard the *France* as planned, on Thursday, October 14. I arrived in Paris the following Sunday to stay for a fortnight before traveling on to Russia via Denmark, Sweden, and Finland. Several times I saw Alberto, Diego, and Annette, whose ill humor had resumed as soon as her husband was reunited with Caroline. The scenes became more and more offensive and violent. Annette even went so far as to mock her husband's emaciated and sallow physical appearance. He nicknamed her The Sound and the Fury.

I was absent on my travels for almost a month, returning to Paris toward the end of November. When I went to the rue Hippolyte, I was again upset by Alberto's appearance. He looked even more unwell than in New York. Though he had never sought praise or honors, they had come to him in recent years, and he had reluctantly accepted an honorary doctorate from the University of Bern to be awarded on November 27, a Saturday. He didn't feel well and hesitated to go, but was characteristically determined to do so anyway because he had contracted a responsibility toward those who wished to honor him. Putting a few things into a suitcase, he went off to take the night train.

In the railway station at Bern, he suffered a heart attack, and though he didn't diagnose it as such, he realized that he was unwell. But the attack passed and he went through with the ceremony and following banquet. What he feared, however, was that the pain he had felt signified a recurrence of the cancer for which he had undergone an operation in 1963. Back in Paris, he decided to go to the Cantonal Hospital in Chur, Switzerland, not far from Zurich, where a complete examination could be made by doctors he trusted. Diego, Annette, and I urged him to consult a doctor in Paris immediately. After much grumbling, he agreed, and an urgent appointment was made with an eminent cardiologist. I delivered him, protesting all the way, to the doctor's door in the rue du Bac.

The next day, sitting on the edge of his unmade bed, smoking a cigarette, of course, he said that the doctor had found no cause for worry. He suffered from chronic bronchitis, but that was news to no one. It appeared that there was an abnormal enlargement of the heart. Nothing to worry about, he insisted. Then, having fallen silent for a moment, he added, "It would bother me a lot to die right now."

"It's absurd to talk that way," I protested.

"Why?" said Alberto. "It's not absurd at all. I still have everything to get done."

He decided to leave for Switzerland three days later, on Sunday, December 5. By a coincidence I had made reservations to fly to New York on that same day. I was worried, and so was Diego. But not Annette. "After all," she said, "Alberto is only sixty-four. If he takes better care of himself, he'll live for a long time still."

On the last Saturday afternoon, I went with Alberto to the artsupply shop of Maurice Lefebvre-Foinet, where he had for decades

purchased all his materials. He bought a few things to take with
him to Switzerland, then we returned by taxi to the studio, passing
along the street that cuts through the Montparnasse Cemetery. Alberto pounded on his knee with a fist. "It seems impossible to do
it," he cried.

"What?" I asked.

"To make a head as I see it. It seems impossible to do it. Between
now and tomorrow, though, I've got to manage."

But he didn't, of course. He sat up late that night in Montparnasse with Caroline and a few other friends. The next day both of
us left Paris.

Thanks to Patricia, news from the Cantonal Hospital in Chur
reached me regularly in New York. There seemed nothing to worry
about. After a week of rest, treatment, proper food, and regular
hours, Alberto appeared very like his usual self. He got out of bed,
walked around the hospital corridors, and telephoned family and
friends, assuring them that in no time he would be back in Paris.
Bruno and Odette, Diego, and Caroline visited the patient and were
encouraged. Even Annette traveled to Chur despite her resentment
of Caroline's visit. But she was obliged to stay on in the dull, cold
Swiss town because Alberto's doctor, a well-known physician named
N. G. Markoff, did not consider Giacometti sufficiently fit to be
discharged. Not present in Chur or even in Europe, I naturally didn't
know what was happening from day to day in the hospital. But I
later learned in detail from all the persons—except Alberto—who
had been there.

A few days before Christmas, Alberto's condition abruptly took
a turn for the worse. His circulation became troubled and the heart
muscle functioned with increasing difficulty, causing serious conges-
tion of the liver. As yet, however, there seemed no cause for alarm.
Alberto kept on telephoning Bruno, Diego, Caroline, Patricia, all of
them reassured by the familiar, throaty voice saying there was no
cause to worry.

But there was. Early in the new year the patient's condition
deteriorated further. Weak and pale, he had lost twenty pounds since
entering the hospital less than a month before. He began to worry.
He telephoned Bruno, asking for help to put his affairs in order,
though he did not explain in what order he desired to put them. He

told Dr. Markoff that it was imperative he travel to Paris for a week, a week only, in order to settle his affairs. He called Pierre Matisse, then with Patricia at his villa on Cap-Ferrat, imploring him to come to Switzerland to assist in making urgent arrangements. "I don't want Annette to touch my things," he told Pierre. "I don't want her to have anything to do with my things."

Now, however, it was too late. Dr. Markoff told the patient that his condition could not permit travel. Alberto had been asked years before to make the arrangements that any sensible person with property of value would make. He had neglected to do so.

On Tuesday, January 11, in the early evening, Alberto looked up from his bed and saw standing round it Diego, Bruno, Odette, Annette, and Caroline. "You're all here," he murmured. "That means I'm going to die." Toward seven o'clock he fell into a coma. Three hours later he lay dead. His heart had failed.

2

In the early morning of the following day I was awakened by the ring of the telephone. It was my friend Wilder Green, calling from the Museum of Modern Art to deliver as thoughtfully as possible the bad news. The last time I'd seen Alberto, thirty-eight days before, he had seemed tired, but that was how he always seemed—on the verge of squandering his last centime of vitality and yet, for this very reason, prepared to expend himself beyond his means in the hope of acquiring in the end the certainty that his investment would be well repaid by posterity. And now the time to start the reckoning had come. It never occurred to me then that I would have any part in the computation.

That gray and chilly day, New York at its wintry worst, fell into my existence with an impact of which even Alberto, despite his almost godlike clairvoyance, could not have foreseen the consequences. I felt bereft, of course, aware that I would probably never again be on familiar terms with a man of true greatness and that the familiarity itself had been supremely worthwhile because that man had been so intimate with the truth. Now that he was gone, whom could I believe in when it came to knowing what was great and right? And yet, while I ambled around the ugly side streets, my sense of loss seemed strangely to have something in common with the sense of thrilling but also frightening good luck that went with having known him. I didn't dwell on this at the time, being too absorbed by the unwarranted distinction of bereavement. But I think of it now, and with more cause, which will be apparent as my story progresses. Indeed, I've often wondered whether Alberto's clairvoyance may not have been more godlike than anyone could have guessed.

To attend or not to attend his funeral was a question I toyed with during that dismal afternoon. Nobody had suggested that my presence would be welcome, let alone appropriate, but presumption was an ingredient of which I had plenty, and this later turned out to be all to the good. If I had known what passions had presided over the final hours of the dying artist—and which were greatly exacerbated by his instantaneous transition into posthumous fame—even I would have probably decided that the best homage I could hope to offer him would be to remain alone with my keen remembrance of the heroic simplicity and indefatigable moral vigilance by which he had lived, and by which, having made his work in the image of his life, he would survive. In the circumstances, anyway, I hardly had the money to fly to Switzerland on the spur of the moment. Moreover, after the vanity of vicarious distinction succumbed to common sense, I saw how little entitled I would have been to pay respects to one so greatly deserving of them. Relatives, friends, eminent representatives of government, those who had helped make the dead man's fortune and reputation were the ones who could, and should, celebrate with befitting dignity his departure from the world.

Before venturing further into the problematic matter of what it was like to live after Alberto, while living at the same time imaginatively with him and for him, I ought to stress yet again that our acquaintance was never a close friendship. He allowed a semblance of intimacy to develop between us, I think, because intimacy offered the most plentiful provision for interest, and Alberto saw, and sought, in everyone an interest so vital that intimacy was virtually beside the point. "You must understand," he once told me, "that I'm just as interested in someone I've known for ten minutes as in someone

I've known for ten years." And maybe the newer acquaintance provided even more absorbing inducements. Alberto's vision rendered
every person, like every thing, unique, and that is why he never had
to step outside his studio to explore the fascination of the universe.
Alberto knew many, many remarkable men—including Picasso,
Sartre, Stravinsky, Balthus, Beckett, Genet, and Francis Bacon, to
name only the more famous—but none of them changed his life.
They added interest to the itinerary without easing or influencing
it. The only persons to do that, and to do it beyond compare until
the end, were the artist's mother and brothers, Diego and Bruno,
to a lesser extent his wife, and in the end his mistress, Caroline. I
couldn't say who had truly been Alberto's friends. Anyway, I was
not one of them. Still, he prodigiously befriended me by allowing
me to look closely at his life and by sometimes looking at me closely
enough to make Giacomettis that were my likeness. And then,
though I never even knew that I had had them, my deepest dreams
began to come true because of him when he was no longer present
to personify them. I still don't know how true, of course, such dreams
can become, or how deep in the first place they really were, but
Alberto's importance in my life became greater and greater after his
death, as if to emphasize the unimportance that was mine while he
lived.

In the snowbound town of Chur on that freezing Wednesday
morning, those who had stood around Alberto's deathbed the night
before awoke to a reality transformed by his absence. The one for
whom the transformation meant most was Diego, but he possessed
the strength of character of a Giacometti; it enabled him to build
upon bereavement a transfiguration of the self and find fulfillment
unobtainable while his brother lived. Annette, the artist's widow,
also entered upon an existence utterly altered by his death, because
the change brought with it overnight both a binding responsibility
and a very liberal opportunity. Bruno Giacometti, the youngest
brother, and his wife, Odette, bound though they were to Alberto
by a lifetime of undisturbed affection and shared experience, never
having been entirely incorporated into his artistic life, did not suffer
from its cessation to a comparable extent. Caroline, however, the
last mistress of the deceased artist and his principal model during
the final period, had been incorporated so completely, it seems safe

to say, that her loss would be the very thing most essential to her in years to come.

It was mid-June before I returned again to Paris, five months almost to the day after Alberto's death. My first thought was to see Diego. I called the studio but there was no answer, so I went to the rue Hippolyte in the afternoon of the day following my arrival. Diego was in his studio, working on a small object in plaster. As the door stood open, I walked in and said hello. Turning, he gazed at me intently—almost, I felt, as if I were a stranger—but he did not speak. That summer afternoon in his dusty studio his countenance bore the mark of a solitude and melancholy more profound than any I've ever observed, save that of my mother standing at the bedside of my dead father. I remained in the studio for fifteen or twenty minutes. It seemed a very long time. Finally I said, "I just wanted to stop and say hello." Diego did not answer or look in my direction, and I realized that the kindest thing I could do would be to leave him in peace.

Annette's response was very different. When I called a couple of days later, she at once suggested that we have lunch together. I went to her apartment at about noon. If anything, the reigning clutter was more general than when I'd been there last. We had a glass of vermouth before going downstairs to the restaurant. It never would have occurred to me to ask her for an account of Alberto's last days and death. To her, however, it obviously was important to relate all those unhappy details. I can't think why. Perhaps possession of so much intimate information reinforced her sense of herself in some obscure way. In any case, she told me a great deal about those days and hours at the Cantonal Hospital, including even details not flattering to herself, such as Dr. Markoff's refusal to speak to her when he called the family to his office to tell them that the end was near, the fight with Caroline in the corridor, and Diego's forcefully preventing her from touching Alberto's hand immediately after his death. Yes, there had been unpleasant scenes, but everybody knew how impossible Alberto could be, and it was deeply mortifying to his wife to have been banished from the room so that he could spend the last afternoon of his life with a prostitute. I couldn't help feeling a certain sympathy for her even as I remembered the foolish, furious behavior frequently inflicted upon a man whose presence had made the world so much more wonderful. During lunch Annette told me what I had already learned from Patricia: that Alberto had died intestate, which meant that she was the principal heir. Did she know, I wondered, that her husband had told Pierre he didn't want Annette to have anything to do with his things? But now she was to have everything to do with them. Diego, Bruno, and Silvio, the son of Alberto's deceased sister, would also receive a small share, something like one sixteenth each. But first there would have to be an inventory. And then there were a lot of things in Switzerland, including houses and land. It would all be very complicated, and there were obviously bad feelings on the part of the Giacomettis. But there was nothing she could do about that, was there? They had not shown her much consideration while Alberto was alive. Well, now that he was gone, now that she was in charge of everything, nobody need expect that she would be passing out gifts. A curator from the Tate Gallery had come to see her and said that Alberto had promised to give the Tate a certain bronze figure. (I happened to know that this was true, because I was with Alberto during his last afternoon in Paris, and had heard him tell Lefebvre-Foinet which bronze he wished sent to the museum in London.) But Annette had said to the curator, "That may be so. I know nothing about it. And Alberto isn't here to give away anything, is he?" People would learn that she had the last word. As the artist's widow she had inherited not only the great majority of his things, but also, and even more important, the moral right—the crucial *droit moral*—to determine how the estate should be administered, what plaster casts should be cast in bronze in editions of how many, what paintings and drawings were genuine, which were not and could therefore be seized by the police, what use could be made of the copyright on Alberto's works, and what exhibitions of them might benefit from her cooperation. Alberto had unwittingly bequeathed to her not only possession of his things but great power over their spiritual significance. And she would exercise that power at her sole discretion.

In the spring of 1968, weary of New York's violence, deterioration, and ever more cloying ugliness, I gave up my apartment there and rented from a distant cousin a large, handsome eighteenth-century house on a hilltop near Old Lyme, Connecticut. In this beautiful, peaceful spot I spent a year and a half, working hard on unpublishable pieces of writing. I corresponded regularly with friends in France and went often to New York, where I usually saw Patricia and Pierre and sometimes stayed overnight in their large apartment. One evening while I was there, awaiting the start of a dinner party, Patricia asked me to accompany her to the lower floor to her bedroom to see a group of new gold necklaces she had laid out. It was the first, and only, time I ever set foot in their bedroom, as the living room, library, dining room, bar, and guest rooms were all on the two upper floors. The gold necklaces, of which Patricia possessed many, were neatly arranged on a low table to the right of the large bed. I admired them, and indeed they were exquisite examples of the goldsmith's art, but I was naturally far more interested to see what hung on the walls. And what was my amazement to discover hanging immediately above the bedside table a drawing by Alberto which I recognized instantly as the superb portrait of Pierre's father which had mysteriously disappeared from the studio nearly fifteen years before. My surprise was so great that I barely noticed the wonderful watercolors by Matisse and other rare works of art in the room. I made some exclamation to Patricia, but she quickly held her finger to her lips. It had been impulsive of her to bring me down here, she said. Pierre never allowed strangers to see their bedroom. And it was very regrettable that I had seen this drawing. Pierre's possession of it was a deep secret which on no account should be revealed to anyone. I did not insist. I spoke of the drawing to no one. To have seen it, however, made the unthinkable almost thinkable, and the mystery seemed more entire than ever.

Later that spring I learned that an important retrospective exhibition of Alberto's work was scheduled for that autumn at the Orangerie in Paris, so I planned to go abroad in November to see it.

One evening in early May the Latin Quarter was suddenly and unexpectedly convulsed by a student riot. And it was a melee that meant business. Automobiles were overturned and set afire, barricades thrown up, and paving stones hurled at the riot police, who responded with tear gas and running attacks with truncheons. This chaotic disturbance was originally motivated by student discontent with the regulations governing the organization of their studies. And it might have amounted to no more than that, exhausting itself in a day or two, had it not been for the eloquent exhortations to anarchy of a few fanatic hotheads who perceived in this excitement an opportunity to overthrow a social structure which they condemned as corrupt and obsolete. Their inflammatory calls to action and appeals to idealistic principle proved contagious, and the riots continued day after day, causing much damage and unprecedented turmoil, paralyzing much of France for almost a month. This was highly embarrassing to the government, which appeared powerless to prevent the duration of widespread anarchy. The appearance was an appearance only, however, for the governmental semblance of indecision was motivated mainly by a determination to avoid serious casualties. The riots were mostly a tumult of the young and ingenuous, but many grown-ups fancied that the dawn of a new order needed their counsel, while others thought that a display of sympathy for the hijinks of the students would be exciting. Annette was one of these. Patricia told me that she received telephone calls almost daily from the rue Mazarine relating the thrills and risks which Annette was sharing with Michel Leiris, their marches together up the rue Soufflot at two o'clock in the morning, helping to chop down the trees that lined the boulevard Saint-Michel and to build barricades in the street that led to the Odéon Theater.

Then in June, when the thrills of May were done for, came the coup de grace. Annette canceled the Orangerie exhibition. Pierre and Patricia were furious, having already gone to much trouble to assist in the multiple arrangements necessary. Patricia gave me a photocopy of the clipping from *Le Monde*.

THE WIDOW OF GIACOMETTI
OPPOSES THE RETROSPECTIVE EXHIBITION
OF THE SCULPTOR'S WORKS

Madame Annette Giacometti, widow of the sculptor, has recently addressed to Monsieur Pierre Moinot, director of arts and letters, the following letter:

"Alberto Giacometti would certainly not have accepted that an official exhibition of his works take place under the present circumstances: police repression against students and workers, expulsion of foreigners and notably of artists.

"I therefore am formally opposed to the exhibition planned for next

October at the Orangerie museum, and suspend immediately the work I had undertaken in order to prepare that presentation."

It was audacious and provocative cultural intimidation reminiscent of the denunciations so beloved by the Surrealists in the heady, long-past days of their ascendancy. I couldn't help wondering whether Annette had written it herself. Headstrong as she was, would she have had the temerity so categorically to state what her dead husband would or would not have accepted under whatever circumstances? And then there was the moral issue of presuming to bring back someone from the hereafter to pass judgment in the present. Alberto had always been on the side of compassion and forgiveness. God knows Annette had good cause to be mindful of that.

Annette had never possessed a mentality capable of logical thought. When I first knew her, she was not yet thirty, and her feckless, vivacious opinions had a certain charm. Now she was forty-five, determined to be taken seriously. Patricia said, "That girl is going to make a lot of trouble for a lot of people. It's a bore, because Pierre has got to get along with her. But not I."

Still, for old times' sake, and—who knows?—perhaps with a blink toward the future, I didn't want to sever entirely my relations with Annette. So when I went to Paris at the end of November, I called her. As usual, she suggested that we have lunch. Her apartment had ceased to be a clutter and become an outright mess. I thought of the old adage intimating that the organization of a person's dwelling accurately reflects the constitution of his personality. We had a drink. She was still excited by the events of six months earlier and couldn't wait to talk about them. It was as if nothing in her life could compare in wonder, fulfillment, and delight with those chaotic weeks. And yet she had spent more than two decades with one of the most remarkable men of the century.

Michel Leiris, she said, had brought her into the ranks of the rioters. Without his daring and encouragement she probably would have missed the most momentous event since the Liberation, with which it had so much in common. She and Michel had marched together night after night, chanting the students' slogans and songs, arm in arm with them, braving tear gas and truncheons. Michel was fearless, and it is a fact that during the early Surrealist years he was, though slight in stature, the most bellicose of the band. Michel was the only one of Alberto's old friends who had shown her kindness and understanding after Alberto's death. There had been moments, she said, when she didn't know what she might have done had it not been for Michel. Michel, Michel, Michel. It struck me that her admiration and gratitude were as excessive as her enthusiasm for the riotous month of May, which, after all, had virtually no subsequent effect on life in France.

During lunch she complained about the complexity of settling Alberto's estate, a business still unfinished more than two years after his death. The delay, she said, was largely due to the vindictive animosity of Diego, Bruno, and Silvio, who hated her and were jealous because she had inherited almost everything. That seemed to me, in the case of Diego, at least, very unlikely, but I let her talk on. There was now an almost-hysterical sharpness to her locution which had never been noticeable before. After lunch she asked me to come back upstairs to meet the young woman who was helping her prepare the catalogue raisonné of Alberto's works. She proved to be American, fluent in French, an attractive and good-natured girl named Julie Burns. I reflected that she had an intimidating task before her. The preparation of a catalogue raisonné requires intimate knowledge of an artist's life and work, infinite patience and politeness, political sensitivity of a rare distinction, and dogged perseverance over a period likely to last half a lifetime. Annette had endured her stint at the Musée de l'Homme for less than a year, and listing African headrests neatly arranged in a museum's cellar was child's play compared to collation of works often unrecorded and scattered across half the world. I didn't consider the Giacometti catalogue raisonné a publication apt to appear in the foreseeable future, and still don't.

I went to see Diego also, of course. He was a little more forthcoming than before, but not much. He asked a few conventional questions, and I made conventional replies, but the miasma of melancholy was still pronounced. However, I was happily impressed by the beauty, whimsy, and originality of the bronze furniture he was making; there was nothing melancholy about it.

It was in February of the following year, 1969, when I had

returned to the United States, that a fateful and unpredictable meeting took place. For fifteen years I had had a literary agent, a likable, long-suffering man whose professional efforts on my behalf had brought him negligible satisfaction or profit. But he was patient. He called me one day in Connecticut and told me that he'd met an editor who wished to commission a biography of Alberto Giacometti. This editor, by his own admission, knew little about art and nothing whatever about Giacometti. But he had seen photographs of Alberto and felt that any man with such a remarkable face must have lived a remarkable life, which, if someone suitable could be found to tell the story, might make a good biography and even a good book. My agent told the editor that he represented just the person for the job. He asked me to come to New York and meet with the editor. I agreed. Now, anybody acquainted with Alberto at all knew very well that he had been, indeed, a very remarkable man and that the story of his life would, if capably related, be remarkable, too. Many of Alberto's friends had been writers, several of them celebrated, but since his death not one had come forward to relate his life. Maybe the awareness of subject matter so remarkable was intimidating, or perhaps they felt that their craving for the world's attention could best be served by creations which owed nothing to the creativity of another man. In any event, I was a writer, I had known Giacometti, and my sole literary production of any consequence till then had been the short book describing his painting of my portrait. So I airily agreed to give the biography a try, and the editor proved willing to take a modest flier on a writer pushing fifty whose principal claim to fame was that he possessed none.

It was with reckless disregard to probabilities that I undertook to write the biography of Alberto Giacometti. When asked by the editor how long the task would take, I said, "Two or three years." He said, "Let's agree on five."

To relate the life history of any man is a virtually insurmountable challenge. Should the man have been a great one, then the challenge would seem to surpass the viable limits of probability. However, I was swayed by my admiration for Alberto and my conviction that he had lived a heroic life which, if related effectively, would interest and inspire anyone who cared about the values of civilization. Besides, I had an advantage: having known Alberto personally and witnessed various aspects of his life, I knew most of the people it would be necessary for me to meet in order to learn more about him, and most of them would know who I was. Furthermore, they were still living, an invaluable asset for a biographer. Nothing can replace the direct testimony of a witness, because even from inaccuracy and prejudice there is much to be learned if witnesses are numerous. And they were. But people die, as Alberto had unhappily demonstrated. If his biography were to be written at all, it would best be done before indispensable witnesses were to join him in the hereafter.

My first thoughts were naturally for Diego and Annette, and I had a pretty good idea what response I could expect from each to a letter broaching the prospect of Alberto's biography. Nor was I mistaken.

From Annette's rambling reply I quote only the relevant paragraph.

As to the biography of Alberto: well, James, I shall ask you to wait. It is clearly premature and out of the question that I be concerned with this for the time being. I speak frankly: Alberto's life is still too close to my own for me to agree to speak of it to anyone at all. A little SILENCE is imperative and does one good. Yes.

From Diego:

Paris, March 10, 1969

My dear Lord,

Forgive me for replying only today to your nice letter written almost a month ago. How time passes!

I have already told you that I think as you do that it would be a very good thing if you undertake to write a biography of Alberto, and of course while Alberto's friends are still here.

For my part, it goes without saying that I will give you all my help and also all my enthusiasm for your efforts.

Discuss it with Pierre—and let me hear from you from time to time.

> Yours very affectionately,
> Diego

Annette presently changed her mind about Alberto's certainty as to the acceptability of an official exhibition of his work and made it known that she was no longer formally opposed to the Orangerie exhibition. Indeed, she was all for it and intended to make every aspect of its preparation her personal business. It would open on October 24, 1969, and close on January 12, 1970. I decided to leave for Paris only on January 6. The first person I went to see the day after my arrival was Diego. I found him seated at a desk in the downstairs room of the little house in the rue du Moulin-Vert purchased by Alberto ten years before. There was no sign now of the oppressive melancholy so pronounced during previous visits. He seemed cheerful and lively. After having chatted about one thing and another, Pierre and Patricia, and our own recent doings, I mentioned the biography and said, "I feel that this book will be about you and for you in a way almost as much as for and about Alberto."

"Well, that's normal," he said. "After all, we did everything together for over forty years." This was said in the simplest imaginable way. No false pride, aggressive ego, or desire to aggrandize his role.

I outlined my feelings about the work before *us* and emphasized that it would have to be a collaboration. He accepted that with perfect modesty. The prospect of becoming closer to Diego by learning about his life was deeply pleasing. There was something endearing about him, a purity and decency, that was quite irresistible.

"I suppose," I said, "that there will be people with whom I'll have difficulties in preparing this work, people who for some reason won't be disposed to help, who won't want the truth to be told, even that part of the truth it would be important to tell."

Diego shrugged. "Aren't you on good terms with Annette?" he asked.

I laughed. He had understood at once. "Yes," I said. "I called her, but she said she was very busy."

"Oh, sure," Diego murmured, shaking his head. "She's busy.

She's always very busy. Since, in any case, it takes her ten times longer than anybody else to do the least thing, she's always very busy."

We talked about the exhibition at the Orangerie, and Diego immediately said, "Why didn't you lend your portrait?"

"I wasn't asked," I said. "I wasn't asked for that or for anything else, and, as you know, I have quite a lot of Alberto's things."

"I wasn't asked, either," Diego said. "I wasn't even consulted until four days before the opening when Jean Leymarie came to me almost in tears and begged me to come to the Orangerie and help with the installation. Annette was driving him insane, he said. She has no idea how to exhibit sculpture but insisted on making all the decisions. The pedestals were all wrong, and only four days left to make things right. We did what we could while she sulked in a corner and smoked cigarettes with her boyfriend."

The next day I went to the Orangerie. To my astonishment and embarrassment, as I entered the first gallery my eyes filled with tears. I went to the window overlooking the Seine and stood there for several minutes, drying my eyes with a handkerchief, overcome by the immediacy and violence of my reaction. Having mastered it, I went into a farther gallery, looking at the sculptures and paintings, many of which I knew, with a passionate sense of identification. Turning, I suddenly saw Annette with two other people, one of whom I recognized at once as Michel Leiris. I went to her quickly and kissed her impulsively on both cheeks, an attention I was instantly aware she did not welcome. "I'm so moved, Annette, I don't know what to do," I said.

She didn't know what to do, either, not having expected me to take her unawares, but made the best of it by introducing me to Leiris, who murmured a vague acknowledgment of having met me before and gave me a rigid, self-conscious handshake. The other person was a tall, slim, swarthy man named Dahan, whose presence went unexplained. All in all, Annette was perfectly agreeable, especially, I noted, after Leiris left us. She asked my opinion of the installation of the exhibition, which I dutifully praised. I told her I'd call her the following week to fix a date for meeting. "Good," she said, "because I'm going to be so busy taking all of this down," as if she would have to pack up every sculpture and remove from the walls each picture with her own hands.

Leaving Annette, I walked back through the galleries, moved beyond words and even beyond awareness, till I came to some chairs in an alcove, where I sat down to write in my notebook. While writing, I glanced up and there suddenly came toward me the obese, bearded, somber figure of David Sylvester. He sat down beside me. I was very glad to see him, because I had felt from the first that he would be a natural and excellent biographer for Alberto and that if he wished to do the job I would withdraw. Here was my opportunity to ask. In addition to Sylvester, there was one other person better qualified than I to write Alberto's biography, and I meant to ask him, too, whether he might contemplate doing so. This was Louis Clayeux's assistant at the Galerie Maeght, a young poet named Jacques Dupin, who had already published a fine critical study of Giacometti's work. When I told Sylvester that I was more or less committed to writing Alberto's biography, he said, "That's impossible."

"Why?" I asked.

"Because you can't tell the truth," he replied.

"Maybe not the total truth," I admitted. "But, anyway, nobody can do that. Alberto himself would have been the first to say so. But one can tell enough of the truth to be true to life. I wanted to ask whether you might consider doing the job, because I won't try it if you want to. You'd do it much better than I."

"I wouldn't dream of trying it," said Sylvester. "But I won't stand in your way. If I can help, I will. There's nothing I wouldn't do to keep faith with Alberto. And with Diego, too."

That assurance gave me courage. Two days later I met with Jacques Dupin and asked him the same question I'd asked Sylvester. He replied that he was too busy with other work to attempt such a complex task and that he didn't envy me all the labor it would entail. Of which, he added, I had no inkling. He also promised that he would do all he could to help me and thus to demonstrate his veneration for Alberto's uncompromising commitment to truth.

Dupin was right, in any case, on the score of labor. I had no inkling of its nature or extent. And probably that was just as well, because I set about my business unafraid. A biography is a written account of another person's life. It is supposed to deal only in facts, which are pieces of information presented as having objective reality.

But it is also supposed to create for a reader the impression of intimate acquaintance with someone no longer alive, whereby objective reality has already slipped through one's fingers. Nobody knew this better than Alberto. "To create a true likeness," he once said, "one would have to be able to dominate reality. It would be total knowledge. Life would stop." But life goes on, and people have a legitimate interest in remarkable men and women who have lived before them. What made Alberto so interesting was the order of interest which he himself as a man and as an artist always held to be the decisive criterion of interest in life itself. "Art," he used to say, "interests me very much, but truth interests me infinitely more." As our unheroic century limps to its conclusion, it becomes increasingly evident that he was the sort of man posterity will hold in awe for having been heroically true to himself. He gave his life for his truth. That, to be sure, is the price great artists have always had to pay. Few possess the resources to do so, and fewer still have the strength of character to expend them with uncompromising magnanimity. It is a thankless job, because the world's gratitude is not its goal and is accorded, anyway, only to the dead. A biographer's task, especially if his subject is a great artist, is also to be more interested in truth than in art and even to try to discern wherein lies the greater interest of truth over art and so to clarify the very essence and definition of the artist's greatness.

One wonders what Alberto would have thought about the prospect of having his biography written. I suspect he thought about it very little, if at all, and would probably have called the endeavor profitless. And yet he had himself been an indefatigable portraitist, one, moreover, who at all periods of his life had scrutinized his own features in the search for enduring interest, and he certainly found it. Also, he was a great lover of words, a brilliant conversationalist, an omnivorous reader, and a not inconsiderable writer: of superb letters, occasional essays, and autobiographical reminiscences. He would have greeted with ridicule and scorn any fuss about the composition or publication of his biography, saying that the life of a passerby in the street could provide a story just as interesting and remarkable as his. He would have been right, of course. He usually was. But at the same time he was too fair-minded not to admit that he had delved very deeply into himself to see what it is that makes men remarkable and had worked with indefatigable passion for half a century to produce evidence that what he had seen was interesting. He went about this in such a way that he became extraordinarily interesting to everyone who met him, or even set eyes on him, and so in the winter of 1970 I rashly set about preparing to write his biography. The effort transformed my life.

Because I was sure of Diego's sympathy and cooperation, my first priority was to remain on cordial terms with Annette, never mentioning the biography yet at the same time endeavoring to obtain a few bits of information which she alone could provide. This proved relatively easy, because she liked to talk and her favorite topic was herself. During the first six months of my research, I had sixteen meetings with Annette. Since I already knew a great deal about her life, it was not difficult to guide our conversations onto grounds where significant information lay. Never once, of course, in all the hundreds of interviews I had with people who had known Alberto, did I use a notebook or the odious tape recorder. Seemingly random conversation always produces the most vivid revelations. In the case of Annette, moreover, it turned out that I possessed for the moment an unexpected advantage for the enjoyment of her trust. Like everyone who knew her at all well, I was aware that for some years— since things had begun to go badly with Alberto—she had been virtually addicted to certain prescription drugs and that they aggravated the wayward and overwrought aspects of her behavior. She tended to believe that people disliked and disapproved of her, belittled her and planned to exploit her. Alberto used to say that Annette could never entirely trust a man with whom she hadn't been to bed. On that score, needless to say, I was not entitled to an iota of trust.

Of the numerous pills that she took, there were mainly two sorts: one to calm her at night, another to excite her during the day. It was the latter variety she found most difficult to obtain, a drug that went by the brand name of Optalidon. The pharmacies in her neighborhood had for a time provided it without a prescription but by the spring of 1970 had grown reluctant to do so. Annette turned to me to try to be persuasive with the uncooperative druggists. I was startled until she explained her reason, which proved what clever cunning she was capable of when it suited her purpose. The decisive factor was nothing more than my nationality. An appeal for some impropriety in the sale of drugs would stand a far better chance of success if put forward by a respectably attired American in Paris on vacation. I happened to be living there, but no matter. It would be well for me to insist that I had inadvertently left at home a renewable prescription for a comparable drug. The proposition was by no means appealing, but I agreed and was on several occasions successful. However, it was a charade for which I had no liking, so I foolishly told Annette that I knew a doctor who might be disposed to give her a prescription. He was a kind, tolerant man and agreed. She was delighted but never thought to provide any tangible evidence of her pleasure. The doctor, in fact, gave several prescriptions, but eventually he, too, like the reluctant pharmacists, refused to continue. This was the beginning of the summer vacation, so I saw no more of Annette till autumn, and then met with her or spoke to her on the telephone only ten times before leaving in January for America, there to continue my researches.

If I had cause to be careful, not to say sly, with Annette, no such precautions were ever necessary with Diego. At first more reticent than Alberto about himself, his past, his emotions, and his aspirations, he was nonetheless prepared to discuss all the details of Giacometti family life, the careers of his father and brother, memories of childhood and youth, and to provide me with invaluable insights into the workaday routine of genius. Albeit an authentic bohemian, he was very little like Alberto, cared nothing for ideas or erudition, did not consider himself in debt to the concept of civilization, and irascibly refused to be regarded or treated as an artist, though fame finally gave the lie to that aberration. Never have I known anyone so easy to like or so ready to return sincere affection as Diego. At the same time he was slow to bestow his entire trust and quick to evaluate the self-serving attentions of any who wanted him to make their weather fair.

The rhythm of my relationship with Diego became established as a routine fairly quickly, because he preferred to work undisturbed during the day, ate very little at noon, but did not enjoy dining alone. For me it was the same. So I would call him to learn whether or not he was free for dinner on a particular day. He usually was, although he had a considerable number of friends, some of whom became mine as well. I would go to meet him at his house between eight and eight-thirty. There we would chat while drinking a couple of whiskys—Johnnies he called them—or a bottle of Champagne. If the latter, he would sometimes gaze sadly at the bottle when empty and murmur, "It's strange how little there is in one bottle." Then we would walk to the taxi rank at the place d'Alésia and ride to our restaurant, Chez Alexandre, located in a short, narrow street close by Saint-Germain-des-Prés. It was run by a Neapolitan rascal named Bartolo, whose heroes were Mussolini and Lucky Luciano, and he frequently whiled away half the evening at our table, much to my annoyance, rambling on about the venality of politicians, the iniquity of Jews, or the bravery of boxers. The food, however, was decent and cheap, the wine so drinkable that we easily finished off a bottle each, with an extra glass or two at the end to wash down our cheese. Then we would go either to the Café de Flore or a bar called Le Village for a nightcap, after which I'd put Diego, by that time often unsteady on his feet, into a taxi for the return home. I walked to the rue de Lille, and why I never fell on the steep flights leading up to my apartment I can't imagine. It was with Diego, anyway, that I learned the pleasures of overindulgence in alcohol.

And little by little my affection for him deepened into a sentiment I happily recognized as love, the ideal feeling one would have for an older brother. He was born exactly twenty years and twelve days before me. I would never have presumed to harbor such a sentiment toward Alberto. I revered him too much for that. Diego I wanted to protect, comfort, and please. Over a period of fifteen years, I saw him more than five hundred times, and he gave into my possession many rare and precious things created by his beloved brother. Only once did I cause him to be displeased.

Among the many, many people I thought it beneficial to speak with about Alberto was the Basel-based art dealer Ernst Beyeler, whom I had already met on several occasions. We dined together on May 29, 1970. During our conversation he mentioned the painting by Matisse which Alberto had taken from his gallery in 1964, promising a work of his own in exchange. He had died, however, before keeping his promise and, moreover, had made a gift of the painting to Diego, in whose bedroom it still hung. Responsibility for keeping the dead man's promise devolved upon his heirs. Now,

Beyeler was well aware that no love was lost between the artist's widow and the rest of his family, especially because she had in her habitual harum-scarum manner been exceedingly dilatory, to say the least, about settling the estate. Consequently he had thought of an honorable arrangement which would allow Diego to keep the Matisse but would not require Annette to do a thing but give her agreement. Beyeler owned a fine standing figure by Alberto which was unique. He proposed that if Annette would agree to allow him to make a single additional cast of this figure, he would consider the affair settled. She refused, adding that if he made an additional cast she would declare it a fake, and have it seized by the police and destroyed. At a loss as to what to do, Beyeler asked my advice. The case seemed simple enough to me. It was the legal duty of the heirs to make good the original promise, and if Annette refused his reasonable proposition, he had no choice but to go before the law to receive what was due him. Though reluctant to do this, he did not want to be the dupe of an obstinate woman. Accordingly, he wrote a very courteous letter to Annette ten days later, requesting her to make prompt and appropriate settlement of a matter that had now been outstanding for six years.

Annette could not be bothered about Beyeler's request until more than six months had passed. What she did then was simply to send a copy of that letter to Diego, demanding that he settle the business of the Matisse directly with the dealer. She knew perfectly well that Diego had received the painting as a gift and was legally entitled to keep it. However, as she repeatedly declared, "I am not disposed to make gifts." Nor did she ever make any save a tiny bronze figurine offered to Michel Leiris. In the quarter century after her husband's death, she never gave so much as a lithograph by him to any museum in the world. From the very day of his passing, in fact, she had demonstrated her reluctance to part with cash by declining to pay any of the costs of his casket or funeral. Diego, of course, being Diego, immediately got in touch with Beyeler, and two weeks later the Matisse was returned to Basel. He also expressed his annoyance to me for, as he viewed it, having meddled in an affair that was none of my business. I was chagrined and contrite but felt that he erred by giving in to the uncompromising irresponsibility of his sister-in-law. But the truth was that he despised her and wanted nothing to do with her. Knowing this, being of spiteful temperament, she welcomed any opportunity to vex him.

While in America I was approached by another publisher, this one wanting to bring out a volume of reproductions of Giacometti's drawings, with a short preface by me. I thought it would not be too distracting from researches for the biography and agreed. It proved, in fact, quite easy to assemble a group of a hundred and seventeen fine drawings of all periods and write a presentable preface. None of this would be worth mentioning had it not added a bizarre twist to the mystery of the superb portrait drawing of Henri Matisse which had disappeared from Alberto's studio only to reappear in the bedroom of the model's son. I very much wanted to reproduce this drawing. Mindful, though, of Patricia's admonition, I hesitated to mention it to Pierre. Still, I knew by this time that a reproof from Monsieur Matisse, as his wife often called him, would ruffle her no more than a springtime zephyr, so I seized an opportunity when alone with Pierre in his office to ask permission to reproduce the portrait of his father by Alberto which he owned.

"But I own no such drawing," he immediately replied. Whereupon I said it seemed to me that I had seen just such a one in his apartment. "Then you were mistaken," he said. "I know what I own, and I own no such drawing." His owlish face was set, imperturbable, and he stared fixedly at me through his thick glasses. There was nothing further to be said. He allowed me to reproduce several other drawings belonging to him, and I never again mentioned to him the portrait of his father. Nor have I ever seen it since, although I know it exists.

Pierre's lie puzzled me until I realized its reason. The drawing had undeniably been stolen, and if Annette had ever learned of its whereabouts, she would have been able to summon the police, demand restitution, and, as a matter of fact, initiate judicial proceedings against the possessor of stolen goods. Pierre was a supremely prudent man.

Annette, after persistent prodding, permitted reproduction of one of her own portraits of Matisse. The mystery of the stolen drawing remained, though I felt certain Jean Genet had taken it, and he later, in his own snide, sneaky way, verified my certainty.

Bruno Giacometti, the third brother and youngest of the brood,

I had never met, but he knew perfectly well who I was and with his wife, Odette, responded cordially to my request for assistance in my preparation of Alberto's biography. Both of them gave it with a certain reticence at first, understandably wanting to take my measure. Apparently they found me acceptable, because the assistance they provided and the hospitality they extended became more and more trusting and friendly as the years passed. Bruno, when I first met him, was only sixty-three, Odette a couple of years younger. As I write these words, I realize with astonishment that in exactly two weeks he will be eighty-eight, happily in excellent health.

In 1970 Bruno was still a practicing architect, well known and admired in Switzerland, where he had designed a number of exceptionally beautiful hospitals, churches, museums, and private residences. Plainly, the Giacometti family was made to bring honor to the vocation of creativity. Bruno's work is like him—modest, not revolutionary in concept but designed with ingenious subtlety of form and lovely concern for the interrelation of various building materials. He and Odette live on the outskirts of Zurich in a comfortable and commodious house designed by him, set in a handsome garden with a swimming pool. Neither Alberto nor Diego, it must be said, would for an instant have consented to dwell in such a residence. Bruno and Odette are wise in the ways of the world, tolerant and perceptive, but they are not bohemian and sometimes looked askance at the carryings-on of the Parisian brothers. I have grown deeply fond of both and regard them also, as I regarded Diego, as part of my family, not exactly the same part but one I nevertheless feel to be indispensable. We talk frequently on the telephone, and in recent years I have gone annually to spend a few days with them in Zurich. When Alberto's biography was finally published, they celebrated the occasion by presenting me with a portrait drawing of myself, one of those I had been too shy to accept when Alberto offered them all, and which had come to them as a part of their meager inheritance.

The other Giacometti whose testimony I needed was Silvio Berthoud, the son of Ottilia, the family's only daughter, who had died giving birth to her child. Handsome and engaging, he, too, received me with cordial goodwill, and told me many amusing, interesting anecdotes about his famous uncle, whom he resembled physically, even vocally, to a truly uncanny degree. A doctor like his father, Silvio had more in common with his Parisian uncles than with the one in Zurich, though on affectionate terms with all.

The conscientious biographer of a person but recently deceased will have a long, long list of people whose testimony he ought to obtain. Of the many still living who had counted for much in Alberto's life, I failed to find only a few before death did. To me the most interesting were Genet, Balthus, Sartre, Beckett, Michel Leiris, and Caroline, the prostitute who had been the mistress and model of Alberto's final years.

Genet, furtive and crafty as ever, was not easy to meet. It was with considerable difficulty that I learned of his whereabouts, spoke with him on the telephone, and obtained consent for a meeting. I mentioned this to Diego and thought at the same time to speak of the stolen drawing which now belonged to Pierre. "It was I who got it for him," Diego said.

"But how?" I asked.

It was simple, he explained. A couple of years after Alberto's death, a young man unknown to Diego presented himself at the rue du Moulin-Vert, showing that he knew more about Diego than Diego knew about him, and said that he had a drawing by Giacometti for sale in case Diego might be interested. It was the portrait of Matisse, the price, payable in cash, two thousand dollars, then the going price. Diego said that he himself was not interested in a purchase but added that he knew someone who very well might be. If the young man wanted to come back in two or three days, he could probably make a sale. This was agreeable. Diego later called Pierre in New York, explaining the circumstances, and was told by all means to buy the drawing, collect the money from Maurice Lefebvre-Foinet, Pierre's agent in Paris, and turn over to him the drawing for shipment. And that is what happened.

"I always thought that Genet must have taken that drawing," I said.

"Well, of course he did," said Diego.

My meeting with Genet took place in the salon of a drab and shabby hotel of the sort which the writer always sought out and frequently left without paying the bill. Well-dressed and courteous, he spoke in a gentle tone of voice with eloquence and cultivation.

We talked about Alberto at length, though there was nothing new or surprising said by either. He laughed frequently, seemed at peace with himself and his convictions, aware of his importance but neither vain nor complacent. I felt his grim charm but, conscious of his fundamental perfidy, didn't like him, and wondered what vicious, perverse, cruel acts he might commit with pleasure. Our conversation lasted for almost two hours, touching, in addition to Alberto, on Rembrandt, Cézanne, Mallarmé, and much else. I longed, needless to say, to ask him about the stolen drawing but didn't dare. It was with a sense of coming out into the fresh air from a closed, stuffy, almost-noxious room that I left him.

Five months after this meeting, as I was walking home late at night from a homosexual haunt in the rue Sainte-Anne, crossing the as-yet-unscathed courtyard of the Louvre, I saw Genet coming toward me. When we were abreast, I said, "Bonsoir, Monsieur Genet."

He looked up at me quizzically and said, "Do I know you?"

"I came to talk to you several months ago about Alberto."

"Oh, yes," he said, "you're James Lord."

Pleased that he remembered, I asked where he was going and he said that he was walking home, so I offered to accompany him a little way and he gladly accepted. He had just spent the evening, he told me, with Jimmy Baldwin and a group of Black Panthers, who wanted his help. He asked whether I knew Jimmy and I said we'd been acquainted for twenty years, having met through Richard Wright. Once again I was impressed by Genet's charm, but there was still, and even more strongly this time, an awareness of the serpent behind the smile. As we walked alone together through the mostly deserted streets, a strange detachment from everyday precedents appeared to prevail, accentuated by the fact that Genet seemed at times not to know quite where we were going, and it was almost as though we'd become lost in the heart of the immense and somnolent metropolis. Maybe this made me bold.

An opportunity so nearly ideal for asking the fateful question was unlikely ever to come again, I thought. It was not easy. Still, I finally managed to say, "There's one thing I wanted to ask you the last time we met. But it's a little awkward."

"What's that?" he inquired, gazing up at me intently.

"You remember when you were posing for Alberto, one of the drawings he'd made of Matisse disappeared."

"No."

"Yes. Alberto had made that series of portraits of Matisse. He had them all in his studio. Then the best one disappeared. Alberto thought you might have taken it."

"I don't remember anything about it," said Genet calmly. "I never took anything from Alberto's studio."

"But don't you remember that a drawing did disappear?" I insisted. "Alberto was not opposed to theft, even used to say he was in favor of it. But this drawing was different, because it was a portrait of Matisse and the best he'd done."

"Simone de Beauvoir mentioned it," said Genet. "I remember. She said, 'How did you get the drawing of Matisse out of Alberto's studio?' "

"Oh?" I said. "But Alberto himself never mentioned it to you?"

"Never."

"And what did you say when Simone de Beauvoir asked you that?"

"The same thing I said to you just now: that I didn't take it. Yes, I remember. It was Beauvoir who mentioned it to me. I was having dinner with Sartre and her, just the three of us, and she made a joke of it, saying, 'How did you get the portrait of Matisse under your coat?' " And he made a gesture as of rolling up a piece of paper and slipping it under his jacket, laughing as he did so.

"But you didn't take it?" I insisted.

"Absolutely not."

"I'm especially interested," I explained, "because at that time you and I were the only two outsiders who had free access to Alberto's studio, who came and went as we pleased, and Alberto said that it must have been one or the other of us who took the drawing."

"Then it was you," said Genet at once, turning toward me with a quick, sly smile.

"No," I said. "I know it was not I. That's why I was so anxious to speak to you about it. I'm sorry, but of course it's because, you see, you aren't exactly a stranger to theft."

"Of course," sighed Genet, "as soon as a cigarette lighter disappears, everybody thinks I took it."

I told him that the drawing had since reappeared and explained exactly in what circumstances. He listened but made no comment.

There was nothing more to be said. About the stolen drawing, at least. Or about much of anything else. Our talk was desultory though cordial until, despite our haphazard itinerary, we presently reached the door to his hotel.

"I've led you far afield," said Genet. "This is not your neighborhood."

"I hope we'll meet again someday," I said. "Good night."

"Good night," said Genet, whereupon we shook hands and he went inside. I never saw him again.

When it was too late, I felt furious with myself for having invited Genet to make a fool of me by allowing me to assume that a man who glorified treachery and lying could ever be led to tell the truth. I should have realized as much when he at first denied any memory of the drawing, then promptly contradicted himself by recalling Simone de Beauvoir's query and joke. He was frankly mocking me. Perfidy being the very quintessence of Genet's ethos, his deliberate pursuit of abjection transformed shame into pride. No remorse, no scruple, no atonement, no confession must ever impair or disfigure the supreme virtue of betrayal. Genet was first and foremost a traitor, recognizing no loyalty or responsibility, acknowledging no debt or obligation, persistently practicing treachery in all its forms. As Sartre painstakingly pointed out in his lengthy book about Genet, the ex-convict consistently stole from his friends because that is the highest form of betrayal. Of course it was he who took the portrait of Matisse from Alberto's studio. The satisfaction would have been irresistible because this was something which his friend particularly prized. He often said after Alberto's death that Giacometti had been the one person he most admired. What greater delight, then, than to betray him? I believe Alberto questioned me rather than Genet about the theft in order to be sure that the thief was, indeed, the latter. He didn't want to be in doubt, because he was wise and noble enough to respect Genet's "truth."

Of Balthus's friendship with Alberto, I knew it would be necessary to speak in detail in the biography. He was promptly responsive to my requests for meetings and willingly talked at length about both Alberto and Annette. He admired Alberto greatly and,

I felt, must have been somewhat envious of him, aware also that his own pretensions to nobility and love for grandeur and ostentation were probably viewed with, at least, bemusement by a rich artist who lived in virtual squalor. This did not prevent him from referring to himself more than once during our conversation as the Count de Rola; and he told me a lengthy, preposterous anecdote about his refusal to attend a reception for General de Gaulle in Rome, because his place among those to be introduced to the general had not been in acceptable accord with his rank.

Of all the people I wanted to speak to about Alberto for the sake of his biography, there was only one who for more than nine years eluded me: Jean-Paul Sartre. And I had been persistent, had written letters, had asked Henri Cartier-Bresson, Michel Leiris, and Gisèle Halimi, Sartre's lawyer, to intervene on my behalf. Several times I called Simone de Beauvoir to request an interview with her and solicit her assistance in meeting with Sartre. She was brusque to the point of discourtesy and bluntly refused either to see or to assist me. I didn't really need her personal views on Alberto, because she had written about him—often inaccurately—in her published autobiography and I didn't believe she would add anything of interest. Sartre, on the other hand, whom I knew to be in failing health and half blind, I was still eager to interview. I had virtually abandoned hope when on Thursday, February 22, 1979, lunching at the Brasserie Lipp with my friend Gilles Roy, I saw Sartre seated with a woman at a table across the room. It was obviously unthinkable to approach someone so celebrated in this public place, but I realized that the law of probability precluded my ever having another opportunity to speak to him. Luckily he and his companion, who was not the redoubtable Beaver, finished their meal before we did, paid their bill, and stood up to leave. Only too aware that my last chance was vanishing, I waited a moment, then followed the pair out onto the impersonal sidewalk, where I introduced myself to Sartre and hurriedly explained my reason for accosting him so unceremoniously. He was immediately responsive, introduced me to his companion, Michèle Vian, said that he would be happy to talk to me about Alberto, gave me his telephone number, and suggested that I call to make an appointment. Then he and Madame Vian got into a taxi and drove away.

Gratified to have finally gotten the promise of a meeting with the last person who counted for much on my list, I waited three days before calling. Sartre was very amiable and businesslike, as if there had never been any question as to the simplicity or suitability of our meeting. He asked me to come to his apartment the following Thursday at eleven in the morning and explained with painstaking precision where to find it. Anxious to be exactly on time, I arrived a little early at the large apartment complex on the boulevard Edgar-Quinet where Sartre lived, and therefore had a few minutes to wait on the landing in front of his door. Through it I could clearly hear a voice which I recognized at once to be that of Beauvoir. She was reading aloud. From my several conversations with her on the telephone, I was aware that she had a singularly graceless tone of voice. She read very, very rapidly but with almost no inflection or expression. It was rather like a machine reading, not a person with any feeling for words or subject matter. I heard enough to infer that what she was reading was a work of fiction. Although I felt it highly inauspicious that she was present, I rang the bell at eleven o'clock precisely. The machine voice stopped reading instantly, then declared, "Somebody's there." She came to the door and without opening it demanded, "What is it?"

"It's for Monsieur Sartre," I said.

She said—obviously to Sartre—"Have you made an appointment with anyone?"

Sartre said, "No."

Beauvoir said to me, "Do you have an appointment?"

"Yes. I spoke with Monsieur Sartre on the telephone last Sunday, and he told me to come this morning at eleven."

"Who is it?"

"Monsieur Lord."

Beauvoir said to Sartre, "It's a Monsieur Lord."

"What is this about?" she asked me.

"To talk with him about Giacometti."

"You have agreed to talk about Giacometti!" she cried with what was plainly a tone of reproach. Then she said to me, "You must wait. Monsieur Sartre is not dressed. Go to the café next door and come back in half an hour."

"Very well, Madame," I said and did as I was told.

When I returned, having recorded the foregoing in my journal, there was music playing behind the door, a Bach harpsichord concerto. I rang—twice—the music stopped, a shuffling step approached, and Sartre opened. He was then so nearly blind that it was apparent he could not see me very well. We shook hands and he very politely asked me to come in. He was short and dumpy, with thin hair, flabby face, thick lips, very bad, cracked and stained teeth, thick glasses, and the walleye, decidedly ugly. The room in which we sat was very plain, with little furniture, the walls bare, and dust, I noticed, on the floor. Sartre spoke somewhat haltingly at first, but then, as our conversation progressed, with more animation and with the evident authority of a highly developed and well-disciplined intellect. Obviously interested in what was said to him, he listened with careful attention. He and Alberto had met, he said, just before the war but had not become really intimate till afterward. From the first, though, he had been impressed by Alberto's powerful personality, enhanced by his remarkable appearance. I asked whether he had felt from the beginning that Alberto was a genius. "I don't like the word *genius*," he said. "It has too many 'loaded' associations. But I felt at once that Alberto was a very remarkable man, that his talent and character were integrated in a most extraordinary and unique way, which made one feel that he was a great man."

"What distinction," I asked, "could be made between Alberto and Picasso?"

"On the 'superficial' level of personal conduct," Sartre said, "Picasso did not have a fine, strong, or exemplary character and that is often apparent in his work, whereas Alberto's remarkable character was clearly perceptible in his work always."

"Do you feel that Alberto had an influence on your thought?" I asked.

"No. Not directly. But indirectly yes, because Alberto's manner of approaching the life experience was very akin to my own. In our conversations my own position was consequently clarified and reinforced."

"It seems to me that there might be a rapport in the fact that Alberto was always, or very often, working at the frontier between being and nothingness, and that is a conceptual domain close to your philosophical position."

"Well," said Sartre, "it was, indeed, very illuminating for me to talk to Alberto about his work and observe his artistic evolution. He had a kind of universal quality. He was a true humanist in the seventeenth-century sense of the term, interested in everything, responsive to everything and everyone. It was a particular quality in Alberto's case that he was able to talk about his work, himself, his experiences, his opinions, and give them an extension beyond himself in such a way that he never seemed to be talking solely about himself but rather about things which had an interest for everyone."

We also talked of things other than Alberto. Sartre was very frank about the inconvenience of his impaired eyesight, which compelled him to dictate his work to a tape recorder. I saw it on a cheap wooden table in a corner. After a time, I prepared to leave. He wished me good luck with my work and I said that I didn't feel up to the task.

"Nobody ever really feels up to his task," Sartre said. "Alberto certainly didn't, and I never have."

"Some people must have," I said. "Hegel, for example."

"One would have to know more about Hegel's life, to be sure."

"In philosophy," I said, "of which I hasten to add that I know absolutely nothing, one does have the impression that the principal writers felt quite up to the task and were confident of their hold on truth."

"Oh," said Sartre, "that's just a trick."

I laughed, we shook hands, said good-bye, and I departed. Nothing Sartre had said about Alberto was new to me, but I was very glad to have heard it from him in person. A year later he was dead.

If it had been very difficult to present myself to Sartre, meeting Samuel Beckett, celebrated for his reluctance to grant interviews, could not have been easier. Somehow I obtained his address on the boulevard Saint-Jacques and wrote a letter explaining why I wished to meet with him. Three days later—it was Sunday, April 19, 1970—the telephone rang. I said, "Hello."

"Mr. Lord?" A deep voice, slightly hoarse, in English.

"Yes."

"This is Beckett."

"Good morning, Mr. Beckett. How kind of you to call me."

"Not at all. I had your letter, and I'll be happy to see you. I'm very busy now. But if you're free this Tuesday, we might meet."

"Certainly."

"Could you meet me in front of the theater where I'm rehearsing? It's the Récamier."

"Yes. I know it."

"If you could meet me there at noon, we can have a coffee together."

"Fine."

On the Tuesday morning I was in the lobby of the theater at eleven-fifty. I could hear a rehearsal of *Krapp's Last Tape* going on inside. Beckett came out after some thirty minutes. I went up to him and said, "Mr. Beckett . . ."

He looked startled, and for a moment I had the impression that he was going to keep right on walking. Then I told him my name.

"Oh, I'm sorry," he said. "I've kept you waiting."

"It doesn't matter," I assured him. We went out together into the light rain, and he suggested that we cross the rue de Sèvres to a small café. We found an unoccupied booth at the back and sat down there, facing each other. Beckett was very tall and thin, his face deeply lined, hair iron-gray, but it would have been difficult to estimate his age from his appearance. Something primitive and eternal about him. He had on rather small but quite thick gold-rimmed glasses which he moved up to his forehead occasionally, then down again, or sometimes took off altogether for a few minutes. His eyes were deep blue, very gentle, welcoming. Far from being in the least intimidated by looking him directly in the eyes, I felt it a uniquely vivid pleasure, as if one might delight to drown in his blue gaze, a sentiment I've never felt with anyone. His attire was nondescript, neither elegant nor shabby. The occasional silences in our conversation were not at all awkward but seemed, on the contrary, natural and right. His voice was resonant but not very strong, with an occasional Irish lilt that was most engaging. A man of immediate, remarkable appeal, though it wouldn't seem quite accurate to say that he was charming.

"You're writing a book on Giacometti," he said.

I answered that I hoped to but was still very far from being prepared to begin writing, being wholly occupied with research.

"You're seeing all of his friends," he said.

I asked how they had met, and he told me that it had been casually at the Café de Flore sometime before the war, adding that he couldn't really tell me very much about Alberto, because most of their meetings had been by chance late at night in Montparnasse, where they would wander about together for hours, talking. And it had been Alberto, he said, who did most of the talking, indefatigably describing the anguish he felt at not being able to do what he wanted to do.

"He was not obsessed but possessed," Beckett said. "I suggested that it might be more fruitful to concentrate on the problem itself rather than struggle constantly to achieve a solution. That is, by accepting the impossibility of what he was struggling to achieve and by developing the inner nature and exploiting the natural resources of that very impossibility, he might achieve a result of greater complexity and richness than by continuing over and over to struggle to do what he knew to be impossible: the creation of an illusion as real as reality. But Giacometti was determined to continue with his struggle, trying to progress even if it was only by so much as an inch, or a centimeter, or a millimeter."

"But in the absolute," I said, "a progress of a millimeter is infinite."

"If possible," said Beckett.

"It has often been suggested," I said, "that there are parallels between your work and Giacometti's, that both illuminate the solitude, alienation, and despair which characterize the world today."

Beckett took off his glasses and paused for a moment, fiddling with his coffee cup, then said, "I've never felt that painting or sculpture can express the same things as literature. I don't see any parallel between the two arts. Often I felt that Giacometti's artistic effort was very like a child's game of trying to catch with one hand a finger of the other, which is determined not to be caught."

I asked whether he had ever known anyone who reminded him of Alberto. After musing for a moment he said, "No."

When I remarked that I'd recently read the biography of Joyce by Richard Ellmann, he said that he admired the book greatly, adding that Ellmann had managed to prevail on people who were usually reluctant to talk about Joyce. He sometimes even used a tape recorder. I said that I wouldn't like doing that, and he said, "I'd never agree to it." I asked whether one could have said that Joyce was "fun." Beckett looked very startled and said, "Never! Joyce was very formal and intimidating. No first names. Even an old friend like Padraic Colum he always called Colum. And for a very long time I was Mr. Beckett, until finally I became just Beckett."

I mentioned that Alberto had been the same, and Beckett said that he had never called him Sam. He, too, I noticed, when speaking of Alberto, referred to him always as Giacometti.

After nearly an hour I said that I supposed he must be very busy and would want to leave. "I'm not always busy, alas," he said. "Just now I am because I'm directing this play." After a few minutes, he did get himself together, insisted on paying for our coffee, and we said good-bye on the sidewalk. I wrote him a couple of times to ask specific questions, and he always answered by return mail.

A few years later we chanced to meet in the street near the Luxembourg Gardens. He asked how the biography was progressing, and I said with difficulty. He nodded and said, "It would, of course." When the biography was finally published, I sent him a copy. He never acknowledged having received it, maybe because I had written at some length of him.

Michel Leiris, like Beckett, was promptly responsive to my request for a meeting. He was attired with almost-ostentatious yet discreet elegance, perhaps as a compensation for the slightness of his stature, and his personal manner was also of distinctive refinement. I remembered Alberto having told me with a certain mockery, natural when coming from him, an anecdote about Leiris's obsession with immaculate attire. During dinner in some restaurant he had spilled sauce on the sleeve of his suit and was extremely upset because of the resulting stain. When someone observed that it would vanish when the suit was sent to be dry-cleaned, Leiris replied, "I never wear clothes which have to be sent to a dry cleaner." Alberto had chortled over this and remarked that the same was true of himself, because his clothes got so dirty that eventually he threw them away and replaced them with others of exactly the same style.

Leiris asked me to meet him for the first time at the Musée de l'Homme, where he had a small office in the basement. There was a cafeteria in the museum where we had a light lunch together. He was exceedingly, almost embarrassingly polite, speaking slowly and choosing his words with such care that one could imagine that they were to be written down later. I had read some of his autobiographical writings and noted that the style was of Mandarin complexity and finesse. He had been the first to write with discerning admiration of Alberto's work, and the two men had been close friends for thirty-five years. He was an erudite intellectual to the tips of his well-manicured fingernails, and I knew him to be a rich man by both inheritance and marriage, living in a large apartment overlooking the Seine and waited upon by servants. It seemed nearly impossible to imagine this exquisite gentleman marching and chanting with riotous students in the middle of the night. This seeming contradiction was peculiarly troubling, and was further aggravated by criticism from others who had no apparent ulterior motives. Leiris enjoyed the reputation of a man of unique integrity. Yet when I mentioned my meeting with him to Diego, he said, "I despise him, He was no true friend to Alberto. A hypocrite. And he encouraged that poor Annette to make a fool of herself in May of '68. I would never shake his hand." Then, some years later, after Alberto's biography had appeared, Leiris sponsored a letter denouncing it signed by forty-odd people who had known Alberto, an act I was at a loss to understand. I mentioned my surprise to Françoise Gilot, who had been Picasso's mistress and had known Leiris well, as Leiris's wife was Picasso's dealer, and his favorite artists were, in that order, Picasso, Francis Bacon, and Alberto. Françoise said, "You must understand that Leiris is a man who wears a mask. He would never allow the world to see the person who's hidden behind it, and that is why all his writings are about himself. The truth about him has got to be *his* truth and nobody else's."

Nonetheless I was interested in Leiris and saw him ten or twelve times during the long years of my work. He had obviously been fond of Alberto and talked of him always with emotion and respect, though he had nothing of impressive originality to say. He never mentioned Diego, but to my surprise on several occasions he spoke feelingly of Annette, praising her intelligence and understanding of

Alberto's aesthetic endeavor, an opinion flagrantly in contradiction with that of her husband. But I didn't presume to differ. Obviously Leiris was fond of Annette. Bruno told me that once, when he and Odette and Alberto were in Stampa, Annette had telephoned from Paris in a rage, demanding that he break off relations with Caroline and threatening, as she often did, to kill herself if he refused. Beside himself with exasperation, Alberto had said, "Well, go ahead and do it then," whereupon Leiris had taken the phone from Annette and severely berated Alberto for his cruel indifference. Clearly, he and Annette had been close.

I enjoyed Leiris's company. We usually had lunch together at a mediocre restaurant in the rue Saint-Benoît called Le Grand Horloge. Only once did he invite me to his apartment for tea. We talked about many topics in addition to Alberto. He was a discerning and unusually cultivated man, his analysis of *The Heart of Darkness* no less profound than that of the iconography of *The Story of the True Cross.*

To contact Caroline, though not quite so difficult as Sartre, required more devious methods. As she was an accredited member of the underworld, the telephone book gave no help, and it was without success that I inquired in the nightclubs and bars of Montparnasse where she and Alberto had habitually spent much time and money. My inquiries, indeed, were received with overt suspicion, especially since my foreign accent marked me as an outsider. In the end I was compelled to turn to a source of information I had never expected to need: a private detective agency. The director received me in his tasteful office with the worldly aplomb of a society physician, asked for an elegant fee in advance, and two days later gave me Caroline's full name, date of birth, present address, and telephone number. When I called, she knew exactly who I was, remembered seeing me with Alberto, and agreed to have lunch with me the very next day. She was striking rather than beautiful, and one's sense of an exceptional personality was immediate. She seemed, if anything, even more eager to talk about Alberto and discuss their relationship than I was. She was very proud of having been important in the life of a great man. With disarming candor she virtually reveled in the details of the life they had more or less shared for five years. That she detested both Diego and Annette went without saying. Her criminal activities were described with relish. But a serious problem bedeviled almost all the revelations Caroline so willingly confided. Just how much was one to believe? I was able to verify a good deal from notes I'd made after conversations with Alberto and from others who had known them together. There were even a couple of letters written by her to him, and all of his that were sent to her, which she willingly allowed me to copy. But much remained uncertain, which in a way was just as well, because Alberto had greatly enjoyed the elusive characteristics of Caroline's personality. I did, too.

Through the years I saw quite a bit of her. She tried to seduce me and I was tempted to succumb, but I feared the quicksands of compromise and intimidation likely to follow. More than once she asked me for money, and I gave her some. She is nearing sixty now, suffers from acute diabetes, and is no longer capable of pursuing the world's oldest profession. Lonely, semi-invalid in her cheap apartment in Nice, the walls adorned only with photographs of Alberto, she must muse with melancholic nostalgia upon those few years when one of the century's greatest artists painted numerous portraits of her, presented her with jewels and automobiles, and proved the depth of his devotion by insisting upon spending the last afternoon of his life alone with her in his hospital room. Hers was not a trivial destiny. On the stage of true-to-life passion, she played an outstanding role and carried it off with panache.

In addition to Genet, Balthus, Sartre, Beckett, and Caroline, I saw many other men and women who were remarkable and interesting: Francis Bacon; Jacques Lacan; Pierre-Jean Jouve; Pierre Klossowski, Balthus's brother; André Masson; and many more. To list or discuss them all would be to exhaust the reader's patience and the writer's stamina. Particular, if parenthetical, mention ought to be made nevertheless of Patricia Matisse. She had known everyone well, having been married to the Chilean artist Roberto Matta before Pierre. She was a delightful, willful pixie, a lover of gossip, and she feared no indiscretion. Without her affectionate cooperation, there is a great deal I would never have learned, and it was a very sad morning for me, when, long before the biography was finished, I found under my door the telegram from Pierre announcing her death from a cerebral hemorrhage, not yet aged fifty.

Needless to say, as I continued my researches, Annette learned that in spite of her injunction I was going ahead with the preparation of Alberto's biography. On November 18, 1975, an exhibition of drawings by Alberto opened at the Claude Bernard Gallery in Paris. Annette was present, of course, also Diego, Bruno, and many others who had known Alberto, dead then for nearly a decade. I said good evening to Annette. She frowned without speaking and turned away. But then she turned back and, speaking sharply, more aggressively than I had ever known her to be, said, "I am very annoyed with you, James."

"Why is that?" I asked.

"Because you are deliberately disobeying my request. I know perfectly well what you are up to, and you know that I disapprove of it."

"I'm sorry you feel this way," I said. "Alberto was a great artist and a great man. His story deserves to be saved from forgetfulness, and if one waits too long, all the essential witnesses will be gone. You know that Diego and Bruno and Silvio all approve of what I'm doing."

"They hate me," she snapped. "You'd better not believe everything they tell you. And I'm warning you. If you continue with this, I'll find a way to stop it. I've got the law on my side. So be careful." With that she again turned away and strode off in the crowd.

When I repeated this conversation to Diego, he said, "She's become a megalomaniac. It's true she has a very powerful lawyer with much influence in the government, a man you'd do well to beware of. And then there's the new secretary, Miss Palmer, also a redoubtable personage, I hear, an American but not a nice girl like the other. Apparently she and the lawyer control my sister-in-law like a marionette. Well, let them. It won't make any difference in fifty years. Only Alberto will matter then."

It was in the late seventies and early eighties, after a decade of increasing intimacy, that Diego began to make me gifts of his brother's works. At first a painting and a drawing or two, then all at once a dozen sculptures in plaster, of which several were of major importance—one of them Alberto's largest, most original Cubist piece; another, also large, the first and more interesting version of the sculpture called *The Cage*; and the head of a man on a high pedestal. I told Diego that I felt that all these pieces were of sufficient interest to be cast in bronze. Not during his lifetime, he said. I was to take good care of them, put them away in a safe place—"well out of harm's way," he said—and after his death I was to do with them whatever I judged appropriate. That would be something, he added, to keep me busy when the biography was finished, and he felt sure that Alberto would be pleased to leave their fate in my hands. For a time I stored these sculptures in my cellar, but then, mindful of Diego's admonition that they be kept out of harm's way and only too aware of Annette's penchant for calling the police, I put them in my car, drove to Switzerland, and deposited them there in a well-guarded warehouse.

At about the same time, I learned from Bruno that Annette was seriously ill. She had suffered an intestinal blockage and was operated on at the American Hospital just in time to save her life. She spent several months in the hospital. Her illness and absence from home were kept as secret as possible by lawyer and secretary, who pretended that she was but slightly indisposed, tired, or out of sorts. If anybody wondered for what reason these evasions and deceptions were practiced, an explanation may have looked like simplicity itself. The business in Giacomettis was booming. His works sold for higher and ever higher prices as his posthumous reputation soared. At his death many pieces had not been cast in complete editions, some not at all. These regrettable lacunae were the ceaseless and vigilant concern of Annette and those whose interests coincided, so to speak, with hers. As a result, a warehouse in Paris was filling up, as if by the ardor of a sorcerer's apprentice, with more and more and more of Giacometti's works, some of which occasionally came onto the market. Cash accumulated with Midas-like spontaneity.

As I approached the conclusion of my long labors on the biography, I began to receive letters signed by Annette demanding to see the manuscript before publication. Behind these demands were barely veiled threats of legal action in the form of reminders that she alone possessed the copyright pertaining to all of Alberto's works and would grant no permissions unless she had previously approved the contents of my book. Censorship, in a word, was what she threatened. I had warned my publisher from the first that Annette would sue if the slightest pretext for such action seemed promising. The lawyer for Farrar, Straus and Giroux, a genial and astute gentleman called Leon Friedman, went over my manuscript with meticulous scruple, but very little was found that needed changing. I had never wished to malign Annette, much less to slander her. My driving desire was to tell the truth, but I knew that that was precisely what she wished to prevent. Annette had made the best, if not the most, of a very trying marriage and did so with loyalty, generosity, virtue, perseverance, and the fortitude of her uncomplicated devotion to a very complicated man. But the biography of her husband could not fail to depict a marriage which no woman would have been able to sustain with composure, let alone contentment. Artists' widows are famous for coming to troubled terms with bereavement and for administering with fretful punctilio the artistic legacies to which they fall heir. Annette proved no exception to this unhappy rule. I wrote evasive answers to her letters.

My unwillingness to show the finished manuscript to Annette did not, however, extend to everyone. David Sylvester expressed a desire to read it. He had known Alberto well, been portrayed by him, and written about him in the catalogs of the exhibitions he organized, and he was, indeed, even then preparing a monograph of his own, which he finally published a decade later to universal and well-deserved acclaim. I saw no reason to refuse his request. On October 4, 1984, he wrote to me from Barcelona, having by that time read three quarters of my text. He said that the biography was a remarkable achievement that he had found highly illuminating, partly because of the new information it contained, partly because of its insights. And, in conclusion, he added that Alberto and Diego were in my debt. This commendation was profoundly heartening for me, coming as it did from one whom I had known and seen with some frequency since he had introduced himself and insisted on hearing my first article about Alberto twenty years before, a man, moreover, legitimately regarded as an expert in the appreciation of Giacometti's art.

Publication of the biography in America was scheduled and announced for the month of September 1985. Annette's lawyer wrote a letter on July 5 that was obviously intended to delay or altogether prevent publication. This letter stated without amenity that Madame Giacometti controlled the copyright for all reproduction of works and/or writings by her deceased husband and would under no circumstances grant permission for reproductions in a book of which she had not been granted the right of review and criticism in advance. The threat of legal action was flagrant. But Leon Friedman had shrewdly foreseen this eventuality. As a publisher's lawyer, he knew every twist and turn of copyright law pertaining to works published in the United States. They are not quite the same as those in force in Europe, and he ascertained that no copyright had been established to prevent unauthorized reproduction of Giacometti's works and some of his writings in America. He sent to Annette's lawyer a brilliant, stringent, unanswerable letter to this effect. The attack, which had been contrived to be lethal, was thus successfully thwarted.

Diego was delighted. His health, however, had for several years caused concern among his friends, who became, of course, increasingly numerous as he grew more and more famous. Articles about his furniture and decorative objects proliferated in glossy magazines on both sides of the Atlantic. His clients were Hollywood stars, Greek shipping moguls, opera singers, Rothschilds, and Mellons. But he stubbornly refused ceaseless offers of exhibitions, insisted that he was an artisan, not an artist, refused to number his pieces or to sign them, and tried as long as he could to go on living the frugal, tranquil life that he had been living in that same neighborhood for more than half a century. But it wasn't easy. The insistence of would-be clients compelled him to install an intercom which controlled entrance to his premises. And he was also compelled, very much against his will, to confront the fact of failing health. He suffered from an ulcer but refused to see a doctor, until I called one despite his obstreperous objections. Then he injured his right hand, making work difficult, if not impossible, for several months. He was obliged to undergo an operation for a hernia. His legs gave him trouble, and he was required to walk first with one cane, then with two. But his good humor, his enjoyment of lighthearted conversation, his gentle simplicity and generosity never failed. And he kept on working.

The assembly-line production of furniture had long since become boring to him. What he wanted was something to challenge his talent and imagination, and just the right thing came along at just the right time. The Picasso Museum had for a number of years been in protracted preparatory stages and in 1983 was beginning to look as though it might eventually open its doors in the magnificent mansion chosen to house it. Lighting fixtures and furniture were needed. The director, an imaginative curator named Dominique Bozo, appealed to Diego to design lamps, chandeliers, benches, chairs. Pleased and excited, Diego set aside all other work and for two years devoted himself entirely to the painstaking and intimidating task of designing things which could withstand with honor the propinquity of Picasso's overwhelming productions. With modesty and imagination he succeeded. His additions to the Picasso Museum hold their own very beautifully beside the work of our century's most remarkable artist. Early in July of 1985 Diego went to the museum, saw all of his things installed there, and came away satisfied. The formal opening was scheduled for September—I, alas, unable to attend because publication of Alberto's biography was to take place in New York at the same time.

Diego had also been troubled by poor eyesight and finally agreed to a cataract operation on his left eye. I had dinner with him on July 8, a Monday, and he entered the American Hospital a few days later. Silvio and his second wife, Thérèse, had come from Geneva to keep him company, because Bruno and Odette were going to their summer home at Maloja. I called the hospital Sunday morning and found Diego in high spirits. The operation had been a complete success and he could read his newspaper without glasses, whereas he had previously needed a powerful magnifying glass. I offered to come and see him in the afternoon, but he said that Silvio was with him and asked me instead to come to his house the next afternoon at three o'clock, as he would leave the hospital before lunch.

The next day was brilliant and warm. I went to the rue du Moulin-Vert at three o'clock, rang the bell, and Silvio let me into the courtyard, where we embraced and went into the house. Thérèse was there but not Diego. I sat down on a stool beside the desk, my habitual spot, and said, "Where's Diego?"

"He's dead," said Silvio.

"What?" I cried. "That's impossible. I spoke to him just yesterday and he was fine."

"I know," said Silvio. "He was fine, it's true. We were with him. But this morning at ten o'clock as he was dressing to leave the hospital, he dropped dead of a heart attack. It was over in an instant. He probably didn't even have time to realize what was happening. You know it's the way he always said he wanted to go."

"I know," I said, choking, and I put both hands over my face. Unable to hold back the sobs, I jumped up and ran outside. After a few minutes Silvio came out and put his arms around me. Then I was able to stop crying. We went back into the house and Silvio explained that he had been aware for several years that Diego's heart was not strong. Because of this weakness, the doctors at the American Hospital had refused to administer general anesthesia for the cataract operation. There was nothing to be done now but inform Bruno, who was even then en route by car from Zurich to Maloja, where he could not arrive for another hour. The wait was terrible, and worse was Bruno's cry of distress when Silvio told him the news. He and Odette would be unable to reach Paris before Wednesday. I had dinner with Silvio and Thérèse that evening and again the next day.

Knowing that Bruno and Odette would arrive Wednesday morning, I waited until that afternoon to return to the rue du Moulin-Vert. When I rang the bell, Silvio came to open the door and told me that Annette and her lawyer were in the house. So I waited with Silvio in the courtyard until they came out. The lawyer, whom I barely knew, greeted me cordially. I held out my hand to Annette, who hesitated, but after a moment with obvious reluctance she allowed me to press her fingers. I was shocked by her appearance and might never have recognized her had I not been forewarned of her presence. Her face was puffy, bloated, and very white, her clothing was shabby, and she had grown almost obese. She did not speak to me but said good-bye to the others, adding that she intended to go at once to see Diego's body at the hospital. After her departure, we all sat around in Diego's small living room, mournfully aware of the absence that dwelt in it, discussing the details of all that would have to be done in succeeding days. Hardly an hour had passed before the telephone rang. It was Annette. Having seen Diego's body, Bruno told us afterward, she thought he looked very handsome, peaceful, content. She evidently asked Bruno a question, because he said very forcefully, "No, Annette, that is not possible." They said little more, and he hung up. She had asked, Bruno said, that her name be included in the list of family members in the newspaper announcement of Diego's demise. We all agreed that it would have been an offense to his memory to publish among the names of those sincerely bereaved that of a woman he despised. But, as usual, Annette was determined to have what she felt to be her due, and she published an announcement of great sorrow under the name, for once, of Madame Alberto Giacometti. Bruno, Odette, Silvio, and his children published a separate announcement.

Encouraged to do so by Bruno and Odette, Gilles and I also went to the American Hospital to view Diego's body. Diego had been fond of Gilles, offering him drawings from his own hand, gifts bestowed very rarely upon anyone. We were glad to have gone, because, indeed, Diego looked in death very noble and serene, very much the image of the man he had been.

He had wished to be cremated. A ceremony took place in the crematorium chapel of the Père-Lachaise Cemetery on Wednesday, July 24, at ten-forty-five in the morning. It was a blinding, very hot day, though the chapel was cool. There were not many flowers but a considerable crowd. All the family. Gilles and I. Pierre Matisse, looking very worn. Diego's loyal and capable assistant, Philippe Anthonioz. Representatives of the French museums and cultural ministry; the Swiss ambassador; and a host of others. Annette arrived with Michel Leiris, Miss Palmer, and her assistant. She took a seat in front, just behind Bruno, Odette, and Silvio. A large wreath bore her name. Short speeches were made by a pastor, the Swiss ambassador, and Jean Leymarie—the last a very moving eulogy delivered extempore. Then there was nothing to be done but leave the cemetery and go to lunch.

A funeral was planned in Borgonovo one week later. Gilles and I naturally expected to attend. Bruno asked me as a representative of Diego's friends in Paris to make a short speech, and I agreed. Once again the day was exceptionally beautiful, though the night before there had been a shattering thunderstorm. The flowers at Diego's grave, close by Alberto's, were far more plentiful than in Paris, the crowd larger, including many who had known Diego almost since childhood. Annette and Miss Palmer this time, at least, had the decency—or was it merely common sense?—to stay away. I was fearful that emotion might overcome me as I delivered my short speech, but I managed it—in French, of course—with only one slip. There were eulogies also in Italian and in the dialect of the valley. After the ceremony a reception was held at a nearby inn. Far from being lugubrious, it was quite jolly. A lot was had to drink. Diego would have enjoyed being present, and in spirit, to be sure, he very wonderfully was. And still is.

In September I went to New York to be present for the publication of *Giacometti: A Biography*, the book begun with so little understanding fifteen years before. By and large it was received with gratifying enthusiasm. Even as I indulged myself in the illusion of having done well by Alberto and Diego, a reception of a very different sort was being prepared for me in Paris. Among the very first copies of the biography sent out to friends were those shipped by express mail to Annette, Bruno and Odette, and Silvio. None of them read English except, with some difficulty, Odette. But Miss Palmer, being American, did. It was felt by many people who were obliged to have dealings with her over the years, which seemed by virtue of her fractiousness to have been considerably more than ten, that Mary Lisa Palmer had come to identify herself with Annette, to share her grievances and resentments as if they were her own, and to arrogate to herself responsibilities and prerogatives which would normally have been Annette's alone. At all events, having read the biography and been outraged by revelations unflattering to her employer, she set out to discredit the entire work. Her method was to prepare a manifesto denouncing the biography as inaccurate, biased, and extremely malevolent toward Annette. On February 21, 1986, she sent out a "confidential" letter soliciting signatures to a scathing condemnation of the biography. The denunciatory text faults the biography for being "wildly distorted" and containing "innumerable factual errors in every domain," and states that one cannot "recognize Annette Giacometti in the distraught, unstable and incapable creature Mr. Lord creates in her guise."

Miss Palmer promised that this text would be sent to all publications which printed reviews of the biography, and asked that statements of agreement be sent to Michel Leiris. That he should have been willing to sponsor this attack against the life story of one of his oldest friends came as only a slight surprise, considering his close relationship with Annette. It was, of course, the long duration of his friendship with the artist, coupled with his reputation as a man of ironclad integrity, that gave the appeal for signatories an aura of unquestionable legitimacy. Some forty persons signed the manifesto. The signatures of David Sylvester and Jacques Dupin shocked me most. Some people had signed the text for base mercantile motives, others because they were beholden to Annette and needed her goodwill. Some signed out of sheer foolishness, and a few, no doubt, out of sincere sympathy for an unhappy woman. More than one, including Simone de Beauvoir, admitted to not having read the book at all; another was totally blind when it appeared; and at least one had never laid eyes on Alberto. The text and signatures appeared but twice, both times as advertisements placed and paid for by Annette, one on February 26, 1987, in *The New York Review of Books*, and the other on March 19, 1987, in *The London Review of Books*, as an adjunct to an unfavorable review by David Sylvester of the English edition of the biography. His letter from Barcelona three years previously had been the kiss of Judas. Leiris's literary executor stated after Michel's death that he had much regretted having sponsored the manifesto and had agreed to do so only after merciless nagging by Annette and her secretary. All in all, Miss Palmer's attempt to discredit the biography was a very trifling passage of wind in the vast teapot of cultural significance. But threats of legal action by Annette, added to ranting intimidation by one of her lovers, were successful in preventing publication of the biography in French. Jacques Dupin complacently remarked to Bruno, "This book will never be published in France." Of all the comment my work aroused, the one that meant most to me came from Bruno, who said, having read the book in French, German, and Italian translations, "Alberto would have been glad that you told all this." He later wrote a foreword for the eventual French edition of the biography and in it amplified this view.

Settling Diego's estate was a complex business of which the major burden fell upon the weary shoulders of Bruno, now retired from his practice as an architect. The heirs were Bruno and Silvio, and they gave to the French National Museums a very large amount of all that had been left behind by Diego, who never threw away anything. Very imprudently, and altogether against his better judgment, Bruno agreed to entrust temporarily to Annette a considerable amount of material which might have some significant relation to works by Alberto. The furniture which remained was divided equally between uncle and nephew, who also shared the contents of a bulging portfolio of Alberto's drawings which Diego had hidden away at Stampa. The house in the rue du Moulin-Vert was sold, leases on the studios at 46, rue Hippolyte-Maindron relinquished, and then it seemed that the sad business was concluded. If only that might have been so . . .

I thought of what might be done with the plaster sculptures by Alberto that Diego had given me. They were safe in their Swiss warehouse, but no good purpose would be served by leaving them there forever. I knew only too well what response could be expected from Annette were I to solicit her permission to have them cast in bronze, even if she, as was her practice, were to retain half of the edition. Therefore I enlisted the cooperation of a friend, an art dealer who knew Miss Palmer, to act anonymously on my behalf. He accepted. Photographs were provided. But the conscientious secretary insisted on seeing the works themselves before a decision could be taken. By whom? we wondered. At all events, my friend and Miss Palmer flew to Switzerland late in May 1986, visited the warehouse, and examined the sculptures. The secretary said that she must consult with Annette and that they would have the matter under advisement. Two days later, the Swiss police presented themselves at the warehouse with a warrant, and all the sculptures were removed in their packing cases to the cellars of police headquarters in Geneva. I was immediately advised of this dramatic contretemps by the manager of the warehouse, who had been compelled to divulge the name of the owner. I in turn flew to Geneva, secured the services of a competent lawyer, requested him to act on my behalf, and returned to Paris.

The following Monday my lawyer called to advise me that Miss Palmer had appeared before a judge in Geneva and testified on behalf of her employer—now become her "friend and collaborator"—that ten of the sculptures were fakes and two others, among them the most important, including *The Cage*, were stolen property, having been illegally removed from the studio after the artist's death. It was a serious charge. As purveyor and possessor of stolen goods, I was liable to criminal prosecution and might also be charged with forgery in connection with the so-called fakes, every single one of which I had received from Diego's hands. I was requested to testify before a judge in Geneva at two-thirty in the afternoon on Tuesday, June 17. Given the circumstances, it is an understatement to say that I was displeased by this turn of events but glad of an opportunity to explain myself and justify my possession of the sculptures. That any of these could be proven fakes was sheer humbug. Still, I took with me a satchel filled with books and catalogs relating to Alberto's art and was more than ready to testify by the time I reached Geneva.

The judge who received me was a most courteous magistrate named Louis Peila, who questioned me with calm and some humor, while every word of my replies was taken down by a secretary on an antiquated typewriter. I displayed my books and catalogs alongside photographs of the sequestered sculptures and asked to be told on what authority Miss Palmer had declared ten of the works to be fakes. She had, said Judge Peila, declared that she did not feel the hand of the artist when studying them. Well, I rejoined, she had never set eyes on the artist, much less seen him at work, whereas I had witnessed his working methods countless times and had documentary evidence to prove it. As for the two sculptures said to be stolen, they presented a more serious charge because Madame Giacometti possessed photographs of the artist's studio in which both were plainly visible. But when, I inquired, were those photographs taken, before or after Giacometti's death? And what proof could be provided of the date? All this discussion lasted most of the afternoon, in the middle of which the judge, his secretary, my lawyer, and I adjourned to a café across the street for a cool drink. By five-thirty we had not nearly concluded all that needed to be said, while Madame Giacometti in person was still to be heard, and Judge Peila requested me to return for further testimony on Monday, July 28.

I had already informed Bruno and Odette of these developments, and that evening I had dinner with Silvio and Thérèse. Silvio,
being one of Alberto's heirs, possessed a copy of the inventory of
studio contents made after the artist's death. We studied it with care
and could find no listing of the two sculptures which Annette maintained had been stolen from the studio after January 11, 1966.
Consequently they must have been removed earlier and could not
have been stolen later. I asked Silvio whether he would allow me
to make a photocopy of the inventory to use in my defense. He
agreed at once, having no fondness for the machinations of his aunt
and her secretary, of which he himself had already learned firsthand
more than enough. The inventory, of course, proved a crucial document in the proceedings that followed. Silvio, meanwhile, had also
read the biography in translation and felt much sympathy for its
portrayal of his uncle, as, indeed, did all the members of the Giacometti family, cousins and cousins of cousins.

I returned to Geneva on July 28, a fiery hot day, and testified
again at length before Judge Peila. During our midafternoon break
he told me that Annette had in the meantime testified before a
colleague of his, adding, which was highly indiscreet, that the colleague had afterward remarked, "Madame Giacometti doesn't seem
to be all there." That this might be so was, with even greater indiscretion, confirmed by Annette's own lawyer, who later remarked
to mine, "You must understand that I'm dealing with the irrational."

To be as brief as possible about an exceedingly protracted business, Annette lost her case on every count, although it was taken
all the way to the Swiss Supreme Court. She had to pay the costs,
and the sculptures were returned to me. I did not press for damages.
In due time I made arrangements to transfer title to the sculptures
to Ernst Beyeler, who contracted with Annette to have a number of
them cast in bronze. I received a munificent settlement. Among the
sculptures authorized for casting were three which had been denounced as fakes, magically reverting to authenticity the moment
Annette had something to gain by the stratagem. I don't doubt that
all the rest will eventually turn up in beautifully patinated bronze
editions.

As if desolation and bereavement intended to dog the Giacometti family, Silvio, in Bern one day on business, collapsed in the street on Wednesday, February 13, 1991. An emergency team arrived in time to resuscitate him, but the brain had been deprived of blood for too long, and he lay in an irreversible coma. Himself a doctor, the friend of doctors, he would have wanted nobody to seriously contemplate pointless delay of the inevitable, and Silvio Berthoud was pronounced dead on February 22. Bruno, who had counted on his robust nephew to carry on his own efforts to protect the legacy of Alberto's genius, was in despair. The funeral took place five days later not far from Geneva in a small country church at ten o'clock in the morning. A pale sun shone. The service was simple, dignified, deeply moving. Afterward, refreshments were served in an adjoining hall. Odette, a lady of stout heart and gentle spirit, did her best to spread cheer and talk good sense to Silvio's children, all three in deep need of it.

With Silvio gone, Bruno and Odette, as she soberly observed, were left alone to hold their own in the front line. And they had only too ample cause for concern. Six years had now passed since Diego's death, but the materials pertaining to Alberto's work which Bruno had impulsively entrusted to Annette had not been returned to him, nor had any explanation as to their specific relevance been provided. He inquired but was put off by Miss Palmer, who said that both she and Annette were too busy to be concerned with this matter for the time being. On another occasion she claimed that she didn't know where the materials were stored. This so angered Bruno that she retracted her claim and revealed where they were but insisted they could not be returned because it had not yet been possible to examine and catalog them. Miss Palmer's practice was always to stall and evade. Whether she even bothered to consult Annette, nobody knew because next to nobody ever saw Alberto's widow, and it was nearly impossible to speak with her on the telephone.

No important exhibition of Giacometti's work had been held in Paris for more than twenty years when the Museum of Modern Art of the City of Paris decided in the spring of 1991 to organize a large retrospective showing. The inaugural ceremonies were to take place on November 29 in the evening. Bruno and Odette had insistently requested a meeting with Annette and Miss Palmer, who with evident reluctance agreed to it. When they arrived at Annette's apartment, they were horrified by what they saw. Annette was physically almost unrecognizable, incapable of a coherent sentence, only occasionally murmuring yes or no, then bursting into tears. It was clearly out of the question for her to leave her apartment. Bruno felt that she had the eyes of a trapped, caged animal. When asked what was the matter with her, Miss Palmer, tough and stony-faced as ever, replied only that she had the flu. Odette asked if there was anyone to take care of her, and Miss Palmer said, "Oh, yes, oh, yes." The situation appeared tragic, and of course it was pointless to attempt to discuss any practical matter. At one moment Annette stood up and rushed away down a corridor, whereupon Odette followed and took her into her arms while Annette sobbed hysterically. When leaving, Bruno and Odette wondered whether they would ever again see Alberto's widow.

Though Annette had always wished to live at arm's length from her family, one of her brothers now began to be concerned about her well-being. He went to Paris, saw his sister and her secretary, and less than a year later Annette was pronounced legally irresponsible. Michel Arm took charge of her affairs, but he knew nothing whatever about them or about the work of Alberto Giacometti and was therefore obliged to depend upon the counsel and decisions of Lisa Palmer.

For some years Annette, her lawyer, and her secretary had endeavored to set up an organization called the Alberto and Annette Giacometti Foundation. What the functions and purpose of this foundation were to be, however, aside from the exemption of paying taxes, were altogether unclear. Works by Giacometti might be loaned to important exhibitions, but there was no provision for showing them on a permanent basis to the public, as in the Rodin and Bourdelle Museums, nor were scholars to be allowed access to the archives accumulated by Annette and her secretary through the years. Now, in order for a foundation to be granted legal status in France, proof must be brought forward to demonstrate that the foundation will be useful to the public—*d'utilité publique*. This the proposed Giacometti Foundation could not provide, and successive applications for approval were denied. Consequently, an Association Alberto and Annette Giacometti was established. Anybody, of course, can set up an association, be it for so trifling a concern as the nourishment of stray cats. The members of the board of the Giacometti Association were to be Annette herself, Jacques Dupin, André du Bouchet, Yves Bonnefoy, the poet, and Sabine Weiss, Annette's photographer. The director would be none other than Lisa Palmer.

The last day of the Giacometti exhibition at the Museum of Modern Art of the City of Paris was Sunday, March 22, 1992. Bruno and Odette had come to Paris the previous Wednesday to visit the exhibition again and once again to see whether there were any hope of ever recovering the materials (the precise nature of which I have deliberately left vague) foolishly entrusted to Annette nearly seven years before. Disillusioned, Bruno had more or less abandoned hope of ever recovering what was, in fact, little by little being stolen from him by persons who were now waiting impatiently for him to die. He called Annette's telephone number, and not Miss Palmer but another woman, someone who sounded American, answered. He asked to speak with Annette, and to his surprise she came onto the wire and spoke fairly coherently. When asked how she was, she said, "Fine, just fine." But her voice sounded peculiar. Then Bruno asked whether she had been to see the exhibition, and she said, "No, no. I don't have time. I'm too busy." When Bruno said he would like to come and see her, pay her a visit, there was simply silence at the other end of the line. If Annette was busy, nobody knew at what. Nobody knew what was the matter with her, what medication she was given, what care, if any, she received. Michel Arm may have had some inkling, but he remained in Geneva, leaving to others the day-to-day decisions concerning his sister's well-being.

Miss Palmer and her assistant, a Monsieur Chaussende, had long since become lovers, though they enjoyed defying convention by remaining unmarried. In due time, thus, Annette's "friend and collaborator" found herself in the family way and the couple became parents of a baby boy they chose to name Tristan. Announcements of the blessed event were sent out to everyone who could imaginably have been interested. Even Bruno and Odette, even I, to my astonishment, received one, noting that the infant's second name happened to be the forename of Annette's lawyer.

Whatever it was that kept Annette so busy gradually overcame her ability to cope with it. On Monday, September 20, 1993, I received a telephone call from Bruno to tell me that Annette had died the day before of both Alzheimer's disease and cancer, having at last been admitted to a clinic some weeks previously. The funeral was to take place a week later, Monday the twenty-seventh, at the Père-Lachaise Cemetery. Michel Arm had asked whether his sister could be interred at Borgonovo beside her husband, and Bruno had refused to allow it. However, in order to show Miss Palmer, the lawyer, Dupin, and others that he was not yet entirely to be discounted, Bruno came to Paris to attend the funeral and asked me to have lunch with him afterward. There was a religious ceremony at the Evangelical Church of the Luxembourg in the rue Madame, a cortège subsequently escorting the hearse to the Père-Lachaise, where a concession is not easy to obtain. The powerful lawyer must have attended to that, unaware that Annette had always wanted to be interred in Montparnasse. Bruno discreetly refrained from going to the church but went to the cemetery, where he was directed to Division Sixteen, Tomb Eighty. There were few flowers and not many people: the lawyer, Miss Palmer and her lover, Dupin and his wife, Jean Leymarie, and three or four others. Michel Arm said a few words, the coffin was lowered, and that was that.

Bruno came with Denise Laurens, daughter-in-law of Henri Laurens, the sculptor revered by Alberto, to meet me at the Hôtel Regina, where he and Odette always stay when in Paris. During lunch there was much talk of Annette. Denise, who had known her from the beginning, made the perceptive remark that she had never grown up. Bruno recalled how truly silly she had been and added that she had been cruelly difficult and devious after Alberto's death, especially in all that concerned Diego. I said that she had had her good points, too, and had greatly served the creation of Alberto's art. We all agreed about that. We talked on until half past four, wondering in particular what provisions Annette may have made in her will and how the vital *droit moral* over Alberto's work would now be exercised and by whom.

The inevitable newspaper notice appeared the next day, reporting that it was with great sorrow that Annette Giacometti's demise was announced by Monsieur and Madame Claude Arm, Monsieur and Madame Michel Arm, their children and grandchildren, and by Monsieur and Madame Bruno Giacometti, Madame Mary Lisa Palmer, Monsieur François Chaussende, and Tristan. Thus, Miss Palmer, her lover, and her illegitimate child publicly became, as it were, members of Annette's family, an apotheosis to which, it must seem, many strange years had been devoted.

The will, when opened, was not easy to administer, because its terms required that the Alberto and Annette Giacometti Foundation be a legally constituted entity, which it was not and may never be. To her brothers Annette bequeathed her two apartments and the furniture they contained but no works of art, all of which were to become property of the would-be foundation. This, incidentally, did not deter the lawyer from selling off at auction a dozen important sculptures and several paintings a year or so later, proceeds of this sale going God only knew where. Miss Palmer, Annette stipulated, was to continue her good work on the catalogue raisonné and exercise moral authority over Giacometti's work. This last proviso was contested by Bruno, because in France the *droit moral* always passes to the surviving next of kin. He had still never regained possession of the regretfully surrendered materials and had little hope of ever doing so. Miss Palmer and the lawyer had also come to a falling out over some obscure issue and resorted to the courts. Annette, I sincerely believe, meant no harm, but her foolishness, vanity, and greed did much damage to everything she would have held most dear had she ever understood the glory of her good fortune.

And that is the conclusion of what I have felt it desirable to say about my relations with the Giacometti family. Except to add that I have never known, and never expect to know: what it was that Alberto saw in me. Why was he from the first so friendly, so welcoming, and so prodigiously generous? What is the explanation of the mystery? His life will not end, as it were, with my account. Every era needs to measure the remarkable men and women of the past in terms of a renewed vision and altered perspective. Both Alberto and Diego were remarkable enough to excite the curiosity and satisfy the interest of people not yet born, whose concept of reality we cannot even imagine. Alberto used to say that he worked primarily to please the dead. Though it is thirty years since he breathed his last, his work survives him with such authority that he himself may seem to rise from the grave to proclaim its eternal vitality and splendor.

Index